Jeff Apter is the author of more than 20 music biographies, many of them bestsellers. His subjects include Johnny O'Keefe, Keith Urban, Daniel Johns, the Bee Gees, and the three Young brothers — Angus and Malcolm (of AC/DC) and George (of Easybeats renown). As a ghost-writer, he has worked with Kasey Chambers, Mark Evans (of AC/DC) and Richard Clapton. Jeff was on staff at *Rolling Stone* for several years and has written regularly about music for *Vogue*, *GQ*, *The Bulletin*, the *Sydney Morning Herald* and *The Australian*. In 2015, he worked on the Helpmann award–nominated live show *A State of Grace: The Music of Jeff and Tim Buckley*. He lives in Wollongong, New South Wales, with his wife, two children, a cat that's so damned cool it needs no name, and a very blue dog named Neela.

www.jeffapter.com.au

Praise for *Friday On My Mind: The Life of George Young*

'Compelling.' —Glenn A Baker

'A fabulous journey from Glasgow to the top of the charts.' —*Daily Telegraph*

'A great book for all Australian music buffs.' —*Canberra Weekly*

Praise for *Malcolm Young: The Man Who Made AC/DC*

'In Apter's hands it is a story as spellbinding as one of Young's guitar riffs.' —Helen Pitt, author of *The House*

'He was a force of nature . . . a powerhouse performer. His Judas in *Superstar* and Pirate King in *The Pirates of Penzance* were pure genius. He was a joy to work with — generous, creative, deadly serious about the task at hand, yet always finding the funny side! His attention to the detail of his stage character, and indeed the show itself, was a beautiful thing! He made us all better at our craft, just by sharing the stage with him. How we miss him.' —Julie Anthony

'I got to know Jon when we started rehearsals for *Jesus Christ Superstar*. We immediately became close. We were both migrant kids from the UK and we were both from the south-western suburbs of Sydney. We both loved the music world we were in and had similar tastes in music. We also had that daft sense of humour that was to be found in *The Goon Show* with Peter Sellers, Spike Milligan, and Harry Secombe.

Professionally we remained close after *Superstar*, indeed I knew all of his family, his wife Carmen and all of the kids. I remember that his Dad Syd had a birthday close to Christmas so they didn't have Christmas in their family, they had a big celebration on his birthday and called it Sydmas.

His performances in *Superstar* were second to none and I have seen and heard many people perform the part of Judas Iscariot over the years, but no-one comes close to his incredible vocal and acting skills.

I'm so fortunate to have had him in my life as a friend and fellow performer and it is fitting that this book commissioned by his brother Jeremy is now complete.' —John Paul Young

'Jon's Judas was brilliantly judged and truly exciting, daring and energetic. I was delighted and not surprised that he remained at the top of the tree for the rest of his career.' —Sir Tim Rice

'Jon was like a rough-cut diamond: he outshone almost everyone; in every room and on every stage he lit up the place. He delivered the best he knew how, always true to himself and true for his audience. His story of triumph and daring, of good luck and bad is gathered from Jon's own writings and the recollections of his loved and loving family, and of his mates and fans. He was an icon for the exciting times he dominated for so long: this larrikin, this dynamo, this gift. This legend.' —Reg Livermore

'I first met Jon in Melbourne after watching his incredible performance as Judas in the groundbreaking production of *Jesus Christ Superstar*. He owned that part! A few months later he and I began a long run of performances together. Jon was always at the top of his game which made him one of Australia's finest stage, TV, recording and live performers. I remember how electric he was on stage which of course encouraged me and my own musicians to take our shows to another level, just to compete with him. Some of my fondest memories are of when we toured Australia and New Zealand together and the many pranks and the laughter we all shared! May he now rest in peace.' —Marcia Hines

'They marvelled at his performance as Judas in the rock musical, *Jesus Christ Superstar*. They danced and sang along to his hits 'Hollywood Seven', 'Handbags and Gladrags', 'Six Ribbons' and 'Turn the Page'. They loved his swashbuckling bravura as the Pirate King in Gilbert and Sullivan's *The Pirates of Penzance*. And they tuned in week after week to see Jon in the hit TV series *Against the Wind*. This is the story of a legendary and hugely talented singer, composer, actor and musician.' —Bruce Elder

BEHIND
DARK EYES

THE TRUE STORY OF JON ENGLISH

Woodslane Press Pty Ltd
10 Apollo Street
Warriewood, NSW 2102
Email: info@woodslane.com.au
Tel: 02 8445 2300 Website: www.woodslane.com.au

First published in Australia in 2021 by Woodslane Press
© 2021 Woodslane Press, text © 2021 Jeff Apter, photographs © as indicated

 A catalogue record for this book is available from the National Library of Australia

Printed in China by HangTai
Cover image: Philip Morris
Book design by: Luke Harris

Special thanks to Nine Network Australia for permission
to cite dialogue from the TV show *All Together Now*.

All inside photos courtesy of the English family, with the exception of Jon and Marcia Hines, courtesy of Peter Rix; Sweden 2013, courtesy of Johannes Lindstrom; *The Rock Show*, courtesy of Brett Stanley.

BEHIND DARK EYES

THE TRUE STORY OF JON ENGLISH

JEFF APTER

CONTENTS

'To my brother John, a true believer.'
— Jeff Apter

ACKNOWLEDGEMENTS

JEFF APTER:

Special thanks to Jane and Jeremy English. The journey we undertook was by turns surprising, funny and often very sad. A huge thanks to both for placing their faith in me. I hope that the end result justifies that faith.

Likewise, a big thank you to the many Js: Jessamine, Jonathan, Julian, Josephine and Jzawo English, who were hugely supportive of this project, in spite of the odd skeleton I unearthed about Jon. I suggest an annual get-together on Dangar Island, just for the hell of it. Jon's sister Jan was also a great help, as was his widow, Carmen. Susan Skelly did a very thorough and thoughtful read of the manuscript. Emma Driver then diligently banged it into shape (yet again).

I'd also like to thank all of the following people who helped me (hopefully) bring Jon back to life on the page: Julie Anthony, David Café, Coralea Cameron, Peter Deacon, Simon Drake, Graham Ford, Simon Gallaher, Mark Gogoll, Dave Hayley, Greg Henson, Debbie Kruger, Reg Livermore, Johannes Lindstrom, Bruno Lucia, David Mackay, Mario Millo, Martine Monroe, Philip Mortlock, Sheila Parker, Peter Plavsic, Marina Prior, Tim Rice, Peter Rix, Stuart Smith, Brett Stanley, Trevor White, Simon Wincer and John Paul Young. A special thanks to Philip Morris for the wonderful cover photo; likewise Andrew Swaffer and all at Woodslane Press for their support and Luke Harris @ Working Type Studio for his stellar design work.

JANE AND JEREMY ENGLISH:

This book is for you, Jon. It's the story of your astounding career. The book that you wanted. Carmen and your children authorised Jeff Apter to write an account of your life as he saw it. This is from us, your Bruv and Sis, a heartfelt gift.

Our thanks to Support Act, Australia's charity dedicated to helping artists, crew and music workers, for the financial assistance towards Jon's funeral held on Monday 21 March 2016 at the Macquarie Park Cemetery and Crematorium. Huge thanks also to Stephen Found for your generosity in providing your Capitol Theatre, including its front and back of house staff, and our deepest appreciation to the Memorial Committee, including Simon Gallaher, Paul Delitt and Paul Rigby, for orchestrating the magnificent Jon English Memorial held on Monday 4 April 2016. Jon's family is forever grateful.

To be a part of the Jon English story, go to facebook's Official: Jon English: http://facebook.com/jonathanjamesenglish/

A proportion of the proceeds of this book will go to Support Act.

FOREWORD

John Waters

Fifty years ago, I turned up to a derelict theatre in Sydney where Jim Sharman, the director of *Hair*, the 'Love-Rock Musical', was holding auditions for the Harry M. Miller production of the new rock opera sensation *Jesus Christ Superstar*. Having played the role of Claude in *Hair* for two long, wonderful years, and knowing both Jim and Harry M. well, I fancied my chances of landing the role of Judas. After a quick run-through with the wonderful Jamie McKinley on piano, I ripped through a fairly muscular and, I thought, impressive performance of Judas's opening song 'Heaven on Their Minds'. Patrick Flynn, also a buddy from *Hair* days, was the musical director, and he seemed well pleased with me.

There were, however, a couple more applicants for the role, and I decided to stay and catch up with all my friends while I watched and listened. After one 'close, but no cigar' effort, the last young man came onto the stage and grabbed the microphone.

He said, 'Hi. My name's Jon English,' and three minutes later I realised my jaw was still hanging open, and my thoughts of full employment for the next couple of years had been modified.

This tall, loose-limbed and athletic man simply blew us all out of our skulls. He huskily growled the first section of 'Heaven on Their Minds' and then, with wild hair flying and dark eyes that penetrated the room like a panther in search of prey, he soared and lifted each successive verse with both his voice and his unbelievable stagecraft until the final, screamed 'JESUUUUUUUUS!' rang out in the almost empty, echoing auditorium, and a stunned silence was the only sound — to paraphrase Paul Simon.

While everyone who had the honour of being there that day recovered their collective breath, I leaned into Jim Sharman's ear and said: 'Maybe I could be one of the other disciples?'

As fate would have it, I did end up playing Judas — in *Godspell*! We played in Sydney at the same time as *Superstar*, and the casts of both shows, which were in theatres a couple of hundred metres apart in Chinatown, used to hang out together. I recall with great fondness the joyous gatherings of the entire rock-opera community, including the cast of the still-running *Hair*. We sang, drank, smoked joints and lovingly embraced each other's talents and gifts. All of us became good friends — Jon and I in particular. We joked about how, in our strangely mirrored roles, we both 'killed God eight times a week'.

We were a few months apart in age, both born Londoners, and we shared a Monty Python sense of humour and a love of performance.

Within a few short years we had both become television actors, both doing work in 'convict-era' period dramas. The parallels then diverged somewhat, as I continued on acting in stage and screen productions while Jon's career as a natural-born 24-carat rock star took him to the very top of the recording and concert industry, not just in Australia but in Europe as well, where he enjoyed chart successes and a huge following. He became, in fact, the Jon English all Australians knew: someone who put every fibre of his being into his electrifying live stage appearances, and whose rock singing voice was up there with the best in the world. No argument.

Jon's friendship was a precious thing to have. We would call each other and discuss life. We advised and counselled each other. When Jon asked me to do a recording session for his own rock opera *Paris*, which I leaped at and love to this day, he told me on the phone: 'I've gotta get you to stop that acting shit for a minute and get you back singing, and I've gotta get the Doc [Doc Neeson, former frontman of The Angels] to do some acting!' He cared for his friends.

As an artist he was always eye catching, and he had a fabulous gift of engaging an audience. Nobody who witnessed his Pirate King, in the reworking of Gilbert and Sullivan's *The Pirates of Penzance* that he did with Simon Gallaher, can ever forget it.

As a man, Jon was grounded. He had enough ego to be the larger-than-life figure he was, and to wear it well, but he was realistic and self-effacing in equal measure. He reached out to me on many occasions where others would retire behind a wall, and I knew I could do the same with him.

I try not to think about the losses that we are all occasionally dealt by the tenuous nature of our grip on this earth but rather about the gains and the riches that remain with us forever. Jon English was a rare treasure. He could be dangerous or gracious, wild or tame; but whichever Jon you encountered, you were never in for a dull day. His relentless energy filled the space around him.

I had the thrill of singing at Jon's memorial. It was a concert in the Capitol Theatre, that once-derelict place where nearly 50 years earlier I had looked for the first time at that unique face. I sang Jon's great rock aria, 'Love Has Power'. And on that day, it truly did.

CHAPTER 1

'I had to [keep smoking].
My voice was starting to clear up!'

Jon English knew how to fill a stage — he'd done it repeatedly for more than five decades, as Judas, as the Pirate King, as the dark-eyed rocker who gave the world such hits as 'Hollywood Seven' and 'Turn the Page'. But today, 4 April 2016, the stage at the Capitol Theatre, the scene of many of Jon's greatest triumphs, was all but empty, apart from a lone acoustic guitar and a tiny black road case, illuminated by a spotlight. Inside were his ashes.

The statement was very clear: Jon English might have died, but he hadn't left the building.

'We love this guy,' said John Waters, first to take the stage at Jon's public memorial, dressed in sombre black. He and English had history — most notably, he'd contributed to the album for *Paris*, a musical that Jon had obsessively worked on for years. (Jon once wrote, only half joking, that he'd come so close, so many times, to having *Paris* produced in the right way, on a large scale, 'that I have calluses on my hopes'.)

'The best thing that we can do,' Waters told the gathering of fans and friends, 'is to give him this send-off that we didn't want to be giving. The best thing we can do is sing.'

With that Waters and the house band — some of whom had backed Jon since *Jesus Christ Superstar* in 1972 — launched into a poignant 'Turn the Page', the Bob Seger–penned song that Jon had made his own back in 1975. (It was his first Top 20 hit.) The lyrics captured how it felt to be on the stage, 'playin' star again'. It was also a story about the downside of fame, the feeling of being alone in some anonymous fleapit, hearing nothing but 'the sound of the amplifiers'. No wonder Jon English recorded it; it told his story.

'Turn the Page' also told the story of Jon's kids, as his daughter Josephine (Josie) revealed when she took to the stage. 'The scent of gaffer tape, fog juice and sweat takes us right back to our childhood,' Josie said, speaking for all her siblings.

Waters would later return to the stage to sing a stirring 'Love Has Power'.

'Wasn't he incredible?' said Trevor White, Jesus to Jon's Judas in *Jesus Christ Superstar*, pointing to an image of a very young English on the screen. 'He used to spit all over me every night, eight times a week.' (Amanda Muggleton, one of Jon's co-stars in *HMS Pinafore*, had a similar experience; while performing, English would shake his head and spray everyone in his vicinity, like a wet sheepdog. 'He loved to get his sweat all over us,' she remembered.)

White spoke about first meeting a very eager Jon at the cattle call for *Superstar*. 'He was this gushing-with-excitement guy.' White still sounded genuinely stunned that he and English got the prime roles: White as Jesus, English as Judas. 'Who would have realised that we [would end up] working together, opposite each other, eight times a week for over 2000 performances?'

It was especially poignant that right at that moment White was standing on the stage at the Capitol, where *Jesus Christ Superstar* had been produced by legendary impresario Harry M. Miller.

Trevor White reflected on how *Superstar* was 'an incredible thing to be part of' and how it had launched his career, as well as Jon's, plus the careers of other cast members such as Russell Hitchcock and Graham Russell (who formed Air Supply), Marcia Hines, Reg Livermore and even a very young Michael Caton, later to be known Australia-wide as Uncle Harry from *The Sullivans* and Darryl Kerrigan from *The Castle*. Many of the members of Jon's bands — Baxter Funt and The Foster Brothers — had come out of *Superstar*. And it wasn't just onstage talent; Brian Thomson, *Superstar*'s set designer, had gone to Broadway and won a Tony Award.

'He grew in stature and confidence,' said White, thinking back to that flashpoint in the early 1970s. 'Mind you, I don't think he was ever *unconfident*, Jon.'

This knowing aside generated a laugh, the first of many that afternoon. English would have hated his farewell to be some grim, downbeat affair; he was, after all, the kind of guy who rarely missed out on a punchline.

Jonathan, Jon's son, channelled his father when he expressed his thanks for 'his fans — "the punters", as he called them. Thanks for helping feed us, clothe us, getting us to school; we also enjoyed some good holidays . . .'

John Paul Young was also a *Superstar* alumnus, and he sang 'Handbags and Gladrags', another song that English had made his own. It had been Jon's first charting single, way back in early 1973.

A video message was beamed in from Richard Wilkins, the entertainment reporter with the perfect hair. He spoke about his first encounter with English in 1980, when Wilkins — at the time Richard Wilde, Kiwi pop contender — was 'blown away and a little bit envious about just how he owned the stage'. Wilkins was hardly alone; English was a hard act to follow. The man had swagger and serious presence. Wilkins also spoke about *Paris*, the rock opera that Jon created with David Mackay. 'He was so passionate about that.'

Peter Rix, Jon's manager from 1977 to 1994, flashed back on 'those wonderful years we spent running amok through the music business'. Rix documented Jon's career: two million albums sold; parallel lives as an actor, singer and composer; 'a titan of the stage'. It was a rare juggling act. Jon's career had been 'extraordinary', Rix said: 'Wherever Jonno went, he was the star.'

Then he observed, knowingly: 'But [Jon was] always a husband and a father — and always captain of the ship, whether I liked it or not.' Rix said that Jon was frequently surprised by his own success, especially on TV, given that, in English's own words, he had the looks of a 'drug-crazed, axe-murdering hippie'.

Another big laugh ensued.

'With Jon,' Rix added, 'you always knew that he was going to go just that little bit further than anybody else on that bloody stage.'

Sometimes off stage, too. Rix likened being on the road with English and The Foster Brothers to the 'end-of-year Bali romp' of Jon's beloved Parramatta Eels rugby league team, but with one key exception: 'The team went for two weeks — but this lot was out there for ten months of the year.' (One of Jon's proudest moments was recording the Eels' team song. 'If you want to see how football's played,' Jon sang, hand on heart, 'come and see the Eels.')

Rix drew what seemed like an unlikely comparison between English and Pete Townshend of The Who, one of Jon's favourite bands. 'You know that [Townshend's] bravado hides great vulnerability, as it did with Jon. He had a fear of failure that drove him to succeed against all odds.'

'Farewell, Jonno,' Rix said in conclusion. 'There will never be another one like you.'

Peter Cupples took the stage to sing 'Words Are Not Enough'. It was Cupples who'd been touring with Jon in the days before he died, suddenly and shockingly, on 9 March 2016. They'd become friends during a New

Zealand tour of *The Pirates of Penzance* and had been playing together —
the Uncorked tour — for some twenty years. Midway through 'Words',
Cupples did his best to reproduce one of Jon's hilarious if politically
sketchy onstage monologues. The subject was Jon's early days: life as a
Ten Pound Pom, fresh off the boat onto the sleepy streets of Cabramatta,
and how he formed his first band 'with a bunch of poofters'.

Cupples looked out at the crowd. 'I told you it was politically incorrect.'

Simon Gallaher, Jon's onstage partner for a lively 30 years, sang 'Six
Ribbons', accompanied by Mario Millo, whose best work with Jon was
collaborating on the music for the hit TV show *Against the Wind*. (Jon
had dubbed him 'Morrie'.) Also performing were Mario's daughter Jess
and, on guitar, Jonathan, one of Jon's four children, who'd spent many
years with his father on the road. Music, clearly, was in the English DNA.

Gallaher described himself as an 'adoring fan' of Jon and *Superstar*,
well before he became a performer himself. He was signed to Polydor,
the same record label as English, and also worked with Millo soon
after 'Morrie' and Jon had finished the soundtrack to *Against the Wind*.
Gallaher first met Jon in *The Pirates of Penzance* in 1984; the original six-
week season ran on (and on) for three years and shut down only 'because
Jon and I each needed to go back to our roots of concerts and recordings'.

Gallaher revealed, with a roll of his eyes, that English would provide
him with sneak previews of *Paris* 'incessantly'. Clearly, it had been his
passion project.

They were an unlikely twosome — the shaggy-haired rock star with
the raccoon eyes and the wide-eyed kid fresh from the Anglican Church
Grammar School in Brisbane. English dubbed Gallaher 'Freddy', a nod
to Frederic, the character he played in *Pirates*. Gallaher accepted that
they were like chalk and cheese, admitting: 'I was the cheese.' They
were also tight, and very successful. 'We were a bankable commodity
for years to come.'

Gallaher related how he and English were smokers, and during *Pirates* they decided to kick the habit together. They did well, too, going smoke-free for six weeks, but then one afternoon Gallaher caught Jon puffing away in his dressing room. He was shocked.

'Mate, what are you doing?'

'I had to,' English explained to him, his face swathed in smoke. 'My voice was starting to clear up!'

They last worked together in late 2014, in the Monty Python creation *Spamalot*, a dream fulfilled for Python nut Jon. 'It was the best fun we could have with our clothes on,' said Gallaher, quoting one of Jon's favourite lines. In the show, Jon sang Eric Idle's darkly comic 'Always Look on the Bright Side of Life', which now flashed up on the video screen at the Capitol.

Somehow, from the great beyond, Jon English had the last laugh.

CHAPTER 2

'I remember getting chased by geese, acorns on the roof, the snow . . .'

Today it's home to a strong Asian population, many of them former refugees. But Western Sydney suburb Cabramatta was a vastly different place in the early 1960s. When the English clan settled in Cabramatta in 1961, it resembled a biggish country town, a far-flung suburb some 30 kilometres to the south-west of the Sydney CBD.

If you stood at one end of the main drag, John Street, looking back towards the railway station, you wouldn't have been surprised if a tumble-weed wedged itself among the fenders of the Holdens parked on either side of the road. There were some signs of life, however: looking left, you'd spot an E.L. Downes menswear store, alongside the local butcher. You could pick up a Lotusland inner-spring mattress — known as the '40-Winker' — for a snip under 20 quid at the nearby Len C. Wilson store. It was a handy acquisition for the many working-class families building new homes in and around Cabramatta, in such suburbs as Canley Vale, Carramar, Smithfield and Fairfield. Yet still the population of the entire Fairfield City area, which encompassed all these suburbs, was not much more than 30,000.

Most of these families were 'New Australians', a mix of resettled Europeans and Brits, seeking a better life after the horrors of World War II.

Some were straight out of the nearby Cabramatta Migrant Hostel, which housed as many as 900 migrants when the English family bought their home in Cabramatta in 1961. The Villawood Migrant Hostel, which would soon spawn the first great Aussie rock group, The Easybeats, was only five minutes away by train. Over time, Jon got to know George Young, Harry Vanda and Stevie Wright, all members of that trailblazing Aussie band. He also met Angus and Malcolm Young, just kids at the time, who'd go on to form the world-conquering AC/DC.

The Easybeats' manic lead singer, 'Little' Stevie Wright, would one day beat the boards with Jon, as would another 'westie', John (Paul) Young, an expat Scot who arrived in Oz with his family a few months after the Englishes. The Youngs' first home was the East Hills Migrant Hostel, then they settled in Liverpool. Young, who was a year-and-a-bit younger than English, could usually be found playing the pinball machines — the 'pinnies' — at Theo's Milk Bar in Liverpool. He was known to his mates as 'Mungy'. Richard Lewis Springthorpe — who'd morph into pop star Rick Springfield — was growing up in nearby Wentworthville; he was the son of a career soldier.

Future prime minster Gough Whitlam, his wife Margaret and their four children had been living in Cabramatta for six years when the Englishes arrived. The Whitlam family home was in Albert Street, walking distance from Cabramatta High School, which Jon and his siblings Janet, Jill and Jeremy attended. Margaret Whitlam helped out in the school's canteen, while Jon sometimes found himself competing against Cathy Whitlam, one of four Whitlam siblings, in the open events at school swimming carnivals. (Jon was crowned Cabramatta High's Athletics Age Champion in 1966.)

Most of whatever action there was to be found in Cabramatta took place at the train station. As Jon recalled, it was there that locals would 'hang around . . . and beat people up'. In 1961, there were two options for a twelve-year-old kid such as Jon — then Jonathan — in Cabramatta: sport and music. 'I opted for sport first,' he said, 'followed by guitar.'

Cabramatta offered 'very few distractions', Jon said in 2009. 'Get into mischief or form a garage band — or do both.'

Mastering his first instrument, a gift from his parents, would remain one of Jon's key memories of growing up in Cabramatta. 'I remember having some great fun at Cabramatta and all points west,' Jon wrote of his upbringing. 'It's where I learnt to play the guitar, after all.'

Of course, the English family story stretched further back than the sleepy suburban streets of Cabramatta.

Jonathan James English was born in Hampstead, London, on 26 March 1949, the second child to his parents, Sydney (Syd), who was 33, and Sheila, who was 25. Jon inherited his 'raccoon' eyes from Sheila; it was one of her family's physical characteristics.

Jonathan's sister Janet had arrived fourteen months earlier. They were named in honour of *Janet and John*, a popular children's book series of the day. The common 'J' was purely a whim of Sheila's, but it stuck. Much of the English clan continued this tradition; at one stage there was at least thirteen J. Englishes, which must have been hell for bill collectors. Jon referred to it as his family's 'endless chain of superstitious alliteration'.

Jon's birth certificate stated that he was born in 'Upper Heath', which, as he'd one day recall, 'was about as close as I ever got to living in a posh suburb of London'. As soon as Jon and Sheila left the Hampstead hospital, it was back to their rented flat in working-class Uxbridge.

Jon's great-grandfather, William, was an engineer, whose work took him to New Zealand and the Far East, on board such steamships as the *S.S. Arawa* (he was the chief refrigeration engineer). William took great pride in telling his family that he was the first man to successfully take a shipment of butter from New Zealand to the UK, a trip that consumed more than 40 days' 'steaming time'.

According to family lore, Jon's grandfather, Sydney Snr, invented the mechanical device known as a 'davit', which was used for lowering lifeboats from ships, but his work was never formally acknowledged.

When he was growing up, Syd, Jon's father, had a cousin called Syd, and the pair were best friends. Jon's father, who stood six feet tall, was duly dubbed Big Syd, his cousin Little Syd. They were mad for machines; their faces would often be pocked by gravel rash, a by-product of frequent spills from a motorbike they shared. They'd compete at the Isle of Man Time Trial, which was strictly for daredevils, and was widely regarded as one of the most dangerous bike races in the world. Big Syd rode in 'the chair', the sidecar, a near-suicidal gig.

Once, when riding in the country, they crashed their bike. Little Syd lay sprawled on the road, while Big Syd was thrown over a brick wall. Big Syd was wandering around the orchard in which he'd landed, in a daze, when he was approached by a local policeman.

'There's been a really bad accident,' the copper told Syd, 'and there's a bloke in here who may be dead or badly injured — could you give me a hand?'

The copper had no idea that it was actually Syd who'd come off his bike.

When World War II broke out, Jon's father joined the British Army — he figured it was better to volunteer, so he might have a little more control over his destiny. Syd was part of the British Expeditionary Force that travelled to Europe in 1940 and was among the retreating forces. He operated a submachine gun on a converted pleasure boat, commandeered by Prime Minister Winston Churchill, and survived two trips out of Dunkirk, where he helped evacuate trapped British soldiers. When the boats returned to the UK, they were almost unrecognisable: they were coated black from smoke, the funnels had been blown clear off, the decks were full of holes.

On the boat's third trip, it was sunk. Fortunately, Syd had been relieved for the journey. He was eventually invalided out of the army and in 1943 found a job at airline BOAC as a driver — first in Bristol, then in London.

The V1s used by the German army — known to Londoners as 'buzz bombs' or 'doodlebugs' — almost proved to be the undoing of Syd. One exploded close by as he and a friend returned from lunch near Victoria Station in 1944. The force of the impact was so powerful that it blew Syd through the locked office door of the building in which he worked. Although relatively unharmed, he was deafened for days.

Sheila's grandmother, Rose, was in the rear garden of the family home in Chiswick when another of Hitler's rockets, a V2, exploded, killing three people and injuring seventeen others. She was blown to the ground but was otherwise unhurt, although the house was badly damaged. Prime Minister Churchill visited the street that day; it resembled a battlefield.

Too young to 'join up' at the start of the war, Sheila (then Sheila Downs) worked briefly at the Vickers aircraft plant, then taught at the Belmont Prep School in London for a year. Once she was old enough to join the services, she trained as a meteorological assistant and forecaster at the RAF Bramcote airfield, learning how to read and decode weather charts. She'd occasionally tag along and fly on 'sorties', the most exciting part of her work. Sheila then served in the RAF at Haverfordwest, a coastal station in Wales. There, her sleepwalking — something she had not been aware of — almost resulted in her being shot by a trigger-happy sentry.

Both Syd and Sheila returned to civilian life at the end of the war; they met, then married in London on 17 January 1946. After the war, Sheila had been living in a hostel in London, with the intention of studying aircraft engineering. But she didn't last long at the hostel; she was turfed out for constantly questioning the house rules. This was not out of character.

'She said it was ridiculous,' recalled her daughter Janet. 'She'd be told, "Well, you can't have a bath tonight." And she'd reply, "Well, of course I can have a bath tonight." That type of thing. So they got rid of her.'

Sheila moved into another hostel, where she met a woman who gave her some advice: 'I know a young man who will look after you.' That, of course, was Syd. 'He'd keep her out of trouble, or at least that's what they thought,' laughed Janet. 'Not that it worked out so well.'

Their firstborn, Janet (Jan) had a running joke — she said that she was a bridesmaid at her parents' wedding. She'd point at their wedding photo and insist it was her in the shot. (It wasn't.) On the day Jon was born in spring 1949, Sheila predicted that he'd be a sports star: after all, his birthday coincided with the staging of the Grand National horse race, two FA Cup soccer semifinals *and* the annual Oxford/Cambridge boat race on the Thames.

'I can't remember much of my birth,' Jon wrote in a memoir he never got to finish. 'I was quite young at the time.'

But the actual day of his birth left its mark on Sheila. Jon said that his mother frequently told the story that he was born 'during a huge thunderstorm'.

Jon was very impressed by this until he heard Sheila repeat the same story about Jeremy's birth. 'Whether we both were born during such meteorological drama, well, it doesn't matter,' Jon wrote, 'because she never let the banal truth get in the way of a good story. Mum always had a flair for the dramatic.'

Syd didn't mind spinning a yarn, either; he could tell jokes that stretched for a good ten minutes, never missing a beat. He was also a competent amateur musician — there was a piano in pretty much every home in which the family lived. Jon believed that his father was a good enough muso to have 'turned pro', although that never panned out. Syd, who was tall and thin, with a terrific head of hair, also participated in amateur theatre.

Jan was enrolled at the Thames Valley Music School, and Jon demanded that he, too, attend. No one seemed to mind that he was only three years old at the time. Clearly, music had already caught his ear. 'People sing more in England,' Jon said, when asked about his musical roots. 'It's part of the culture. I didn't think much about it until I got to Australia.'

By the age of ten, Jon was attending primary school and singing in the choir at the comprehensive Lord Knyvett's School (now Thomas Knyvett College), whose founder had foiled the Gunpowder Plot of 1605, which led to the arrest of the treasonous Guy Fawkes. Jon and the choir once performed 'Jerusalem' at St Paul's Cathedral in London. He was a natural-born show-off, although he understood that outlets such as music didn't rate too highly in his very working-class world. It was an indulgence; men had other more important things to do in their lives, such as providing for their families.

'It was like, real men don't do that stuff,' he told a writer from *The Australian* in 2010. 'That's for girls.'

For one mad moment, though, Jon had his mind set on becoming a stunt performer, as Jan recalled. 'He learned things like pedalling his bike twice as hard and hurling himself off sideways.' While still in primary school, Jon attempted what was known as the 'western roll' during a high-jump event. 'He literally ran up to the bar and hurled himself over headfirst,' Jan laughed. 'The teachers were horrified.'

Jon's upbringing, in many ways, was that of a typical working-class English kid. In summer, he and the family would go 'apple-scrumping' — wandering orchards looking for apples that had fallen from trees and not been collected. In autumn, they'd search for conkers at the bottom of chestnut trees. As winter set in, Jon donned his gabardine raincoat and stepped gingerly over the frozen puddles that seemed to be everywhere in his neighbourhood.

Every year, on 5 November, the Englishes would celebrate Guy Fawkes Night. 'I remember penny bangers going off in my hands and near my ears, making them sting for five minutes,' Jon wrote in a column penned in 1974 for Sydney's *Daily Mirror.*

But not everything the Englishes did could be described as typical. Sheila was a strong-willed, free-thinking woman, proudly anti-establishment and, in 1953, when Jon was aged four, with a post-war housing (and baby) boom in full force, she and Syd opted for a very different lifestyle. Syd bought an Albion bus that he converted into a caravan. He fashioned a small kitchen, a double bed for him and Sheila, and bunks at the rear for Jon and Jan (Jeremy and Jill were not yet born).

Sheila was granted permission to park the van on the Grove Park Polish Camp, in south-eastern London, which had been used as a resettlement camp for refugees since the end of the war. The camp was dotted with horseshoe-shaped Nissen huts, similar to those of Australian migrant hostels. The Englishes parked their 'gypsy caravan' on the edge of the camp, in a field. They paid a small rent for the space, much less than they would have paid for more traditional accommodation.

Although he was very young, Jon retained vivid memories of living in the camp.

'I remember getting chased by geese' — owned by their neighbours, the Zabel family — 'acorns on the roof, the snow,' he said, when asked about their unusual lifestyle during an episode of TV's *This is Your Life.* 'It was great.'

As Jan recalled, 'It was a great place for kids to live. Jon and I loved it.'

She was right: the camp was full of children and animals and was a very lively place to grow up. The family was never short of company, or the kids short of adventures. Yet it was no five-star lifestyle: at first they had to cart water to their bus in buckets and Sheila washed their clothes by hand. Over time, Jon's parents added a timber kitchen extension onto the bus, made from old wooden boxes, while Syd arranged for running water and electricity to be connected.

'Quirky' best described the Englishes' Christmas tradition. Rather than the usual celebrations on 25 December, they'd hold off until Syd's birthday on 16 January and host what they called 'Sydmas'.

'Sydmas was my mother's idea,' said Jan. 'We were living in the country and didn't have any extended family so my mother decided we wouldn't have Christmas, that we'd leave it until the middle of January. That way we could all buy presents in the January sales and our friends could come and share the celebrations. That went on for years.'

'We even had a "Sydmas tree", made of old car axles, a busted piano and used guitar strings,' Jon wrote in a blog in 2010. 'It was very cool, with none of the hypocrisy and hype that's attached to the real thing these days.'

Jon's father liked to read his children bedtime stories, mostly from a book of Greek myths, along with other stories of mythology. 'I think my parents wanted us to grow up to be philosophers or something,' Jon recalled.

Jon loved these stories. He would say to his father, 'Read me some more about the battles and the heroes', and Syd would duly read him the story of the seven labours of Hercules.

'Read about the monsters,' he'd ask Syd, who'd then recite the story of Jason and Argonauts. Jon simply couldn't get enough. Some of these stories, especially the one about Helen of Troy and her lover, Paris, seeped into Jon's subconscious.

Jon knew the tale of Helen of Troy so well he could just about recite it verbatim. Many years later he would describe it as 'the story of the greatest armada the world had seen, a thousand ships, the great siege of Troy that lasted for ten years, the wooden horse, the subterfuge, the great heroes, the great battles'. As for the doomed couple, well, they did have their flaws. He could see that, but that just made them more fascinating. 'If you took the gods out of it, Paris and Helen turn into randy, rutting, irresponsible royals who managed to cause a ten-year war and destroy an entire nation (or even two, or three).'

These stories — and those of the Norse gods, too — resonated with Jon throughout his life. 'I learned somewhat later how this mythology still remains with us today in everyday life, and how we never really left it behind.'

Jon's love of stories proved handy, because there was no TV in the English bus. The first time they watched TV was in the community room at the Polish camp, dubbed 'The Men's Room' by the family, where the kids took in a couple of hours viewing every Sunday afternoon. Cowboy Roy Rogers and flamboyant piano man Liberace became faves of Jon and Jan, although, admittedly, they weren't picky: TV was still a novelty and pretty much anything, from the test pattern onwards, was worth a look.

When Sheila was pregnant with her third child, Jon and Jan came down with sore throats. The local doctor — who also cared for the Duchess of Kent — diagnosed them with a minor throat infection. But when skin started to peel off their hands, it was apparent they were suffering something far more serious. Jon and Jan were diagnosed with scarlet fever, a highly contagious, potentially fatal, condition. They were quarantined — even the books they'd been reading had to be 'baked' for fear of contamination.

Because of her children's illness, Jon's mother was sent to a special maternity hospital where she, too, was quarantined. Her only communication with Jon and Jan was by letter, so she wrote to them every day. Her third child, a son, was born in the midst of a thunderstorm (or so Sheila would insist) and for a time she considered calling him Thor. But family tradition prevailed and he was named Jeremy.

When the family was finally reconciled, Jeremy (often known as Jem) spent his early days sleeping in a chest of drawers inside the caravan.

After three years at the Grove Park camp, the family moved on, resettling on a new housing estate in Stanwell, roughly half a mile from Heathrow Airport — Syd still worked at BOAC. (They'd also live in Staines and Hounslow, suburbs populated by 'airline families' like the Englishes.) It was known as the Airways Housing Estate — later it acquired the even more clumsy title British Airways Social Housing (aka 'BASH').

'It was built by BOAC and BEA, before they were amalgamated,' said Jan, 'and it was to house all their staff. Housing was a nightmare after World War II. They did it on a rent-to-buy system, which was very forward thinking.'

One day, while Sheila was washing the family's clothes on a rented machine, she asked Jon to go to the BASH estate's shops to buy some washing powder.

'Can you take Jem with you, please?' she asked.

Jon soon returned with the powder, but without his two-year-old brother.

'Where's Jem?' Sheila asked.

Jon shrugged; he had no idea. It turned out that he'd left his brother at the shop. It took some hours before Jeremy was found, cheerfully wandering the streets of the estate, a risky proposition at any time of the day.

Jeremy was a 'terrible wanderer', according to Jan. 'If you took your eyes off him for five minutes, he'd be off. The police got him on one occasion; they picked him up riding across a major crossing, against the lights — on his tricycle. He was three. My mother found him at the police station, where he was completely happy. They'd given him some biscuits.'

Random acts of forgetfulness were a family trait. Sheila gave birth to their fourth child, a daughter named Jill, on 11 November 1958, while the family lived on the BASH estate. Out shopping, Sheila braked her pram outside the grocer's. She was walking home, shopping done, when she heard a woman loudly calling to her. Sheila had left Jill outside the store; when she returned, the baby was sleeping peacefully.

Jon's first day of secondary school was a tough one to forget. An older and much bigger kid, simply known as 'Spider', strolled up to him at recess and punched him in the nose, completely unprovoked. Jon bled all over his crisp new white shirt. But Spider got his comeuppance: two days later, on his way to school, Jon picked up a roof tile from a building site and, as he recalled, clobbered Spider with it, 'hospitalising the bastard when he wasn't looking'. Jon was given sixteen strokes of the cane, one for each of Spider's stitches. Jon laughed as his hands began to swell. Revenge could be sweet, even if it was painful.

CHAPTER 3

'[Seeing the Beatles] was an epiphany. It was earth shattering, the stuff of mythology.'

Sheila was the first to start thinking about emigrating. Syd, with no small amount of encouragement from Sheila, had brought home pamphlets from Australia House, which enticed Brits to 'come over to the sunny side' and emigrate to Oz. They agreed that the idea of starting a new life Down Under had some appeal. But the mere sight of the brochures left Jon's grandmother in tears; she had no intention of leaving the Old Dart.

In 1960, Syd flew out to Australia in search of work and landed a job with KLM, the Dutch national airline. The position, running their cargo division, was based at Sydney Airport. It was a big step up for Syd, a great opportunity.

The family followed him six months later, on the *RMS Orion*; it was a six-week journey to Oz. Once on board, Sheila was asked to surrender the family's passports, a routine part of emigrating. But she played dumb and said that she had lost them. This, of course, wasn't true; she'd actually pocketed the passports, because she knew that this would enable her and the children to go on shore when the boat stopped at various ports. 'That's how you deal with bureaucracy,' she told her kids. (Years later, if Jon's children had trouble with their teachers, he'd offer this advice: 'Tell them to fuck off.' Sheila's influence had clearly rubbed off.)

The Englishes reached Port Said in Egypt, which had been a hotspot during the 1956 Suez Crisis, and disembarked while the ship was in port. Jon remembered seeing 'lots of soldiers with machine guns', which was a first. They also stopped in Aden, a port city in Yemen, where Jon was stunned by the sight (and smell) of 'goat dung in the streets and a man sitting on the wharf with a tin cup, and empty sockets where his eyes should have been'.

The family reached Sydney on 1 April, travelling via Western Australia. Jon celebrated his twelfthth birthday on the boat, a couple of days out of Fremantle. He also had his first kiss while on board. 'It was a real adventure,' he said of the trip. 'It was a hell of a thing my mum took on.'

But the concept of long-distance travel wasn't foreign to Jon. When he was ten, he'd travelled with Jan to meet family in Canada, flying via New York, where they caught the train north. They had stayed in Canada for six weeks.

'My mother decided it would be good if we visited her sister in Canada,' said Jan. 'There were no direct flights, so we went to New York, where we were met by an old friend of Syd's from BOAC.' They spent the night in Manhattan; it was the first time either had seen a skyscraper. 'It was mind blowing,' said Jan.

Clearly, they were independent kids.

———

Jon knew little of Australia beyond what he'd read in the pamphlets Syd had brought home from Australia House, but he adapted very quickly. Jon would admit that while he was 'English by birth', he became 'a dinkum Aussie by choice'.

Jan, however, didn't acclimatise so easily. 'I loathed school, any school. I particularly didn't like this one [Cabramatta High] because I hated the uniform. Jon liked it, I didn't; I hardly went to school. I just wanted to go home, hated everything, whereas Jon fitted in straightaway.'

Syd's new job was a step in the right direction financially, and the family took out a mortgage on their first home, in Coventry Road in Cabramatta. It was like most of the local homes — sewage had yet to be installed, so when nature called the family had to use the backyard dunny, which was numbingly cold in winter, unbearably hot in summer, and crawling with insects and spiders. That outdoor toilet, emptied by the local dunny man, remained one of Jon's strongest memories of his childhood in Cabramatta (in more ways than one), as did the sheer size of the quarter-acre block on which their house was situated. 'It was huge compared with England.'

Syd was a car-lover, like Jon in later life. The yard of their home in Coventry Road resembled a car yard. Peter Plavsic was a schoolfriend of Jon's, who'd go on to become his bandmate, too. He remembered the English family home as 'like a spare parts yard — there'd be all these cars with grass growing over them'.

But not too many of Jon's friends visited the house. They found Sheila intimidating.

'He loved his mother like Elvis loved his,' said Graham Ford, another schoolfriend and bandmate of Jon's. 'But the love was not really returned. He wasn't the favourite child and it really bugged him.'

Peter Plavsic agreed. 'He was seeking approval from her all the time, but she was tough.'

The relationship between Jon and his mother 'was very up and down', says Jan. 'A lot of it, I thought, was because they were very similar. They both had a short fuse in some situations, they were both anti-establishment, they were always right.'

Syd, however, was more easygoing. Often he'd come home, still in his KLM uniform, sit down at the piano and plunk out a tune. Things changed for Syd, however, in 1962, when KLM ended the cargo run and he lost his job. Syd eventually found another role, working in cargo with Qantas, but he was no longer a boss and the pay was less. He would slowly work his way back up the ladder before retiring in 1976.

Though undeniably his mother's son, Jon inherited a couple of traits from Syd. One was his reluctance to deal with confrontation. He just wanted everyone to be happy: a noble aim but often an impossible task. In Syd's case, if a drama arose, he'd either noodle away quietly on the piano or head off to the garage to tinker with his cars.

Another trait that Syd would pass along to Jon was his inclination to perspire. 'He'd hardly have to move at all,' said Jan, 'and it would pour off him.' Jon's sweatiness would prove to be a curse for his fellow musicians.

While at school, Jon befriended the Plavsic brothers, Peter and Alex. Both were budding musicians. A bond was formed — a bond that strengthened even further when Jon, like so many other teenagers, had his 'Road to Damascus' moment in 1964, inside the tin shed they called the Sydney Stadium.

No phenomenon rivalled The Beatles in 1964: not all-conquering, fast-talking prize fighter Cassius Clay; not Hollywood's royal couple, Elizabeth Taylor and Richard Burton; not even the early moves of the space race, as Russia and the US stretched their Cold War rivalry all the way to the Moon. Nothing came anywhere near the global appeal of The Beatles. They were, in the words of their own John Lennon, 'the toppermost of the poppermost'.

And their timing couldn't have been better. Almost a decade earlier, swivel-hipped Memphis truck driver Elvis Aaron Presley had gyrated his way into the hearts and minds of teenagers the world over, but now Elvis was stuck on the Hollywood treadmill, making embarrassing B-grade movies, his future rotting away thanks to the short-sightedness and paranoia of his manager, 'Colonel' Tom Parker, and Elvis's growing dependence on pills. And the star of many of Elvis's peers had also faded: pompadoured screamer Little Richard had found God (while crossing the Hunter River in Newcastle, no less), piano pounder Jerry Lee Lewis had been 'outed' for marrying his underage cousin and was in disgrace. Buddy Holly and Richie 'La Bamba' Valens, meanwhile, were now playing in rock'n'roll heaven, having both boarded a doomed Beechcraft Bonanza on a snowy Iowa night in 1959. Johnny O'Keefe, Australia's first homegrown rock'n'roll star — who'd come to play a role in the Jon English story — was also in decline, a victim of mental health issues, generational change and a horrible car crash that just about killed him.

The time was ripe for a new sensation and The Beatles, four mop-topped, working-class Liverpudlians — who were much savvier characters and better musicians than many people realised — absolutely exploded into the pop stratosphere in 1964. Their sound had been honed in the bloodhouses of Hamburg; it was raw and primal and unashamedly sexual. John Lennon and Paul McCartney could make a simple 'yeah yeah yeah' sound like the raunchiest come-on ever heard.

The Beatles were funny and they were cool, at a time when that word was more typically used to describe the weather. Blokes wanted to dress like them and learn how to play the electric guitar, while girls wanted to — well, they made their intentions clear at The Beatles' chaotic shows, where they'd scream themselves hoarse, or seek adventures in numerous hotel rooms and at the back of stages as the 'Fab Four' traversed the globe like modern-day Roman conquerors.

When the Beatles toured Australia in the winter of 1964, fifteen-year-old Jon English would become their latest convert. He and Jan saw them play at the Sydney Stadium. Until then, Jon had been a Shadows man, a big fan of the English instrumentalists led by the bespectacled Hank Marvin, a master of the Fender Stratocaster. But now Jon was a Beatles convert; The Shadows were yesterday's men.

The 1964 Beatles tour featured a couple of key future players in the Jon English story. The Australian promoter who secured the tour was Kenn Brodziak, from Aztec Services, who had famously booked the band, purely by chance, in 1963, before they became global stars. The prescient Brodziak acquired them at the fee of £1500 per week — an absolute steal by mid-1964. (Beatles manager Brian Epstein dug in and upped the fee to £2500, which was still incredibly low — they were being offered 40 times that amount for American shows.)

Competing with Brodziak for The Beatles tour had been a rival company named Pan Pacific Productions, run by an ambitious Kiwi, now based in Sydney, named Harry M. Miller. Back in New Zealand he'd promoted tours by Del Shannon and The Everly Brothers; he'd also brought The Beach Boys to Oz as part of the Surfside '64 tour. Miller, whose business partners were Keith and Denis Wong, owners of the Chequers nightclub and numerous other Sydney venues, was a very persuasive man, the kind of operator who could sell ice to the Eskimos — and at a healthy profit. But he lost out on The Beatles to Brodziak, who was currently the luckiest guy in the entertainment biz.

Harry M., however, would hit the big time in the next few years, when he shifted his attention to the theatre.

One of the bands supporting The Beatles on their Australian tour was an instrumental outfit known as Sounds Incorporated, managed by Brian Epstein. Just a few years later a fresh-faced Brit named Trevor White would join the group and, when they fell apart during a tour of

Australia, he'd decide to stay. White, like Harry M. Miller, would play a prominent part in the world of Jon English soon enough.

Beatle George Harrison remembered their 1964 Sydney shows as 'a drag' — the band were almost torn to shreds when they ran through the crowd to reach the stage — but what Jon could hear beyond the screams, and see through the chaos brought on by rabid fans and a clunky revolving stage that sometimes refused to revolve, was life changing.

'I want to be one of them,' he told Jan as they left the stadium, the audience's screams still ringing in their ears.

'Bang,' Jon recalled in 2009, 'it was an epiphany. It was earth shattering, the stuff of mythology.' And Jon wasn't alone; at the same show were the Gibb brothers — Barry, Maurice and Robin — as well as migrant hostel boys George and Malcolm Young. They all, too, underwent a life-changing experience that night.

Back at home, he and Jan would dissect The Beatles' songs, working out their harmonies. Syd would tell them what chords the band used, then show Jon how to play the songs on guitar. Jon also started listening to a lot of other British pop: The Who became a particular favourite. Jon saw them play at the Sydney Stadium, with the Small Faces, in 1968. The Who's lanky, windmilling guitarist Pete Townshend became one of his heroes, as did their husky-voiced, streetwise vocalist Roger Daltrey.

Talk-show host Ray Martin once asked Jon about his rock'n'roll conversion. 'When the first Beatles record came out puberty was running rampant in my body, with the pimples and the hormones going nuts,' Jon explained. 'I was starting to look at girls in a different way — and starting to listen to the radio. "She Loves You" was a hit and I was just gone from that point on. There I was, in front of the mirror with the tennis racquet. I got lost to rock'n'roll.'

It also didn't escape Jon how frantically The Beatles' female admirers reacted to the group and their music. When Jon became a musician, he found the job came with its benefits: 'I found I could pull more birds.'

Now in his teens, Jon (still known as Jonathan) was attending Cabramatta High School. To him it was all about 'dust and flies in summer . . . no school lunches and big, echoing classrooms with young teachers'. He also recalled 'walking to school in 120 degrees of midsummer swelter when my voice was breaking and I was too embarrassed to talk'.

Jon started growing his hair, in part to hide his big ears, which led to plenty of teasing. ('Hey Dumbo,' was the usual taunt.) But Jon's shoulder-length mane led to some lively encounters, as the west of Sydney wasn't the most enlightened place in the early 1960s. 'I can remember running like a dog through Canley Heights,' he told *After Dark* TV show host Donnie Sutherland (whose midnight eyes almost rivalled Jon's), 'because I had long hair.'

It may not have won favour with some of the locals, but Jon's looks — not just his shaggy mane, but his dark, soulful eyes and tall frame — won him his share of female admirers at high school. He was also something of a gun sportsman, which didn't hurt. On top of that he was a prefect and a house captain, a big man on campus. And so what if Sheila treated these privileges with a snort of derision?

Still, Jan, who described the teenage Jon as 'tall, dark, untidy, [with] a broken nose', was a bit shocked to see inscriptions carved into desks at Cabramatta High that read: 'I love Jonathan English.' She couldn't quite believe it was the same Jon English.

Jon's broken nose was the result of a clash on the footy field; his passion for league would be lifelong and profound. He played for Cabramatta High, and was picked for the NSW Schoolboys team. Parramatta would always be his team, even if they were perennial cellar-dwellers in the highly competitive Sydney first-grade comp of the 1960s. (They won just two of their eighteen games in 1960 and only three from eighteen in 1961.)

'It's a tough stigma, following Parramatta,' Jon said. That would improve in the years to follow.

Basketball was another good outlet for Jon; it helped him shake off his usual teenage concerns about how people saw him, and what they thought of him. Jon wrote about how he spent many high school years 'freezing and sweating my way through 100,000 different basketball games, where you could lose juvenile anxieties in the madness of the moment'.

While in high school, Jon showed his flair for writing, penning a bizarre, futuristic short story that drew on his interest in sci-fi. It was published in the 1967 edition of *Thuruna*, the Cabramatta High School magazine. It ran alongside reports from the school's swimming carnival ('Cathy Douglas and John English [*sic*] were very happy to receive the trophy for the winning house' — Jon was house captain), essays ('Has poetry a place in modern society?', 'The supposed origin of detective stories', 'Should final exams be abolished?') and ads for such local companies as Toyland and M. Fiorelli of Cabramatta, 'wine and spirits merchants and continental delicacies'. Jon's story, titled 'Automatic funeral', was a world apart from everything else in *Thuruna*:

When Johnny finally came staggering home, the machinemen were there to meet him. They had taken over and no-one noticed. After all, machines and computers are so much more efficient than bodies and brains. 'Progress' I believe it's called by the big boys. But what of the 'lay'? Around here it's called 'instant depression'. But that's another story completely, to the little bowler-hatted men with wheels where brains used to be. They are the organisers.

Everywhere are the silent electronic miniaturised black-box judo champs. Everyone is a set of programmed reactions saying, 'Hold me baby, you fuse me!!' Your factory needs you.

So Johnny marries a nice respectable girl and settles down. Until, one day, the blower hats come round to change his wife's tapes. And Johnny runs screaming into the street where there are twenty thousand identical nationalities — 32 folk singers are holding a song fiesta. They sing him to death.

Jonathan J. English, 6B

Jon met Carmen Sora when they were both students at Cabramatta High; Jon was in Year 12, Carmen in Year 11. It was raining when they first met, and Jon and his mate Lonnie shared their umbrellas with Carmen and her friend Sandra. Carmen knew about Jon but they'd never spoken before. 'Everyone knew Jon — he was quite striking looking, a good sportsman,' she recalled. Jon, despite being a big man on campus, couldn't bring himself to ask Carmen out, so instead he deputised Alex Plavsic, who was in many of Carmen's classes. 'Jon was too nervous to do it himself,' Carmen laughed.

Up until then, as Jan recalled, 'We used to say that any girlfriend took third place, after basketball and music.' That soon changed. Carmen's family was Estonian and quite traditional: Estonian food was served at home, and her people were religious (unlike Jon's). Most of Carmen's closest girlfriends were also Estonian.

Carmen's parents, her father Lembit and mother Benita, had met in Germany in a displaced persons camp; when they emigrated to Australia in late 1949, they had three children, a son and two daughters. Carmen was born in the Parkes Migrant Hostel, the family's first Australian home, in May 1950. Soon after, the Soras settled in

Cabramatta, on a quarter-acre block. Carmen's father, who'd learned the building trade after they relocated to Australia, built the family home on Lord Street. The Soras fitted comfortably in Cabramatta, populated as it was with 'new Australians' — Latvians, Estonians, Italians, Greeks, Germans.

'It was a very cosmopolitan area,' Carmen said. 'I grew up speaking Estonian and learned English later. From the age of about five, we'd go into Surry Hills every Saturday morning to Estonian House. There'd be lessons for the children about Estonia, the culture, the language. There were choirs. I joined the Brownies and then the Girl Guides; they were all Estonian kids from around Sydney. We did live partly in the Estonian society, but once I started going to school, my main language was English. I'd only speak to my parents in Estonian.'

When she started dating Jon, Carmen got on especially well with Syd English. Everyone got along with Syd. When Carmen came to see Jon, she'd spend just as much time in the garage with his dad as Syd tinkered with his cars. 'That was his escape,' Carmen recalled. 'He'd wake up, have breakfast and then straight out to the garage. I learned a lot about motor mechanics.'

Sheila, however, was a tougher nut to crack — Carmen admitted to being 'terrified' by Jon's mother. 'She could be quite nasty. It took a long time for me to feel comfortable around her. She was quite a volatile person, but very intelligent.' It took years before, in Carmen's words, Sheila 'really mellowed out' and they grew reasonably close.

Dave Haley was another budding musician; he was dating Carmen's friend Sandra and spent a lot of time with Jon and his new partner. 'He was very much in love with Carmen,' Haley said. 'That was the big one.' As for Jon, Haley remembered him as 'good company. You'd have great, deep philosophical conversations with him about music, politics, religion. You always looked forward to seeing Jon.'

CHAPTER 4

'This is the dawning of the age of a hairy ass . . .'

It wasn't strictly The Beatles who inspired Jon to learn about music and start playing in bands. His friends from the Villawood Migrant Hostel — Scottish-born George Young, who was dark and short, and Dutchman Johannes van den Berg, who was blond and tall — had formed a band with Stephen Wright, who lived near the hostel, drummer Gordon Fleet, a resident of the East Hills Migrant Hostel, and Dingeman van der Sluijs, another Dutch expat not long out of the hostel. Fleet rechristened himself 'Snowy', van den Berg became Harry Vanda, van der Sluijs morphed into Dick Diamonde, and The Easybeats were born.

By 1965, on the strength of the breakout hits 'She's So Fine' and 'Wedding Ring', and some savvy handling by Ted Albert, the scion of the Alberts music empire — its fortune built on selling sheet music and the Boomerang harmonica — they'd become Australia's answer to The Beatles.

'Easyfever' swept the country like wildfire; the hysteria and mayhem at their shows rivalled the mayhem seen during The Beatles tour. Their live sets rarely made it to the 30-minute mark without stage invasions, police intervention and a hefty body count of fans who'd passed out from the sheer thrill of seeing their idols up close. To Jon, this was different from The Beatles, because he actually knew these guys. They had similar backgrounds; they were suburban battlers, working class. Jon had once jammed at the hostel with Harry Vanda — his friend Peter Plavsic had even been offered a spot in the band before George Young joined. The Easybeats were more tangible, more real than The Beatles. And they were also good musicians, something that was sometimes overlooked amid the madness.

'They were a shining light,' Jon said. 'See, we can do it. Radio will play local product.'

The Easybeats' success motivated Jon to take the big step from bedroom guitarist to aspiring muso. He'd already written his first song, a ditty named 'Old Wives' Tale', when he was fourteen. But the big business, especially in the suburbs of Sydney, wasn't in originals; it was a covers circuit, where groups were expected to master, and mimic, the hits of the moment.

Jon's first band was called Zenith — they were all students at Cabramatta High. The first song Jon played on stage was The Beatles' version of 'Twist and Shout'. Zenith found regular work at a local venue called the Blue Fountain, in Fairfield (near where a plinth now stands, dedicated to Jon). 'We used to play there three or four nights a week,' Jon said in 2011. 'We weren't very good, but there was a market for it, people wanted to come out and dance to live music.'

When Zenith ran out of puff, Jon began playing with his friend Peter ('Pep') Plavsic on bass, Graham Ford on guitar and Richard Lillico on drums. Jon sang and played rhythm guitar. Ford was the first to experience what would become a bugbear for all of Jon's guitarists: his extreme sweatiness. 'Jon would always sweat a lot,' said Ford. 'As a lead guitarist, we would share microphones. His hair would be covered in sweat, his nose would be running and then he'd go *whoom!* and shake it all over me.' (Jon didn't just sweat on stage, as his son Jonathan recalled. 'Dad would sweat at inopportune moments of slightly careful thinking. If he had to check the oil in the lawn mower, or something like that, he'd sweat buckets.')

Jon, even then, was a heavy smoker. A smoke, to Jon, was a 'snout'. 'Hey, Fordy,' he'd say to the guitarist, 'let's go have a snout.'

'I've never seen anyone smoke as much as Jon, and I'm a smoker myself,' said Ford. 'He'd go through 60 a day. Non-stop.' Jon's eating habits were almost as voracious as his smoking: 'Jon could eat a hamburger in one mouthful,' Ford insisted.

———

Two key events took place in Jon's life during 1969. He and Carmen were married in September, settling into a granny flat at the rear of a house in Cabramatta, near the train station. Meanwhile, on the music front, Jon's latest band, the Sebastian Hardie Blues Band — or simply Sebastian Hardie — was hired to back local rock legend Johnny O'Keefe. Both Plavsic brothers were now in the band — Alex played drums — along with Jon and Graham Ford.

JOK, as he was known to many Australians, wasn't quite the star he'd once been back in the heady days of the Sydney Stadium, when he'd frequently upstage big international acts. He'd recently been hit with a hefty tax bill of $70,000 and his first marriage had ended badly. His career wasn't in much better shape — he had been usurped at the top of the pile by a wave of new, younger, 'hipper' acts, among them Billy Thorpe, Johnny Farnham and Russell Morris, whose remarkable single, 'The Real Thing', was the biggest local hit of the year, spending almost six months in the charts. In the past few years, JOK had cut just one hit single, 'She's My Baby'. But JOK was a workhorse; he'd play upwards of 200 gigs a year, which is where Jon and the others came in.

In order to reduce costs, O'Keefe hired young, hungry musicians, and Sebastian Hardie was the latest in a succession of backing groups. O'Keefe was a hard taskmaster and always made very clear to his musicians what their obligations were to him and to the audience. 'This is the Johnny O'Keefe show,' he'd state. 'It has to be bigger and better than anything else they've seen before.'

Ever the control freak, he'd even school his backing bands in the art of the 'long chord'. 'After each song,' he'd instruct, 'I will speak the last words of the song — say, "She's My Baby", for example — and then you guys play a long major chord, while I take a bow. Got it?'

If someone like Jon was brave enough to question O'Keefe, he'd put them straight: 'You have to understand an audience,' he would say. 'A long chord tells an audience that the song is over and it's time to applaud. With most other kinds of ending, they're not sure if the song's over. Then they don't clap as loudly — they get confused. And I don't like soft clapping.'

JOK might have been a rock'n'roll dictator, yet it proved to be an invaluable experience for Jon and his friends. While backing O'Keefe, they'd play rural tent shows, which required short, sharp twenty-minute sets — O'Keefe boasted of having played 28 sets in one day at the Sydney Royal Easter Show. They'd also play far-flung clubs and country fairs, wherever JOK could get a gig. They really got the chance to refine their craft — and also witness a master entertainer from close range.

Jon would sometimes speak about JOK with his brother Jeremy. 'He always said that the stint with Johnny O'Keefe was where he first got a sense of how you can work a big crowd,' Jeremy recalled. 'It was definitely a bit of an eye-opener. It was the first time he was exposed to a real old-style entertainer. No one was there to see the band — they were there to see JOK.'

Most gigs would open with Sebastian Hardie playing a few songs, then

Jon would hand the mic over to O'Keefe. Jon would move to keyboards and sing backing vocals for the rest of the night. It wasn't strictly a comfortable fit; JOK needed a show band, nothing flashy, while, according to guitarist Graham Ford, 'we were trying to be the Stones'. And JOK had strict rules for his backing band — he insisted they wear dinner suits on stage. Jon, ever the rebel, wore his with sandshoes, only just hidden by his billowing flared trousers.

JOK didn't take to Jon; to him, he was just another longhair trying to steal his limelight. 'JOK didn't like having Jon around,' said Jan. 'He wanted the rest of the band, not Jon — Jon sang better than him.' But Jon did learn one vital lesson from the old master: no matter how small the crowd or how dingy the venue, O'Keefe did not leave the stage until he had the audience on their feet.

Being part of Sebastian Hardie brought out different sides of Jon's musical personality. Given the band's love of early Stones records, Jon learned to play a mean blues harp, modelling himself on Brian Jones. This really came to the fore when they covered such songs as 'Little Red Rooster', which had been a breakthrough hit for the Stones in 1965.

One of the bigger gigs that Sebastian Hardie got to play was an open-air concert staged in the suburb of Liverpool. Headlining the show was pop band Sherbet, whose star was beginning to rise. Jon and the band took the stage and began to play, but they could barely hear themselves; the sound was terrible.

'Turn the fucking foldback up!' Jon roared into the microphone, but nothing happened. Things changed, however, when Sherbet took the stage.

'Suddenly,' said Graham Ford, 'it was like a plane taking off.'

Jon was incensed; clearly, Sherbet had sabotaged their mix. And he intended to sort out the problem. As Ford recalled, 'I saw Jon walking over to the side of the stage, shouting. It was the first time I'd seen him angry.'

———

Jon first met one of his most frequent and successful collaborators on New Year's Eve 1969, during a Sebastian Hardie gig in Wollongong, at Wonderland, a converted bowling alley. Mario Millo was a curly-haired guitar prodigy from an Italian family living in Sydney's western suburbs. He was not yet fifteen. Millo was playing with The Menu, a covers act that worked with Jim Towers' Cordon Bleu booking agency, who also booked gigs for Sebastian Hardie. The young Millo had started playing live around the same time as Jon and in the same neighbourhood, treading the boards for the first time, aged nine, at Canley Vale nightclub The Village.

The paths of Jon and Millo had almost crossed a few months earlier, when both bands signed up for the 1969 2SM Pepsi Pop Poll, a precursor to the Hoadley's Battle of the Sounds band competition. When Millo noted that Sebastian Hardie was among the competition, he shrugged and accepted his fate: 'I thought, "Wow, this band sounds fantastic; they'll win for sure." They were already a working band.'

But Sebastian Hardie didn't make the final at Sydney Stadium because they were booked to play on a cruise liner and dropped out of the running. The Menu won the event.

On New Year's Eve in Wollongong, Millo was standing side stage when Sebastian Hardie began playing. 'There's this gangly, tall guy with black eyes, and I'm mesmerised,' said Millo. 'They were playing "Aquarius" from *Hair* and I did a double take because at the chorus, Jon has gone: "This is the dawning of the age of a hairy ass."'

Millo wasn't sure he'd heard right, so he waited until the next chorus, and sure enough, Jon did it again.

'He had a deadpan face; he didn't react. I'm pretty sure it went over the audience's head. I was just a kid and I thought, "This guy's cool."'

Jon would also tweak the lyrics of Traffic's 'Hole in My Shoe'; rather than singing the line 'Was letting in water', he'd keep a poker face and declare, 'I'm fucking your daughter'.

'We were young and we had such confidence,' said Graham Ford. 'That night we walked on stage and it was all over for everyone else. It was incredible what Jon could do.'

Jon was just as impressed when The Menu played, because part of their set was playing the entire second side of The Beatles' *Abbey Road*, a challenge for any band. Jon's jaw dropped; they were pretty damned good. And who was the kid on guitar? Jon introduced himself after their set.

'And that's how we met,' said Millo.

From that point on, the two bands shared a lot of bills, playing in various Sydney suburbs and some high school shows, mainly on weekends. As for Mario Millo, he became an important English collaborator, and a close friend.

There was a considerable age gap — Jon was 20 and Mario not even 15, but 'there was a mutual respect,' said Millo.

CHAPTER 5

'If they ever put that show on,
I want to play Judas.'

J on nurtured dreams of playing Judas Iscariot in *Jesus Christ Superstar* long before the stage show made it to producer Harry M. Miller's wish list. Jan had returned from a trip to visit family in the UK with a copy of the soundtrack album from the original 1970 recording and Jon fell hard for the songs of Tim Rice and Andrew Lloyd Webber.

The British pair were struggling songwriters and had composed the entire 'rock opera' in a week — famously, Lloyd Webber had scrawled the idea for the title track on the back of a napkin. Tim Rice admitted that he thought the Bible's version of Judas was a 'cardboard cut-out figure of evil', so he strived to humanise Judas more for *Superstar*.

'In the Bible,' Rice told a reporter, 'there is absolutely no motivation for Judas, other than that he is sort of a 100 per cent figure of evil. And it seemed to me that that was probably not the case.'

Jon was particularly drawn to the way 24-year-old Londoner Murray Head — later of 'One Night in Bangkok' fame — immersed himself in the character of Judas and such standout numbers as 'Superstar' and 'Heaven on Their Minds'. These were songs Jon could imagine himself singing; soon enough he'd be doing just that during Sebastian Hardie gigs.

Jon wasn't even vaguely religious, although he wasn't then an atheist.

'I like an each-way bet,' he admitted. (Later in life, though, according to his brother Jeremy, Jon would call himself an atheist.)

Jon preferred at that time to think of himself as a polytheist, someone who accepted that there could be any number of deities. Jon had read the Bible but thought of organised religion as little more than 'mythology', 'great fiction' and 'not something to build a life around'. He was more intrigued by the relationship and the conflict between Judas and Jesus, a central theme of *Jesus Christ Superstar*.

'[Judas is] the guy with the questions and Jesus is the guy with the answers,' Jon said. 'They're both more or less pawns in a game, a game designed to make Jesus a martyr in order to unite the Jews.'

Lloyd Webber and Rice had trouble pitching their show to Broadway producers — one potential producer told them that the concept was 'the worst idea in history'. The original Broadway production of *Jesus Christ Superstar*, which opened in October 1971, came about only because the album had been a success: it topped the US *Billboard* charts and peaked at number 6 in Australia, charting for almost three years. In the decade after its initial release, it went on to sell eight million copies worldwide.

Superstar was still running on Broadway when murmurs of an Australian production started to circulate in 1972. The Broadway production featured some radical choices; to play Judas, the producers chose popular actor Ben Vereen. (He'd also appeared in *Hair*'s original Broadway run.) Casting an African American was a bold move, something that caught the attention of Harry M. Miller when it came to finding the right talent for the Australian production of *Superstar*.

Miller's fortunes had improved significantly since missing out on The Beatles in 1964. He'd bought out his partners, the Wong brothers, in 1967, and renamed his business Harry M. Miller Attractions, partnered up with his old adversary Kenn Brodziak, and promoted shows by such hot international acts as The Monkees, Eric Burdon and the Animals, and Jon's heroes The Who (in a 1968 tour that ended in such chaos that prime minister John Gorton reportedly wrote to Pete Townshend and insisted that he and his band never return). Perhaps a tad scarred by that experience, in June 1969 Miller shifted his gaze from rock'n'roll to rock opera, staging the debut Australian production of *Hair*, whose cast included John Waters and Reg Livermore. They'd both go on to become household names, as well as peers and friends of Jon English.

Hair broke local box office records, at the same time drawing A-list crowds. And the show generated unbeatable publicity with its onstage nudity, drug use and other controversies — even a legendary creator of controversies like Miller couldn't have dreamed of better press. Due to its strong language, the cast album was banned in Queensland and New Zealand. *Hair* was a must-see show, not just for regular punters but for artists, celebrities and politicians. Sydney's *Daily Mirror*, upon spotting numerous familiar faces in the foyer, declared that *Hair* offered 'two shows for the price of one'. It was an *event*.

Among the cast of *Hair* was a sixteen-year-old African American named Marcia Elaine Hines, who'd been spotted by director Jim Sharman when he was in the US scouting talent. Hines had an interesting bloodline: her cousins included future US secretary of state Colin Powell and gender-bending performer/model Grace Jones. Because of her age, Hines agreed that Miller would become her legal guardian. Miller recoiled, however, when he was described as a 'father figure' to Hines. 'For a start,' he wrote in his memoir, *Confessions of a Not-So-Secret Agent*, 'I'm only nineteen years older than her!'

Hines discovered that she was pregnant while working in *Hair*, and gave birth to a daughter, Dohnyale (Deni), in September 1970. She was back on stage nine days later.

Twenty-five-year-old NIDA graduate Sharman, whom Miller would hire again to direct *Jesus Christ Superstar*, had an equally unusual background. He was the son of legendary 'boxing tent' impresario Jimmy Sharman, a formidable character who'd often step into the ring and referee the fights he staged all over the country. Midnight Oil and Cold Chisel would write songs in honour of Sharman's boxers.

Hair ran in Australia for two years and gave Miller all the motivation — and money in the bank — that he needed to stage *Jesus Christ Superstar*.

It was Jon's brother Jeremy who spotted a casting call for a local production of *Jesus Christ Superstar* in the newspaper. Jon had been expressing his love of *Superstar* for some time.

'If they ever put that show on,' Jon informed Jeremy, 'I want to play Judas.'

Carmen, too, understood Jon's love of *Superstar*. 'He would play the soundtrack nonstop so I knew he was desperate to either be in it or see it.' Jon was no fool — he could see that Judas had all the best songs, such as 'Heaven on Their Minds' and 'Superstar'. It was a great role. But what chance did he have of being cast? He was an unknown.

At the time Jon was biding his time in an office job at Mauri Brothers and Thompson, an import/export company in Waterloo, a few kilometres south of the city. Somehow he snagged a job in the accounting department, which to this day makes Carmen laugh: 'God knows why, because he was hopeless with money.' He was also playing Sebastian Hardie gigs at night.

After school he'd enrolled at uni, but later claimed it was nothing more than a ruse to avoid being conscripted into the army and shipped off to Vietnam. He had enrolled through a teachers' scholarship program at the University of New South Wales, which paid $35 a week, but he rarely (if ever) showed up for classes — although he played intervarsity basketball for the university team.

But he gave up on his teaching degree after a year, when he had a moment of career clarity. 'I found myself looking in a mirror trying to imagine myself being a teacher,' Jon said when interviewed on the TV show *After Dark*. 'That was enough. It wasn't going to happen. I walked out of the class and got the bus back to Cabramatta.'

He'd actually left uni before conscription was abolished, but put his faith in what his mother, Sheila, saw as the hopelessness of bureaucracy. Whenever another letter would arrive, requesting that he attend a physical, Jon would tear it up and throw it in the bin.

There was, however, a little more to the story, as Jan English explained.

'What Jon did was that every time he'd be told to be somewhere and do something regarding conscription, he'd say, "Don't worry, I'll be there" — and he'd never turn up. He did that about four or five times. He passed the medical the first time, but after not showing up four or five times, they gave him another medical and failed him.

'They said he couldn't breathe properly because of his broken nose, and that his arches were too high. If he wore army boots it would be really bad for his feet. But I think they just gave up.'

Jon took every possible step to ensure he didn't get conscripted; he even told a recruitment officer that Carmen couldn't handle the stress of him being in the army. 'I had to go and have sessions with a psychologist,' Carmen recalled. 'There was nothing wrong with me; it was just a ploy to get him out of the army. We were all anti-Vietnam.'

'I hid for a while in plain sight,' Jon explained in 2009, 'and then waited for Gough [Whitlam] to get elected.'

He may have joked about it, but conscription was a matter of deadly concern for Jon and his friends, as Dave Haley admitted. 'We were anti-war, even then. Our parents had gone to war, but this was wrong — we knew it was wrong. Jon wasn't going to go under any circumstances.' Public sentiment about the war was shifting, too; Jon's attitude wasn't unusual.

'We were freaking out,' said Graham Ford. Fortunately, none of them was called up.

Jon's father Syd, and Sheila to some extent, had trouble understanding Jon's resistance, but Jon would argue about what he saw as the pointlessness of the Vietnam War. 'Of course our parents didn't really understand this,' said Jan, who was studying at the University of Sydney and marched in the anti-Vietnam moratoriums. 'They'd both fought in World War II. They couldn't understand why Jon wouldn't want to fight, and he'd say, "I don't agree with it. It's got nothing to do with me." Syd would say, "But your country is at war, you should go and fight." Jon simply said, "No."'

Jon's Cabramatta neighbour, Gough Whitlam, was elected prime minister in 1972 and promptly abolished National Service. Jon was now out of the firing line, quite literally, and ready for *Superstar*.

Jon harboured no grand plans for his *Superstar* audition, or for any type of professional career in showbiz. Neither did his Sebastian Hardie bandmates. 'As a band, at that age, all we wanted to do was play,' said Peter Plavsic. 'To get paid was a bonus.'

Jon once spoke about what might have happened if he'd even suggested a life in music to his school's career advisor: 'He would have laughed.' Both Jon and Peter would get home from Sebastian Hardie gigs, sleep for a few hours and then head off to work. (Plavsic was a high school teacher, barely older than his students.)

'I never thought of music as a career,' Jon explained. 'I always thought of it as a bit of extra pocket money. I never dreamed that high.'

Carmen remembered it that way too. 'Jon was in a garage band. He wasn't really dreaming of being an entertainer.'

Superstar was about to change all that, although Jon went into the auditions with low expectations. 'Off we toddled to see what would happen,' Jon once wrote about his *Superstar* audition in a blog, 'with dreams of maybe getting into the chorus, or at least running into someone famous.' His brother Jeremy decided that he would also audition.

They woke early one Saturday morning and drove into the city, a long haul from Cabramatta, eventually reaching the site of the auditions: the Phillip Street Theatre. But the theatre was closed. The brothers stood outside, wondering what the hell was going on. Had they missed out?

They had the day wrong. The audition was on the Sunday. When they arrived at 11am on the right day, they were greeted, as Jon wrote, 'by a rather hassled looking woman at a desk taking names of auditioners and other assorted hopeful people. Jem and I dutifully gave our names and Mum and Dad's phone number, imagining that it would go no further.' On the form, Jon wrote that he'd like to audition for Judas. He didn't know that some 2000 others also applied for the role.

Jon and Jeremy walked into the foyer, which was packed, and found themselves surrounded by, in Jon's words, 'hairy, biblical types, all standing on their heads or doing some other sorts of weird hippie-type yoga stuff. They all seemed to know each other, which really added to the complete sense of isolation.'

There were, however, 'quite a few guitar player/singers there as well,' Jon wrote, 'so there were the obligatory happy-clapping impromptu singalongs. This, along with the drifting scent of dope and tobacco gave the whole thing the impression more of a party than a serious job opportunity.'

Jon found himself seated next to Trevor White, a fellow expat Pom, who'd been living in Australia for the past few years. ''Ow you going? All right?' Jon said to White.

'We got chatting,' White recalled, 'and he was very outgoing. We probably calmed each other's nerves. The most striking thing about Jon was how friendly and enthusiastic he was. I got a sense of his energy.'

The mood changed when an ABC TV crew arrived. After conferring with one of Miller's staff, a producer asked the gathering: 'Who's auditioning for Jesus? And would anyone mind being filmed while they audition?'

'The whole atmosphere went from being a sort of egotist's convention to a sentencing hearing,' Jon later observed. 'I found out later that it was not the done thing to interrupt your audition with cameras, interviews and other distractions while you were trying to woo the producers.'

Jon was the only one to raise his hand. Jeremy motioned to stop him — he was about to remind Jon that he was auditioning for Judas when Jon covered his mouth with his hand. To hell with the others, he figured, this was too good an opportunity to miss. It was TV!

His audition, though, proved to be tricky. When Jon's name was called, the accompanist asked what music he'd brought with him.

'Erm, none,' Jon replied with a shrug. 'I thought I was supposed to do something from the show.'

'No, not necessarily,' he was told. 'We just want to hear you sing. So do you have any music?'

Jon went ahead and sang two pieces from *Superstar* that he knew inside out: 'Gethsemane', one of Jesus's songs from the second act, and 'Heaven on Their Minds', as the ABC camera rolled. When a report on *Superstar* ran on the evening news, Jon's singing voice could be heard quite clearly in the background.

Jon may have been forced to wing his audition, but as a relative unknown he didn't realise how lucky he was. Producer Miller and director Sharman, who were seated in the theatre that day, had agreed that *Superstar* wouldn't work with well-known actors; they sought a more unique look for their cast. 'We had decided that most of the actors in Australia sucked,' stated Miller. 'We decided to go out into the street where the real people were.'

Purely by chance, Jon's timing was perfect — he was untrained as both a singer and an actor, and those dark eyes gave him a certain sinister quality. No one looked like Jon; he was a genuine curiosity. When he stepped onto the stage for his audition, wearing what Miller remembered as a 'weird suit, stovepipe trousers and winkle-picker shoes', Jon had exactly the out-there look that both producer and director felt was perfect. Jon wasn't some jaded thespian; he was every inch the rocker on day leave from his band.

Miller and Sharman nudged each other in the darkness of the theatre.

'There's our Judas,' Miller said, motioning to Jon on the stage. Later, he said that he was drawn to Jon's 'haunted look'. 'And he sang wonderfully,' Miller clarified.

That may have been true, but Jon wasn't offered the part straightaway. One of the staff casting the show pulled Jon aside after his audition.

'We've got you on a recall — can you wait for five hours?'

'Yes,' Jon replied without a moment's hesitation.

(Jeremy was given a 'We'll be in touch' response, which he knew was a rejection, but he still had to wait around for Jon.)

Jon was his mother's son in some ways; he always enjoyed embellishing a story. In one version of events that he'd relate, he insisted that after his first audition he never returned to his office job. In another variation, he was wearing his work clothes during the audition, with his long hair pulled back. (An odd outfit for a Sunday.) Neither was quite the case.

After his second audition, Jon was told, 'Look, we're interested ... can you hang by the phone for the next six weeks?' Casting was to take place all over the country; Sydney had been one stop of many.

Jon went back to Mauri Brothers and Thompson, and to his band, and grew increasingly impatient. When he did finally get the call, he was in for a shock.

'We've got some bad news for you,' Jon was told. 'We can't offer you the role of Jesus' — the casting director had mistakenly thought he craved the lead role — 'but think you'd be right for Judas.'

'I was expecting a role in the choir,' Jon said, 'but I played it cool and said, "If you give me a lot of money I'll be happy." We reached a compromise.' (Jon was originally paid a weekly wage of around $150 for eight shows a week.)

Many years later, Jon said that he got the role, 'Because (a) I could hit the notes enough to do it, and (b) because I look like I could murder my mother.'

Jon's fellow cast members included Trevor White, whom he'd met at the audition, who was cast as Jesus (and would be paid $250 a week for his services). White was just as surprised as Jon when he got the call — when he had said that he wanted to audition for the lead role, a production assistant had actually burst out laughing.

As Jon got to know White, he recognised a kindred spirit; they were both 'expat Pom cynics, who'd gotten into Monty Python at exactly the right time. Things were always funny first.' The famous Python sketch featuring the Gumbys, dimwits whose catchphrase was 'My brain hurts!', was a particular favourite of the pair. The bond between Jon and Trevor made the daunting prospect of eight shows a week just that bit more palatable.

Another key cast member was John Young — soon to become John Paul Young — who'd recently graduated from his days as a pinball prodigy to the pop charts, thanks to a hit cover of Harry Vanda and George Young's 'Pasadena', which they'd co-written with British actor David Hemmings. He was cast as Annas, the high priest of Judea. (Writing in Go-Set, Molly Meldrum described Annas as 'the little priest who hobbles

a lot'.) Stevie Wright, the former Easybeats singer, was cast as Simon
Zealotes, one of Jesus's apostles. 'He was fine, he was great,' Jon said of
Wright, his old buddy from the migrant hostel days. 'He smoked a bit of
dope but it didn't seem to affect him.'

Jon liked a drink but steered clear of pot, unlike much of the cast and
crew. 'It didn't agree with me,' he said. A memo circulated among the
Superstar cast insisting that there be no pot-smoking backstage — with
the exception of Stevie Wright, who best remembered his lines when he
was stoned.

As unlikely as many of these casting choices seemed, they all fitted
perfectly with Miller and Sharman's shared vision of using 'real people'.
Stevie Wright's latest project had been running the menswear department at The House of Merivale. Trevor White had been drifting between
gigs. John Young had only recently retired from a suburban factory
floor — he had the hairnet to prove it. Jon had been doing nine to five
in Waterloo. None had been trained to act.

'But then, I've never taken any singing classes, either,' Jon told a
reporter.

The one thing Jon had failed to do was tell his bandmates in Sebastian
Hardie about his new gig. Until *Superstar* came calling, they'd been working steadily, playing six nights a week, making $80 each — reasonable
money for the time; they'd also been trying to gain the notice of various
local record companies, hoping to sniff out a deal.

One night, when the rest of the band were playing the Sydney venue
Chequers, John Young arrived and told them that Jon had been hired and
that he was finished with the band. They were all a bit stunned.

'Jon was a beautiful guy, and he liked us very much,' explained guitarist
Graham Ford, 'but didn't want a bar of confrontation.'

The relationship between Jon and the guys in Sebastian Hardie
stayed cool for some time, although Jon did persuade Ford to accompany

him to Harry M. Miller's office when he was required to sign his *Superstar* contract.

'Pretend you're my manager,' Jon whispered to him. Ford didn't say a word during the brief meeting; nor did Miller, who gave him the once-over and then focused entirely on Jon, his new star. 'Who is Jon trying to fool with this guy?' he thought.

Jon's casting as Judas Iscariot was his first time in the type of role he'd come to frequent: there was a darkness to the character that Jon found easy to project. Those raccoon eyes didn't hurt, either. 'I think Jim Sharman liked my eyes,' he admitted.

Many, many years down the line, Jon would one day speak about Judas at an event called Men of Letters, staged at The Basement in Sydney's CBD. 'He's a sympathetic character in *Superstar* and the "betrayal" is shown as an inevitability, as in: someone had to do it in order for things to progress,' he observed. 'I'm sure there are many eminent theologians with explanations and theories about the events, but it still remains a bit of a mystery to me.'

Jesus Christ Superstar's Australian debut was set to take place on 16 March 1972, at the Adelaide Festival of Arts. It would be an outdoor, semi-formal event — black tie was optional — before an audience of about 10,000. The show would briefly travel the country before beginning its season in May at Sydney's Capitol Theatre, which would be the first time audiences got to witness the full theatrical production of *Superstar*.

'It's a fairly original, contemporary conception of the role of Jesus and the role of Judas,' Jon said, when it came time to speak with the press. 'Jesus is more or less played as a man and Judas is just played as a guy who likes to see the right thing done.'

He was asked if he thought *Superstar* might return society to a time when religion was conveyed through the theatre as well as the churches. 'I don't think so,' he answered. Jon had a far more pragmatic take on *Superstar*'s intentions. 'In this case it's just a money-making venture. But it is at least making people think about Christianity again.'

And what were his feelings about Christianity and *Superstar*?

'It's bringing Christianity back to the people,' Jon replied, 'rather than having some witchdoctor ritual performed in the church on Sundays. Which is really pretty boring.'

Opening night in Adelaide was going well until the end of the first act, at the moment when Judas betrays Jesus. At this pivotal moment in the story, Jon caught sight of a huge black bat sweeping across the sky, right in front of the illuminated cathedral that overlooked Adelaide Oval. The image was spooky, ominous: was someone trying to tell him something? Then Jon ripped his pants on stage, and not for the last time. (His mother Sheila referred to him as 'bulgy bollocks'.)

These distractions, as it turned out, meant nothing; not even a traffic jam that delayed the opening by an hour could diminish the audience's enthusiasm. They loved *Superstar*. There was no backstage area, so after the show the cast was forced to walk through the crowd, with Jon and Trevor in the lead. As they made their way through the audience, a child's voice could be heard saying, 'Hello, Jesus.'

White was tempted to reply, 'Bless you, son,' but instead smiled and kept on walking.

After the show, Jon laughed that he'd just performed in front of '10,000 penguins' — many took up the black-tie option — but he also admitted that it had been a massive thrill. 'It was a terrific feeling,' he said, even though he nursed a sore throat and a bleeding nose, the result of spending too much time in the Adelaide chill during rehearsals. 'It was knowing it was something I'd always wanted to do but never had the guts to do — and then doing it and knowing it was where I belonged.'

'I've never been part of anything quite as big,' he admitted. 'It was extraordinary.'

'I could see how popular he was in *Superstar*,' said Carmen, who'd found a job in the crew as a dresser, making sure that the costumes for all the principal performers were clean and ready at show time. 'And I knew he absolutely loved it, but I don't think he knew how big it would become.'

Superstar was also a hit with the press, although not so much with the protest groups who'd gathered at the Adelaide site. Protests would shadow the production for much of its life, despite the fact that *Superstar* was doing a good job, albeit accidentally, of selling Jesus and Christianity to a younger, more cynical audience.

'All the loonies came out of the woodwork,' Jon said. 'It was quite a controversial show.' He had actually gotten a taste of what lay ahead after the sound check for opening night. Walking back to their hotel, Jon and Trevor White spotted the group of anti-*Superstar* protestors, who were waving placards and causing a ruckus. Jon, who could be, in White's words, 'a provocative bugger', walked over to the gathering.

'Have you seen the show?' he asked, fully aware that this was impossible.

'Erm, no.'

'Well, what are you protesting about then?' Jon asked. With that, he and White walked away.

US evangelist Billy Graham had railed against the original Broadway production, insisting that 'it bordered on blasphemy and sacrilege', while Melbourne rabbi Prete Swalh, when asked about *Superstar*, offered this: 'I can only say that I deplore the mean and vulgar representation of certain Jewish characters.' Interestingly, Rabbi Swalh did have a good word for Judas: 'To find him shown as a sensible man, a man given to deep thought, rather than the typical traitor, is greatly refreshing.'

Covering *Superstar*'s Adelaide premiere for *The Canberra Times*, W.L. Hoffmann stated that it was 'an unforgettable premiere . . . 120 minutes of shattering sound and kaleidoscopic colour', easily the highlight of the Adelaide Festival.

Yet while Hoffmann praised Trevor White's Jesus ('his performance grew in stature as it proceeded') and Michele Fawdon's Mary Magdalene ('appealing and musically excellent'), Jon didn't impress him.

'Jon English's Judas was hardly up to the standard [of the other principals], a rather wild performance lacking in sufficient depth to sustain Judas as the motivating character.'

Proving that one man's underwhelming Judas was another man's superstar-in-the-making, a reviewer from *The Sydney Morning Herald* picked Jon as the standout. 'JC Superstar . . . should be renamed Judas Iscariot Superstar,' the review claimed. 'Judas, played by Sydney pop singer Jon English, stole the show . . . Leaping around the tiered stage like a demented Mick Jagger, English overwhelmed the gentler character of Jesus.'

The review's headline said it all: 'Judas scene-stealer of the Festival Superstar show.'

Another critic described Jon's performance as 'Judas with balls'. He was even said to outshine Murray Head, who had played Judas on the original soundtrack; that would have given Jon a great thrill. 'The show is worth seeing just to hear this guy sing. Within the confines of the stage, he managed to insinuate his presence like a very fluid spider. Excellent!'

At an afterparty in Adelaide, Jon first met drummer Greg Henson, who was part of the *Superstar* band — they'd go on to play together for the next 40 years. ('I thought, "Who the hell is this bloke? He looks like Dracula,"' Henson remembered.) Another graduate of the Sydney suburban rock circuit, most notably a band named Levi Smith's Clefs, Henson had gotten the job after convincing *Superstar*'s musical director,

Patrick Flynn, that he could read music, even though that was far from the truth. He had studied the *Superstar* album closely by ear and then pretended to read the sheet music during his audition. The gig was great for Henson — he was initially paid $80 a week, a big step up from the $5 per night he got playing live shows in the 'burbs.

Henson was enjoying the free champagne in Adelaide when he stumbled backwards into some foliage, his sheet music flying from his grasp. 'Who picks me up,' Henson recalled, 'but Margaret Whitlam and Bob Hawke. That's where I lost my charts.'

When he told Flynn about his missing sheet music, Flynn 'freaked out', said Henson. 'Don't worry,' Henson reassured him, 'I'll wing it.' Henson didn't miss a note in rehearsals and afterwards Flynn pulled him aside. 'You,' he said, shaking his head, 'are a genius.' Flynn didn't suspect that the drummer had been bluffing all along.

Playing in the band gave Henson a prime position for watching Jon in action. 'Jon was definitely the star of *Superstar*,' said Henson. 'His charisma was incredible. His ego was incredible. That's what drove him. He wanted to be loved by everyone, even if it was the cleaner or the bloke who ran the fish and chip shop around the corner.'

Tellingly, after the rave reviews for *Superstar* were published, almost all praising Jon, the record companies were soon circling. Jon told a *Sydney Morning Herald* reporter that he'd had expressions of interest from eight labels — and he was all too aware that they'd had a change of heart since seeing him in *Superstar*. 'These are the same people who didn't want to know about me when I was knocking on their doors before I got the role.'

Jon intended to get cracking on a solo album when he returned to Sydney. But he had no idea how long *Superstar* would run, or how crucial it would be for his career.

CHAPTER 6

'It was an unreal period.
As long as I kept in my mind it was a job,
I was OK. Don't believe everything
written about you.'

The next step for Jon and the rest of the *Superstar* team was a series of concerts, rather than the full-blown rock opera with all the trappings — they'd keep that on ice until they settled into their Sydney season. After the Adelaide run, these concerts were staged through mid-April, at Perth's King's Park Tennis Club, Festival Hall in Melbourne, Launceston's Princess Theatre and Hobart's City Hall. The Launceston venue, allegedly, was haunted — a piano would sometimes start playing by itself and spooky visions were known to materialise in the actors' dressing rooms. This seemed strangely appropriate for *Superstar*, a controversial show with its fair share of ghosts.

Final concerts at Brisbane's Festival Hall, on 14 and 15 April, were the last before the cast began their season at the Capitol Theatre in Sydney on 4 May.

In theory, these concert-style shows were designed to iron out any kinks before the Sydney run, but the truth was a slightly different matter, as Jon later wrote: 'I think there was a delay in the set being built in

Sydney so [Harry M. Miller] thought he'd earn some money out of us while he was waiting!' Carmen travelled with Jon during the mini-tour, still working as a dresser.

To spruik the Sydney season, Harry M. Miller appeared in a TV ad for *Superstar*, promoting its broad appeal, at the same time doing his best to lessen the controversy it was bound to create. (He'd also used TV to put out a casting call for the show, so he understood the power of the medium.) 'Perhaps once in a lifetime,' Miller said direct to camera, with due portentousness, 'there comes an entertainment phenomenon, a show that gets to the heart of all people, and really moves them.' And then the kicker: *'Jesus Christ Superstar* is such a show — and I think it's important that you see it, with your children.'

In a few smartly chosen words, Miller had made his pitch: *Superstar* was a show for the whole family. This brilliant marketing strategy did the trick and advance sales for the Sydney season quickly reached $425,000; more than 1000 people were unable to get tickets for opening night.

Miller was clearly pleased by his handiwork. 'I have the copyright on Jesus,' he cheekily told a reporter.

He wasn't kidding; when Miller learned that a group of nuns was planning an amateur production of *Superstar* in Newcastle, he hit them with an injunction and had the show shut down.

Miller didn't just have the copyright on Jesus; he also had control of the Capitol Theatre. The Sydney landmark, by then almost 50 years old, had started to slide into financial and physical ruin in the early 1970s. Harry M. acquired the lease of the Capitol from Greater Union Theatres for $2000 a week and ordered that the outside of the theatre be painted *'Superstar* brown'. The theatre was saved.

Jon was struck by Miller's sheer bravado. 'There was a massive ego on the guy — he had three pages in the program.' (And a full-page portrait, cigar clenched between his lips, looking every inch the impresario.) Jon barely rated a few paragraphs, although he did get the chance to learn a few truths about Harry M. in due course.

'Harry's very publicity minded, he was always playing the role of the producer, but he didn't really know what was going on,' Jon told writer Debbie Kruger. 'I'd say, "We need some foldback," and he'd say, "What's that?" And he'd say, "What do you need microphones for?" "We just do, Harry."'

Superstar's production and staging were bold and innovative, far more visually striking than anything staged before in Australia. The designer was Brian Thomson, who'd worked on *Hair* and also ran the London production of *Superstar*, which opened three months after Sydney's.

'There's not much sex and there's not much bloodshed in the life of Christ,' Jon explained to a reporter, once again speaking without a filter. 'You've got to have something to get the people in.'

That something came in the shape of a dodecahedron — a twelve-faced, three-dimensional, hydraulically operated sculptural form that would dominate the Capitol stage. It was mounted on a platform some 1.5 metres high and could be rotated a full 360 degrees. It cost almost $100,000 to create, roughly a third of the production's entire budget. Symbolism aside, the 'dodeca' was also a handy stage device, allowing cast members to materialise on stage or quietly disappear off stage. In a scene in which Jesus preaches to his followers, the dodecahedron would open, like the petals of a flower, allowing the disciples to sit and listen to Jesus speak, as if they were on a hillside. (Director Stanley Kubrick had considered using one as an alien artefact in his film *2001: A Space Odyssey*.)

There were other curios, like the converted golf buggy that was driven by King Herod. It had a custom-made gold fibreglass skull mounted on the front, its headlights wedged into the eye sockets.

As Judas, Jon had his fair share of challenges. Probably the most physically demanding was a sequence in which he was to hang suspended some 25 metres above the stage — and he failed to inform anyone that he had a serious fear of heights. To achieve this 'magical' act of levitation, the crew set to work making what Jon called 'a sort of flying harness'. The original model was made of canvas and metal, and before Jon got to test-fly the harness, it was thoroughly tested — except for the buckles. His first trip went smoothly, but on his second run-through, the buckles snapped and Jon was left hanging — quite literally — from the theatre's scaffolding, high up in the air, screaming for help.

Fortunately he was saved, but afterwards director Sharman had a quiet word with Jon.

'Don't scream too much,' Sharman told him. 'It frightens the crew.'

Jon later said that in all their time working together, the director gave him just one note, and it came very early in rehearsals.

'How do you think Judas feels?' Sharman asked him.

'Horribly frustrated,' Jon replied.

'Oh, that's good,' Sharman said, and walked away.

Sharman, however, did spend some time with Trevor White, whom he gave three pieces of advice in order to prepare for his role. The first was to see the 1964 film *The Gospel According to St. Matthew*, a sometimes brutal telling of Jesus Christ's story, directed by Italian Pier Paolo Pasolini. The second was to read the Gospels. The third was to read *The Last Temptation of Christ*, a controversial novel written by Nikos Kazantzakis, best known for the story *Zorba the Greek*.

As for Jon, he liked to talk shop with Patrick Flynn who, in the words of Trevor White, was 'outrageous and unorthodox'. Flynn moonlighted producing jingles and would slip some work to Jon and Trevor and some of the other principals — after a day of *Superstar* they'd spend their downtime flogging biscuits and soft drink. (Flynn would later work as conductor for the American Ballet Theatre.)

Jon and John Young also spent some time together off stage. They'd first met when Young sang in a suburban band named Elm Tree; they played many of the same venues as Sebastian Hardie. During rehearsals for *Superstar*, Jon would collect Young from his home in Liverpool and drive him to the theatre.

Jon's Sebastian Hardie buddies, despite their disappointment at the way he handled his departure from the band, watched Jon go through his paces during rehearsals at the Capitol. It was only then that they were struck by how big a leap Jon had taken. 'The guys were very happy for me, but they couldn't actually believe it until they saw me in rehearsals,' said Jon. 'They were like, "Fuck!"'

'It wasn't until *Superstar* that I realised his hunger,' said Graham Ford. 'He didn't lack confidence in himself.'

Jon had come a long way from playing the Blue Fountain.

———

Just prior to *Superstar*'s opening night, Jon and the cast squeezed together on the footpath outside St Mary's Cathedral for a group shot. Jon sat in the middle of the group; his dark eyes seemed to burn a hole right through the camera lens. He was ready.

In the audience at the Sydney opening was *Superstar* co-creator Tim Rice, who, by his own admission, was 'a little nervous', particularly after seeing the Broadway production: 'although bravely ambitious', Rice had said, the production 'did not quite work'. Sydney was only the second staging of *Superstar*, as it hadn't yet opened on the West End.

It's almost a given that opening nights never go smoothly, and Sydney was no exception. Groups of protestors gathered outside the theatre, waving placards. Then there was a long delay at the beginning of Act 2, allegedly because a protestor had somehow managed to sneak backstage and cut the main closed-circuit TV cable that connected the conductor with the orchestra. Jon, his fellow disciples and Jesus were left standing on the stage, waiting for the musicians to take their places. Tim Rice, writing in his memoir, *Oh, What a Circus*, had another theory: perhaps Jim Sharman, he joked, 'had decided at the last moment to include a biting attack on slow restaurant service'.

Writing in *The National Times*, Kevon Kemp noted that during the delay 'the cast, by no means all of them seasoned professionals, were noticeably on edge'. Another reporter said it was 'an amateurish lapse'.

But the show — eventually — went on. And Kemp, like most people inside the Capitol, became a convert. '*Superstar* is a triumph,' he declared. 'Not to be missed.'

As for Tim Rice's concerns, they disappeared after the Sydney opening.

'It was a great relief that the Australian production, the first version after Broadway to be staged in English, proved to be a thumping success,' he said, via email. 'This was in part because of Jim [Sharman]'s imaginative and exciting direction — which led him to be signed up for London — and in part because of the exciting cast who understood that this was a rock show rather than a traditional musical.'

'No one realised this more than Jon, whose Judas was brilliantly judged and truly exciting, daring and energetic,' he added. 'Jon was a great Australian rocker, larger than life — and a top bloke to boot.'

Jon's sister Jan was also in the audience that first night. 'I thought it was great, amazing. I'd seen Jon perform in a band but never like that, acting — well, hamming, really.'

Harry M. hosted an opening-night afterparty, splashing out $5000 on the gathering. The party was held at the Summit revolving restaurant, on the 47th floor of Australia Square, with its sweeping views of the city skyline. As Molly Meldrum reported slyly in *Go-Set*, 'I've never been to a party that's been so high.' The La De Da's and Tamam Shud provided the music, while members of the cast mingled with the 400 guests, among them Tim Rice and expat Aussie impresario Robert Stigwood, manager of the Bee Gees and noted bon vivant (he'd helped Miller secure rights to the show). Miller even managed to find a few local clergymen who weren't offended by *Superstar*, so he invited them too. One was the Reverend Alan Walker, an evangelist, who spoke with Miller, suggesting that a 'higher force' had inspired him to stage the show. (During one of the early Sydney shows, the entire front few rows were occupied by nuns. They were the first people at the stage door after the show, asking for autographs.)

One review of the Sydney premiere described *Superstar* as 'a sort of electronic miracle . . . the set by Brian Thomson is a mechanical wonder . . . Judas wore brown and managed not to upstage Jesus nearly as much as the [Adelaide] version.' Another reporter said this of the staging: '*Jesus Christ Superstar* . . . is not so much a rock opera as an exercise in the technological theatre of the 1970s. If it can be opened and shut, it opens and shuts, and if it can fly through the air — then it flies.'

While accepting that the dodecahedron was 'incredible, an awesome sight to behold', Jon took umbrage at the notion that *Superstar* was more about technology than music. 'One critic said that *Hair* was people and *Superstar* was machines. I don't think this is fair,' he said. 'The machinery is just there to help the something that is really a very human drama.'

The dodecahedron was almost the undoing of Jon. During one show it snagged his microphone cable, which grew increasingly shorter as the 'petals' started to close. Jon was forced to move closer and closer to it as he sang. Somehow he managed to get through the scene before his mic cable completely disappeared. (Stevie Wright actually had his mic cable sliced in two by the dodecahedron.)

Not everyone, though, was sold on Harry M.'s theatrical miracle. A writer for *The Sydney Morning Herald* said English's Judas 'was the only relief in what was for me a couple of hours of crashing boredom'.

A TV crew did some vox pops outside the Capitol, and an older woman was asked about the show. 'Judas was wonderful,' she replied without a moment's hesitation. And then, almost as an afterthought: 'Oh and Jesus Christ, too, of course.'

The show was a runaway hit, and Jon threw himself into his role, sometimes quite literally. During one performance, he accidentally knocked the hat clear off the head of John Paul Young's character, Annas, a move that was definitely not in the script. A stunned Young didn't know how to react.

'I was trying to look cool, with all this long hair tucked up under a hairnet,' said Young. 'There was nothing I could do.'

Despite his spotlight-grabbing performance, Jon did have at least one peculiar post-show encounter. He was having a quiet beer when a woman approached him, clutching a program.

'You were so good as Peter!' she exclaimed.

'Erm, I actually play Judas,' Jon replied.

'No,' she insisted, 'you played Peter, didn't you? You know, the one who hung himself!'

Jon wondered if he and the rest of the cast should wear name tags.

The anti-*Superstar* protests continued throughout much of the early part of the Sydney season. Prior to one show, Jon was spotted on the street and was heckled and jostled by an angry mob. While on stage, a sharp-shooting antagonist in the balcony flicked a handful of twenty-cent coins repeatedly at Jon; one bounced into Jon's eye and he needed five stitches during intermission to repair the damage. During another show, a Molotov cocktail was hurled on stage, landing at the feet of Trevor White. 'The wick came out, fortunately,' Jon reported in a surprisingly casual manner. It almost became a regular occurrence for the entire cast to be hustled out of the theatre as the bomb squad responded to yet another threat.

These protests led to some stealthy moves on the part of Jon and the cast in order to avoid the protestors camped outside the Capitol. The cast would sometimes use the back alleys near the Capitol to gain access to the theatre, where they'd hang out between shows, dressed in full stage gear. A nearby pub closed at 7 pm, and drunken regulars would stumble into the street to be confronted by Roman guards, people on stilts and some bloke dressed like Jesus.

During the interval in the show, all the principals — Judas, Jesus, King Herod, Pontius Pilate and the others — shared one dressing room. There was an agreement that the first person to reach the dressing room had to put the kettle on for tea. That, too, would have been a sight for the unprepared. 'It was great,' said Trevor White, who admitted that sometimes he and Jon snuck in a bottle of port: 'Purely for medicinal purposes, of course.'

There was another problem brought on by *Superstar*: Jon was becoming a very public figure. Hordes of admiring young women could spot his dark eyes and long hair from a mile away, which led to some awkward encounters. Jon regularly received up to 300 fan letters a week, many simply addressed as 'Dear Judas'.

A reporter asked Jon how he handled women throwing themselves at him. He replied with a joke — 'I dropped a lot of them' — but also accepted that it was a strange time. Jon knew that he had to keep his head, otherwise he would have been in danger of disappearing up his own backside.

'It was an unreal period,' he later reflected. 'As long as I kept in my mind it was a job, I was OK. [I kept telling myself] to never get carried away. Don't believe everything written about you.'

Carmen readily admitted that she had her share of uncomfortable moments; after all, they'd been married for only a few years. 'I used to get quite jealous,' she said. But it would be some time before Jon succumbed to the temptations of his many female fans.

Jon's newfound fame became starkly evident to his family, too, when he was booked to appear at a suburban shopping centre. He'd asked his mother to collect him afterwards, and was very insistent about one thing: 'You have to be there at the right time,' he told her. 'Not a minute later.' Sheila agreed, but couldn't grasp why he was being so demanding. Jon's sister Jill also came along.

The reason became very clear when the event finished. Jon came racing out to the street, jumped into the Kombi, slammed the door shut and yelled, 'Go!' The car was quickly mobbed by screaming fans; it was like a scene from The Beatles' movie *A Hard Day's Night*.

Jill described it as 'a big moment of realisation for the family'. Jon was a superstar.

As the Sydney season of *Superstar* rolled into 1973, Jon reconnected with his former bandmates — and schoolmates — from Sebastian Hardie. The band had re-formed and would in time recruit guitarist Mario Millo, the kid from The Menu who had been won over by Jon's bawdy reinterpretations of rock classics. Inspired by Yes and the Mahavishnu Orchestra, Millo had started composing rock with a symphonic bent, which over time would make this a vastly different Sebastian Hardie.

Sebastian Hardie was holding down a residency at an inner-city venue called the Stagecoach, run by the Wong brothers, Harry M.'s former business partners. When *Superstar* was done for the night, Jon would head down to the Stagecoach and sing with his old band. Millo, who was playing in a band called The Clik, would finish his gig for the night and also head to the Stagecoach on his bike, guitar slung across his back, and jam with Sebastian Hardie.

'The place was packed,' Millo explained, 'because of Jon's presence in *Superstar* … he had an incredible presence.'

Jon and the *Superstar* cast, meanwhile, had recorded an Australian cast album, which had been released in October 1972. Featuring Jon, as well as Stevie Wright, John Young, Trevor White and Rory O'Donoghue — who was in the process of unveiling his Thin Arthur character on what would become the iconic *Aunty Jack* TV show — the album peaked at number 20 in the *Go-Set* charts and eventually went gold (sales of 35,000). Over time, the stage production of *Superstar* also launched the careers of Marcia Hines, John Young, Graham Russell and Russell Hitchcock (Air Supply), as well as Reg Livermore. It seemed that everyone involved with the show was on their way to stellar careers, especially Jon English.

In and around his *Superstar* commitments, Jon found the time to record his solo debut, *Wine Dark Sea*, which was released in March 1973. The cover image of *Wine Dark Sea*, shot by Nicholas van der Ley, was striking: Jon was immersed in water, with only his face above the surface; his eyes were closed. It was as though Judas had just been baptised. The record was released on Warm and Genuine Records, a label set up by Jon and G. Wayne Thomas, whose single 'Open Up Your Heart' had been a Top 20 hit in April 1972. (Major label PolyGram would promote and distribute most of Jon's albums.)

Thomas, like Jon, had been a sportsman before turning to music, having played 1st XV rugby for Canterbury, in his native New Zealand. He'd then written jingles with Patrick Flynn, *Superstar*'s musical director, before producing the music for the cult surf flick *Morning of the Earth*, the first Australian soundtrack album to 'go gold'.

Thomas was the executive producer of Jon's album, which brought together some English originals — including the title track and 'Tomorrow' — and a selection of wisely chosen covers. Among them was a Rice/Lloyd Webber song, 'Close Every Door', which featured in their first musical, *Joseph and the Amazing Technicolor Dreamcoat*. A surprise cameo came from Jon's father, Syd, who played piano on 'Sweet Lady Mary', a Rod Stewart cover. *Wine Dark Sea* also marked the next stage of the long association between Jon and *Superstar* drummer Greg Henson, who played on the record.

Henson recalled spending 'two or three weeks in the studio' on *Wine Dark Sea*. 'We did think about what we were doing. The songs we'd played live, so they were ready.'

'It is a peculiar sort of album,' Jon admitted. 'There are moments when it has a touch of *Superstar* about it. Otherwise it is purely original.'

The standout song was the haunting, melancholic 'Handbags and Gladrags', which had been written by Mike d'Abo of Manfred Mann and turned into a US chart hit by Rod Stewart on its second release in 1972. It was a moderate hit for Jon, reaching a national peak of number 50, but more importantly it established Jon's winning formula: he didn't so much interpret the song as reclaim it as his own. It didn't hurt that he and Stewart shared a vocal raspiness and a knack for bringing stories alive in song.

Jon's likeness to Rod Stewart was noticed by critics when they tuned in to *Wine Dark Sea*. Writing in *The Sydney Morning Herald*, Gil Wahlquist twigged to the fact that Jon 'has a tendency to sound like Rod Stewart', then noted that 'his style starts with Stewart but becomes his own in other songs'.

Naturally, no review of Jon English circa 1973 would be complete without a nod to *Superstar*. 'The debut of Jon English confirms, on record, the talent which he has shown as Judas,' Wahlquist summed up. He felt that English handled 'Handbags' 'brilliantly'.

In his hometown of Sydney, 'Handbags' reached the Top 20 of the 2SMusic Top 40 Survey — 2SM being the leading pop radio station in the Harbour City. Jon was keeping some good company, too: Elton John ('Crocodile Rock'), Joni Mitchell ('You Turn Me On I'm a Radio') and the King himself, Elvis Presley ('Separate Ways') were his chart-mates, as were The Who. (Pete Townshend's 'Behind Blue Eyes' was a song, just like 'Handbags', that Jon would reinterpret so well that he could just about claim it as his own.)

The *Wine Dark Sea* LP was only a moderate success, peaking just outside the national Top 50 in April 1973, but it was a solid start. The parallel career of Jon English, recording artist, had begun.

CHAPTER 7

'[Stevie Wright] was the only person we knew who'd ever been in a knife fight.'

The first Sydney season of *Superstar* closed on 10 March 1973. *Superstar* had been a staggering success, and the making of Jon English. His passion for the role of Judas hadn't diminished one bit during its run, made abundantly clear by a review of the final night's show. As Jon sang the words 'I don't know how to love him', in the words of *Go-Set*'s Darel Nugent, 'tears dripped from his blackened eyes'.

'Perhaps Jon wasn't the sole person in the theatre to shed tears,' Nugent wrote. 'Jon English . . . was superb.'

Some 21,000 punters turned up for the final ten Sydney performances of *Superstar*, bringing the total to about 500,000 during the Sydney season alone. These were amazing numbers, exceeding Harry M.'s wildest dreams for the show — and proving that his $350,000 investment was money well spent. Harry had even agreed to increase Jon's wage during the run, although he was still earning little more than $200 per week.

As far as Jon was concerned, the reaction to the show grew more enthusiastic the longer that it ran. 'The last few weeks of *Superstar*,' Jon told journalist Jennie Turner, 'when the crowd went crazy, were great . . . I had reached an emotional and physical high and it takes a while to come down after that.'

Jon had little time for recovery because the *Superstar* roadshow now headed to Melbourne. Prior to *Superstar*'s southern debut at the 3000-capacity Palais Theatre on 30 March 1973, Jon put in an appearance on Graham Kennedy's TV talk show. Kennedy wasn't the gushiest of hosts, but that night he was full of praise. This was a particular thrill for Jon, because Kennedy was one of his idols.

Before Jon came on set, the man known as 'Gra Gra' raved about the show. 'I can talk about [*Superstar*] until the cows come home,' he exclaimed, his bug eyes just about popping out of his head. Kennedy had seen *Superstar* in Sydney and was in the process of recording his own version of 'Herod's Song' for a record called — imaginatively — *Graham Kennedy Sings the Shows*.

His co-host, Pete Smith, hinted that Kennedy might have had a financial interest in the show, but he deftly dodged the question. Kennedy joked that 'already two cheques have been in', as well as 'a couple of Poles and three Italians.' (Harry M. Miller also represented Kennedy.)

'Jon English?' Kennedy gasped, switching subjects. 'Is he here?'

The studio lights dimmed and Jon sang 'Heaven on Their Minds' with all the gusto and intensity, if not quite the pitch-perfect voice, that he brought to the stage. The Channel 9 cameras couldn't get enough of English, zeroing in on his face for much of the performance. It didn't feel quite right to see Judas wearing a wristwatch, but it hardly mattered: the studio audience loved him. So did Kennedy, who invited Jon over for a chat.

The lanky singer, just days shy of his 24th birthday, towered over both Kennedy and Smith and smiled nervously as they spoke.

'How's the voice standing up?' asked Gra Gra.

'Pretty well,' Jon said. 'I've had two weeks off, been larking about.'

After a little small talk he shook hands with Kennedy and Smith. A week later *Superstar* opened at the Palais. It'd be home for Jon and his *Superstar* peers until 28 July.

Just as in Sydney, some big names turned up at the Palais on opening night to see what all the fuss was about. ACTU leader Bob Hawke was in the house, as was fashion designer and socialite Dame Zara Bate (the widow of former prime minister Harold Holt). Sir Maurice Nathan, the former lord mayor of Melbourne, also attended the opening. *Superstar* was *the* must-attend show.

Harry M. rented out Luna Park for the opening-night afterparty — where Jon found himself sharing a merry-go-round ride with none other than Graham Kennedy. 'Harry's guests,' reported society columnist Leslie Walford, 'frolicked like happy children, dashing from the bar to the fairy-floss machine to the merry-go-round.'

The headline in the press the next day read: 'Full-length mink at the hot-dog stand'. Again, Jon was singled out for attention. 'Jon English, as always,' wrote Walford, 'made his role as Judas a show-stopper.'

Writing in *Go-Set*, Molly Meldrum, however, wasn't so thrilled by Jon's performance. 'I'm a great Jon English fan but luv . . . I did think that Jon over-acted his part.' (It wasn't long, however, before Meldrum wrote a grovelling retraction. '[I was] unfair . . . your performances have been A-1.')

It was an incident in Melbourne that almost stopped *Superstar* in its tracks. It happened during the opening scene of Act 2, just as the table for the Last Supper was lowered into place and the cast, Jon included, were in what he called their 'Dali poses', ready to sing 'The Last Supper'. The cast was both still and silent — this was a big *Superstar* moment — when a very loud fart boomed around the hushed theatre. Ripples of laughter spread through the audience, and Jon and the cast tried to keep straight faces. It wasn't easy.

As Jon recalled, 'We couldn't wait for the loud music [to kick in] so we could roll about laughing. [But] I was laughing so hard I could hardly sing.'

Jon also insisted that it wasn't him — he blamed a gassy audience member.

As if the eight-shows-a-week grind of *Superstar* wasn't enough, a few weeks into the Melbourne season, Jon (and Trevor White) agreed to appear in another Harry M. production, *West Side Story*. They'd fly to Canberra for rehearsals, somehow finding the time in their heavy schedule. Fortunately, this was a one-off performance, in early June, as part of the Canberra Winter Youth Festival. In a commendable act of 'keeping it real', some of the cast, including Jon (who played Bernardo, leader of the Sharks gang), were asked to work with real knives during the gang-fight sequences. Jon knew just the person to bring authenticity to the scene: Stevie Wright. He wasn't in the cast, but Jon asked him to give him tips because, as Jon said, 'He was the only person we knew who'd ever been in a knife fight.'

They also staged a midnight concert, backed by the 'Superstar rock band' and the Canberra Youth Orchestra. Elsewhere, Jon appeared on a TV special with John Farnham and made an appearance on Channel 7's *True Blue Show*.

Jon was everywhere.

In his journal, Jon scrawled this note about *Superstar*: 'Finished July 28 [1973]. Returned to Syd[ney] August 16th. *Finished.*'

That wasn't quite the case. Jon and *Superstar*, now with Marcia Hines in the role of Mary Magdalene, returned to the Capitol in Sydney and continued running until February 1974. Casting a black woman in the part — a first — was another smart and undeniably attention-grabbing move on the part of Miller and director Jim Sharman. It also made Hines a star.

'I think Harry was clever enough to realise it was controversial,' Hines told TV's Peter Luck in 1997, when asked about her casting.

Even then, *Superstar* was hardly done with him. Jon would readily admit that of all the roles he played — and there would be many over the next 40 years — Judas was the one with which he was most closely associated. In 1983, he talked this over with TV host Mike Walsh.

'It took me longer to get out of the Judas from *Superstar* image than it did for the Jonathan Garrett one later on [in *Against the Wind*]. I'd get a lot of, "I remember you, you were Judas in *Superstar*. What's your name again?"'

———

This was a golden time for Jon. He and Carmen became first-time parents; their daughter, Jessamine, was born on 10 May 1973 while the Englishes — including their cat, Ruth — were in Melbourne for *Superstar*, staying at the Riverside Apartments on the Yarra. Ruth clearly didn't fancy sharing Jon and Carmen's affection, because she ran off soon after Jessamine returned from the hospital, never to return.

When *Superstar* was done, the Englishes settled into a brown-painted house with mustard walls in the Sydney suburb of Surry Hills, in Riley Street. Not yet the inner-city hub of cool that it would become, Surry Hills did have two things going for it: it was close to the city and it was cheap. Crime was the downside. Casa de English was frequently broken into.

'We were the first family at our school to have the first VCR,' Jon's second daughter, Josephine (Josie), later remembered. 'It got nicked — we got robbed a lot.'

Jon's next challenge was to search out a role with the same impact as *Superstar* — and to provide for the ever-expanding English clan, as Carmen was soon pregnant with Josie (who was born on 3 April 1975). Jon was definitely done with the nine to five, as Carmen recalled. 'He was never going back to the office.'

His next big move was intended to be a star turn in *Ned Kelly: The*

Musical (also known as *Ned Kelly: The Electric Music Show*), a co-creation of Reg Livermore, who wrote the book and lyrics, and *Superstar* musical director Patrick Flynn.

In theory, Ned Kelly seemed to be the perfect follow-up role for Jon — after all, the man in tin was, like Judas, a conflicted character, reviled by some as a common crook and revered by others as an anti-establishment cult hero. It was a role that offered plenty of challenges for Jon, not the least being how he could cast his dark-eyed spell over an audience while wearing Ned's ever-present visor. And he got to again die every night, only this time on the gallows.

'What we've done,' Jon said after being shown Livermore's book, 'is turn Ned into a kind of Australian Robin Hood. That's what this country needs.'

'[I've been] a husband, then Judas, then a father, now Ned Kelly,' noted Jon. 'I wonder where it will end — and who I really am.'

Livermore and Flynn had big plans for the show; it would be Australia's first homegrown rock opera. Taking their cue from the *Superstar* playbook, Livermore and Flynn first cut an album, prior to any stage production; the plan was to have a hit record, which would then encourage backers to get behind the stage production. The album was released in mid-1974. Jon sang on the record — in the title role of the (almost) bulletproof bushranger — as did fellow *Superstar* alumni John Paul Young and Trevor White. White sang the role of the notorious informer Aaron Sherritt.

An innovative marketing plan was set in action to launch the album: a man dressed as Ned 'held up' the York Street branch of the National Bank in Sydney, but rather than clear out the vault he handed over copies of the LP. Yet the album wasn't a hit. It barely scraped the Australian top 50, charting for just three months. Its sales were nothing like those of the original *Superstar*, which had been a worldwide smash.

News of *Ned Kelly: The Musical* broke at the end of May 1974; the rock opera would 'almost certainly go into production next year', according to a report in *The Sydney Morning Herald*. Sir Robert Helpmann, no less, was tagged to direct the production, which would feature Jon as Kelly, and Livermore as Superintendent Hare, the high-ranking policeman wounded during Ned's last stand at Glenrowan. It was to be a co-production between JC Williamson's Hamlyn Group, which had been making a big splash in local publishing for the past ten years — they'd also released the soundtrack album — and Clyde Packer, the eldest son of the Packer media empire. Clyde had recently begun dabbling in the counterculture: he even dared to wear a kaftan in public, much to the horror of his straitlaced father, Sir Frank. Packer owned the rights to the show and Jon hoped that he'd bring Harry M. into the mix.

'It has to be done big,' Jon told a reporter.

Clyde Packer boldly told the media that Ned Kelly would be 'as big as *Hair*'. Kevin Weldon, managing director of the Hamlyn Group, went one step further, assuring a writer from *The Canberra Times* that Ned Kelly would be 'the biggest thing yet in Australian musical history'. But Ned Kelly was still a long way off being produced. As Reg Livermore wrote, Ned Kelly 'took years to fashion . . . and it involved way too many people for far too long — none of whom were remotely capable of actually getting the show off the ground'.

Nothing came of it for another three years, and then not with Jon's involvement. He'd moved on.

Jon didn't have a full-time manager but was being courted by American Tommy Amato, who worked with wholesome country boy John Denver. Amato caught Jon playing a live set at the Manly Silver Screen theatre and smelled money.

'He's like a diamond in the rough,' Amato said.

They met and Amato talked up the opportunities for Jon in the US; he said that he'd even ask John Denver to write for him. It was a lot for Jon to take in — after all, just a couple of years before he'd been dodging conscription and playing suburban pub gigs.

While Jon was flattered, he didn't quite buy into it. Yet Amato persevered, peppering Jon with messages, insisting that Denver had written some songs for him and that the US was waiting.

'It's great,' Jon said, 'but I don't believe anything will come from it. I mean, you know people, and especially Americans. They're generous and lavish with praise but you have to take it with a grain of salt.'

He was right, too; despite a trip to the US to meet with Amato, nothing came of it. Jon's roots were too firmly entrenched in Australia — he talked up his 'dinkum Aussie-ness' at every chance. Unlike such peers as Rick Springfield, the Bee Gees and Olivia Newton-John, Jon wasn't obsessed with the notion of heading overseas to conquer the world.

'I figure that if I'm going to be a success,' he told a journalist, 'I'd rather do it here.'

With his next big theatrical role eluding him for the time being, Jon continued playing live with his band, Baxter Funt, which included some of the players from the *Superstar* band, including drummer Greg Henson and guitarist Mike Wade. Their name was a nod to a cartoon character created by Wade, a keen artist. Decked out in a long black cape and silky silver shirt, Jon stepped out with the band at Sydney's Paddington Town Hall, looking like a cross between a kids' party magician and a dark-haired Roger Daltrey. He was hosting *Rock and Roll Ballroom of the Air*, a series of four gigs broadcast on ABC-TV in early 1975.

It was a curious mash-up of local musos — Jon and Baxter Funt, soul singer Renée Geyer and Sydney group Ayers Rock — who were sharing the bill with ballroom dancers and the tango dancing champions of Australia, Alex Schembri and Adele Fraser. This was rock'n'roll cabaret. The audience was encouraged to dress as wildly as possible, to up the 'outrageous' tone of the event (although to some that simply meant slinging a tie over the obligatory jeans and T-shirt). The guys of Baxter Funt opted for full monkey suits, all matching in deep blue, with oversized burgundy bow ties.

Jon was in good voice, belting out 'Snakeyes', a slow-burning, sinewy number from his next album, which was still being recorded. 'That's not easy,' he said at the end of the song, gasping for air, holding onto the mic stand for support. 'You should try and sing it some time.'

Jon's career juggling act continued, as he balanced live performances with some theatre work — he was both beating the boards and treading them. Six months prior to the Paddington Town Hall shows, during June and July 1974, he'd appeared at the opening of Sydney's Nimrod Theatre in a production called *Bacchoi*, billed as an 'Australian-Greek rock musical'. That was definitely a first.

'I'm really still coming down after *Superstar*,' Jon said, 'and I needed another show to help me along.'

Bacchoi was an updated version of Euripides' *Bacchae*, an ancient Greek play with the type of story that Jon had devoured as a kid, so the appeal of the role was obvious. He starred alongside singer Jeannie Lewis, under the artistic direction of John Bell and Richard Wherrett, both on their way to becoming Australian theatre legends. Jon took movement and acting lessons at the Nimrod to prepare for the role. On stage he wore a brilliant blue wig and animal skins, his face coated with war paint, in a production that culminated, as one reviewer noted, 'in an erotic orgy where bare nipples and pulsating bodies twined with snakes dance and writhe across the stage'.

Bacchoi was well received — 'It's Super-Bacchus,' declared the *Daily Telegraph*, 'Jon is back in musical orgy.' Another headline read, 'Rocking around the Acropolis'. But it was a short season, nothing like *Superstar's* epic run.

Jon's next move was a surprise, even for someone who was fast growing into a multitasker. Jon was approached by composer Roy Ritchie, who'd been musical director for the original *Rocky Horror Show* stage production, which had also been directed by Jim Sharman. Ritchie told Jon that he was working on a piece for the Sydney Dance Company and he wanted Jon to sing.

'Where are the words?' Jon asked.

Ritchie shrugged and admitted that they hadn't been written. Jon duly went away and composed lyrics for a piece they called *Phases*, which was performed at the recently opened Sydney Opera House, with Jon singing from the orchestra pit. It was proof that Jon had little trouble shifting between sweaty beer barns and upscale gatherings. But that next big role still eluded him.

CHAPTER 8

'I was a very good drug-crazed, axe-murdering hippie.'

The November 1974 release of Jon's second album, *It's All a Game* — its working title had been *Against the Grain* — marked his emergence as a genuine commercial force. It was again overseen by G. Wayne Thomas (although he wasn't as actively involved as he'd been with Jon's debut) and featured such regulars as Jon's old Cabramatta High/ Sebastian Hardie buddies, brothers Peter and Alex Plavsic. Mario Millo, who'd joined Sebastian Hardie permanently in late 1973, played guitar on several tracks. Jon even added lead guitar to 'He Could Have Been a Dancer', which was a first.

Writing in *The Sydney Morning Herald*, Gil Wahlquist managed to give due credit to Jon's second LP despite his prejudices about *Superstar*. 'English . . . has emerged from the plastic nonsense [of *Superstar*] to create a personality for himself,' Wahlquist wrote, singling out 'He Could Have Been a Dancer' for special attention, describing it as one of the album's 'most complex' tracks. 'It is the first song I can recall about an abortion,' he added. As a lyricist, Jon was starting to push the boundaries, just a little. 'I'm just trying to make amends,' Jon sang, as a slow, sad melody played. 'God knows there'll be other chances someday / . . . Your dad and your mama would have crucified me.'

While not a runaway smash to rival current chart-hoggers Skyhooks, *It's All a Game* did well enough, charting for four months. It also served to remind listeners that Jon could tell his elbow from his funny bone. The track 'Space Shanty' was a faux Irish sea shanty/singalong, Jon desperately resisting the temptation to rhyme 'Venus' with the obvious, while various studio noises — a throat being cleared, a drumstick dropped, a sly chuckle — were left untouched in some songs. Actor Arthur Dignam, yet another *Superstar* cast member, read out the credits at the end of the album, speaking with both the plumminess of a BBC newsreader and the wit of John Cleese. He thanked Brian Cadd 'for not turning up' and gave due respect to the studio tea lady, 'Boo Boo' (Jon's wife Carmen), as well as thanking the local police department for their parking tickets, while casually throwing such big names as Gough Whitlam and Harry M. Miller into the mix. Jon clearly bought into the old showbiz adage 'Leave 'em laughing'.

'It's more raunchy and funky [than *Wine Dark Sea*],' Jon said on the LP's release. 'And [it] has more of my own material.' Jon wrote all of the album's tracks, bar one — and that was the song that brought about his first mainstream hit.

American rocker Bob Seger wrote 'Turn the Page' in 1972, inspired by an incident at a roadhouse somewhere in the US Midwest, where he and his bandmates were given a rough welcome by unfriendly truckers. (The name of the band Seger was playing with at the time — Teegarden & Van Winkle — probably didn't help his situation.) Seger didn't release it as a single, but it became a live staple and a crowd favourite.

Jon's knack for not so much covering a song as inhabiting it once again came to the fore: he made 'Turn the Page' his own. He had done enough time on the road to relate to Seger's lyrics — things could get lively for a touring group of longhairs in rural Australia — and perhaps even drew on the various *Superstar* controversies to get in the appropriate 'freaks vs straights' mindset. It was a keeper, too; he'd still be singing the song 40 years down the line.

Released in the lead-up to the appearance of the album, 'Turn the Page' was Jon's first Top 20 hit (number 2 in Sydney) and charted for more than six months. Another phase of his career — chart regular — had begun.

The emergence of ABC-TV's *Countdown*, which started broadcasting in colour during March 1975, a few months after its launch in black and white, intersected neatly with Jon's post-*Superstar* career. He first appeared on the show in late April 1975, singing 'Turn the Page', and fast became a *Countdown* regular thanks to his talents as a performer and a raconteur.

Molly Meldrum was now a Jon English convert. 'The moment he walked on stage, he was in the spotlight,' Meldrum recalled. 'He had that presence. He had those piercing eyes.'

And he was 'a natural on TV', added Meldrum. 'An all-round entertainer.'

Jon's *Superstar* peer, John Paul Young, whose nickname was 'Squeak', was another natural fit for *Countdown*; he and Jon would sometimes fill in for host Molly Meldrum as they forged their careers beyond Judas and Annas. Yet another *Superstar* alumnus, Marcia Hines, was poised to become a solid-gold hitmaker, again with the help of nationwide exposure on *Countdown*.

It was a hot period all over for Australian music, with other acts such as Richard 'Girls on the Avenue' Clapton, Sherbet frontman Daryl Braithwaite and Jon's *Superstar* colleague, Stevie Wright, whose propulsive 'Guitar Band' was making a splash in the charts and on the airwaves. They'd all do time on *Countdown*, too, some more reluctantly than others; Clapton famously sparred on air with Meldrum, struggling to make Molly understand that he didn't feel that *Countdown* was especially credible. But everyone fully appreciated the impact and reach of the show.

Jon's *Countdown* audience was slightly different from most, as his drummer Greg Henson recalled. 'Jon was maybe more rock'n'roll. But he loved being a pop star.' Jon's future manager, Peter Rix, had a similar take on it. 'Jon wasn't Hush on *Countdown*. He wasn't Sherbet. He was seen as more of a grown-up. The twenty-year-olds liked him, not the fourteen-year-olds.'

This continued when he went out on the road, first with Baxter Funt and later on with The Foster Brothers. It wasn't teenage girls who'd hang about after the show, seeking out Jon and the band. 'It was the local doctor's wife,' Rix remembered. 'Older women.'

Harry M. Miller hadn't quite finished with Jon, and in early 1975 the call came in: how did he feel about resurrecting Judas? Jon had no problem with the idea; he'd come to see steady work such as *Superstar* as a necessity. He did, after all, have a family to feed.

'It was as close as you get to having a real job, and the money was there,' he explained. And Jon knew the role inside out.

Harry M., in typical style, didn't hold back on the hype when news of *Superstar* Mk II broke. He revealed that he'd dropped $600,000 on getting the production right, which was almost twice the budget of the original show. Miller described it as 'the last of the great spectaculars' and 'one step removed from a movie'. It opened in Newcastle on 14 June 1975 and then travelled to New Zealand, where it ran from July to November 1975.

'Everything I've ever learned, every clever person I've met, is in the show,' Miller stated. 'It really is the culmination of twenty years in the business for me.' He estimated it would take in $4.5 million by year's end.

Miller again engaged Jon and Trevor White, the two leads from the original *Superstar,* for the revival. White wasn't long back from an unbilled singing role in the film of *The Rocky Horror Picture Show,* as well as a tour of the US with The Kinks, where he'd experienced the dubious distinction of almost being throttled by the volatile Dave Davies. (The Kinks' guitarist blamed White, in error, for playing a practical joke on him.) The stunning Chrissie Hammond — she of the big voice and even bigger hair, who was soon to form Cheetah with her sister Lyndsay — took on the role of Mary Magdalene.

Jesus Christ Superstar was a hit all over again.

———

Away from music, Jon joked that there was one role for which he was perfect: 'a drug-crazed, axe-murdering hippie', mainly due to his dark eyes and undeniable physical presence. He was duly cast in several TV appearances over the next few years, including a *Homicide* episode entitled 'Stopover'. Crawfords, who produced this and many other Australian TV dramas, felt the script was strong enough to be granted 90 minutes of screen time, rather than the usual 60 minutes.

Jon was cast — typecast — as a rock star. 'It was a whodunit,' Jon recalled. 'What was interesting was that the people cast as extras were musicians and we did a lot of stuff live.'

One of Jon's co-stars was Aussie actor Charles 'Bud' Tingwell, who impressed Jon both as an actor and a human being. Tingwell handed along some solid advice. He told Jon that while on set he should keep his eyes open and his mouth shut. 'Acting is reacting,' Tingwell told Jon.

Jon was also impressed by the Crawford method of TV production; for one thing, they shot on film, just like a feature film, while the writing and production was first-class. 'It was a good school to go to,' Jon said. He also appeared in an episode of *Matlock Police*, which screened in September 1975, playing a character simply known as Quinlan in an episode entitled 'The Grass is Greener'. The sometimes Norman Gunston, Garry McDonald, was Jon's co-star.

'I love playing villains,' said Jon. 'There's an edge to them.'

While working with Crawfords, Jon met Bronwyn Binns, a researcher with an active interest in Australia's convict past, and a producer named Ian Jones. They'd both come to play a huge role in Jon's upcoming acting career.

Jon wasn't so taken by his stint in Channel 10's sexy soapie, *Number 96*, where he undertook a two-episode stretch as Mr Master, a cultish drug lord. Jon thought the dialogue was 'fucking appalling'; at one stage he stopped and asked the director, 'Do you really want me to say this?' He was convinced he was speaking on behalf of the entire cast. 'It was grotesque,' Jon said. 'And not just my lines; everybody's.'

Jon soon added yet another string to a bow that was growing ever longer, seemingly by the day. He and Baxter Funt had begun sharing some bills with the 'new' Sebastian Hardie, on the suggestion of their shared booking agency, Cordon Bleu. He'd grown particularly close, once again, to Sebastian Hardie's guitarist Mario Millo.

'We'd become personal friends, close friends,' said Millo. 'We watched each other's kids grow up, we'd holiday together, picnic together, all sorts of fun things.'

Sebastian Hardie held down a residency at the Savoy Club in Newcastle, playing Thursday, Friday and Saturday nights. Jon would join them on stage; he'd sing a couple of *Superstar* numbers, as well as 'Turn the Page' and some of the older tunes he'd sung with the band back in the day, such as Bob Dylan's 'Like a Rolling Stone' and the Spencer Davis Group's 'Gimme Some Lovin''.

Sebastian Hardie also held down a regular gig at the Kirk Gallery in Surry Hills, not far from where Jon, Carmen and the children lived. Millo had recently finished writing a sweeping, symphonic musical suite that he called *Four Moments*, which Sebastian Hardie premiered at a Kirk Gallery gig. Jon was in the audience. 'Shit,' Jon said to Millo afterwards, 'when did *that* happen?'

Jon had worked with the band when they played the 'burbs and stuck to covers; now they were channelling such prog-rock acts as Focus and Yes.

Jon was hell-bent on getting the band a record deal. He went to PolyGram, his label, and urged them to sign Sebastian Hardie. Jon knew that he was the label's 'chosen one' at the time and that he had some pull.

'Jon was like their unofficial A&R because of his status through *Superstar*,' said Peter Plavsic.

The label agreed to sign Sebastian Hardie, much to the surprise of the band, because they were not the kind of group to write three-minute pop songs, and that's what most major labels expected from their new signings.

'Three minutes to us wasn't a song,' said Plavsic. 'That was just warming up.'

But there was one proviso from the record company: Jon had to co-produce the band's first album. This wasn't a bad idea — it'd give Jon the credibility of being involved with a band on the rise, while also bringing in new listeners for Sebastian Hardie. Jon duly produced the record with the help of Richard Lush, another expat Pom. Not only was Lush experienced, but he'd worked with The Beatles at Abbey Road while they were recording *Sgt. Pepper's*. How could Beatles-obsessed Jon possibly say no?

'I made [the band] stand there and [did] whatever it is producers do,' Jon explained, sort of, in 2009. 'Richard [Lush] was there to help me. It was very smooth and great fun to do. Lots of laughs, a good atmosphere, no one bothering us. And Polygram was delirious.' He and Lush became good friends and colleagues.

Four Moments was released in August 1975 and became a surprise hit, peaking at number 13 and 'going gold'. Writing in *The Encyclopedia of Australian Rock and Pop*, Ian McFarlane praised the album's 'seamless, dramatic arrangements and impeccable musicianship . . . Millo contributed some of his most epic and graceful guitar playing'.

Later in the year, Sebastian Hardie embarked on a 63-date Australian tour, as their following grew.

Jon had helped launch the next stage of Sebastian Hardie's career: clearly, this was a band to which he felt strongly connected. And his working relationship with Mario Millo would reach even loftier heights in the very near future.

Jon loved a good story song. He was an avid reader, a huge fan of Stephen King, author of such creepy bestsellers as *Carrie* and *The Shining* — one day he'd write a song actually called 'The Shining'. So it was no surprise that he was drawn to songs with strong narratives —previous singles 'Turn the Page' and 'Handbags and Gladrags' both span poignant tales.

'I like moody story songs,' said Jon. 'Songs with a point.'

They also played well live, giving Jon the chance to introduce a little theatricality, learned from *Superstar*, into the beer barns of Oz.

His latest single, 'Hollywood Seven', definitely fitted that mould — and it came with a curious backstory. It was a bespoke piece, originally intended for Canadian singer (and budding environmentalist) Terry

Jacks, who in 1973 had had a big hit with his weepy ballad 'Seasons in the Sun', which sold 14 million copies. American Gloria Sklerov was a staff writer for Garrett Music, and she was asked to come up with 'an urban story song' for Jacks. She was driving home in LA when she passed a motel named 'Hollywood Eight'.

'I started to think about who might be checking in there,' Sklerov later wrote.

She sat down to write with her regular partner Harry Lloyd. They quickly realised that 'Hollywood Seven' 'sang' better than 'Hollywood Eight' and the song grew from there. When it became clear that Terry Jacks wasn't going to record the song — its dark themes would have been a stretch after the maudlin 'Seasons in the Sun' — it was sent out to various music publishers, including Essex Music Australia, where John Bromell gave it to Jon.

'Hollywood Seven', a tale of a Hollywood hopeful who meets a grisly demise, wasn't quite a hit on the scale of 'Seasons in the Sun'. It peaked in Australia at number 13 in June 1976, but it marked Jon's growing consistency as a charting singles artist. It also continued his solid working relationship with Sebastian Hardie, who backed him on the track — Mario Millo came up with the song's distinctive guitar riff.

Jon's wasn't the only rendition of 'Hollywood Seven' — one of its many covers was by Brit Dennis Waterman, better known for his role as the-hunk-with-the-muscle on TV's *Minder*, who'd one day work with Jon — but Jon's was very much the defining take. He sang it as though he'd lived it, as if he really was the Hollywood Seven resident with coffee and sympathy on tap, who one morning makes the kind of gruesome discovery that wouldn't have been out of place in a Stephen King novel.

Co-writer Sklerov saw that, too. 'I was very proud of Jon's version.'

CHAPTER 9

'I'm very good at [playing] mumbling boys from Essex.'

The story of TV miniseries *Against the Wind* had its roots in the late eighteenth century, the convict era of Australian history. The lead character of Mary Mulvane was based on an eighteen-year-old woman who'd been transported to New South Wales for seven years after having committed the 'crime' of protecting her own property — the family cow. The backdrop to Mary's story of suffering and struggle was made up of real historical events like the 1798 rebellion in Ireland, the Castle Hill convict rebellion of 1804 and the 1808 Rum Rebellion. It was a big story, something like an Australian answer to *Roots*, the massively successful 1977 US miniseries based on Alex Haley's bestselling novel, which, at its peak, drew an incredible 80 million viewers per episode.

Thirty-five-year-old Bronwyn Binns, who'd met Jon during his various Crawford cameos, was now an independent researcher and producer, and she'd been piecing together the character, and the story, of Mary Mulvane. Like Jon, Binns was a suburban Sydneysider, a 'westie' who'd grown up near Castle Hill. As a child she'd heard the stories of the flashpoint at Castle Hill in 1804 — Australia's first uprising, where at least 39 convicts died — and the Rum Rebellion.

As she dug even deeper into the story, Binns learned that the original house on the site where she lived had been visited by rebels on the night of the Castle Hill uprising. And an old building in Kellyville where she often tethered her horse while out riding was once a tavern where the rebels met. The story of *Against the Wind* was pretty much in her DNA.

Jon, too, knew about this often overlooked slice of Australia's past. As a history aficionado, Jon felt the failed uprising at Castle Hill, known as the Battle of Vinegar Hill, had the potential to be 'our Valley Forge, our War of Independence'.

In 1978, as Binns began plotting what would become a thirteen-part TV series, spanning fourteen years, she discovered that the lines between fact and fiction were blurring. 'The staggering thing,' she told *The Canberra Times* in October 1978, 'was that, in some cases, my continuing research showed that I had "imagined" precisely what had exactly happened.'

To Binns, *Against the Wind* wasn't simply about rebellion, or just a love story. 'It's also about people whose ideas and attitudes were crushed in their own day and virtually lost to history.'

Binns's husband was writer/producer Ian Jones; they'd worked together at Crawford. He'd been the original writer for the hit cop show *Homicide*. Jones had a lively interest in Australian history and was a leading Ned Kelly historian. He convinced Binns to let him present her story to Channel 7. The network loved the idea and paid Binns to continue with her research; she eventually presented a richly detailed 70-page dossier, complete with notes, character bios and outlines of the episodes, along with a one-hour script for a pilot that Binns and Jones had co-written.

The green light was given and they set to work on what would be, at the time, the most ambitious historical drama ever made for Australian TV. Shooting would consume the best part of eight months; locations selected included Old Sydney Town, the faux-convict tourist spot near Gosford, just north of Sydney, and various Victorian locales with an appropriately 'ye olde Australia' character: Belgrave Heights, Geelong, Colac and Emu Bottom.

Jon figured that he'd never be cast in something like *Against the Wind*. He thought that Henry Crawford saw him as a rock singer and a part-time 'drug-crazed, axe-murdering hippie' — but not a dramatic actor. Yet Crawford had clearly changed his mind because the chance arose for Jon to travel to Melbourne and do a screen test for the part of Jonathan Garrett — and he seized the moment. Jon loved the script.

Despite a strong audition, Jon was surprised when he got the call telling him he'd been cast as Garrett, the illiterate emancipated convict who falls in love with Mary Mulvane (like Mary, Jonathan was based on a real-life figure). Jon thought the role would go to a more established local actor.

He told Mario Millo: 'I don't know why, but they want me to act.'

Yet at the same time Jon was thrilled. His character, Jonathan Garrett, entered the story during the third episode and remained for the entire series. This was a part Jon could really sink his teeth into and bring to life.

'It wasn't just a guest role,' Jon said. 'It was something I could build slowly. Jonathan Garrett was a mumbling boy from Essex who gradually gained confidence — and I'm very good at mumbling boys from Essex who gain confidence.'

Jon described his character as 'surly'. 'He didn't say much, he'd mumble, and not make eye contact, which could easily be translated as being nervous. It worked perfectly, because I was nervous until I got used to it. He grew as a character.'

Director Simon Wincer worked on six of the show's thirteen episodes, which each took two weeks to produce, and he described Garrett as a 'character of few words'. Wincer felt that Jon was absolutely right for the part.

Irish actress Mary Larkin was cast in the lead role — curiously, Jon(athan) and Mary had been cast as Jonathan and Mary. 'I have to say that *Against the Wind* was the hardest working, hardest drinking experience I've ever had in my life,' said Larkin. 'And I thoroughly enjoyed every minute of it.'

Larkin's real-life husband was the highly regarded Irish actor Jim Norton, and he was cast as a character named Cunningham. But more importantly — at least for Jon — Norton would serve as a very handy on-set mentor. First Bud Tingwell, now Jim Norton: Jon was learning from some high achievers.

'By god he was a lot of help, as an acting coach for me,' said Jon. 'He was terrific.'

'Jim was fantastic,' said director Simon Wincer. 'Jon would have latched onto him — everyone was drawn to Jim because he knew his craft so well and was so experienced.'

Also in the cast were locals Gerard Kennedy, Bryan Brown, Frank Thring, Lynn Rainbow (who had been a *Number 96* regular) and Chris Haywood, all in the middle of solid careers or working their way up the ladder. The crew was just as strong: the two directors were Wincer and George T. Miller, who'd both go on to stellar careers. Miller was known as 'Noddy' to avoid confusion with the 'other' George Miller, future director of the *Mad Max* films. Both Noddy and Wincer had spent time in the Crawfords' school of TV production and knew how to deliver a series like this on time and within budget.

Old Sydney Town was a key location for the series, as was the Montsalvat artists' colony in the Melbourne suburb of Eltham. The Emu Bottom homestead, which was just outside Melbourne near Sunbury — the site of one of Australia's most famous rock festivals — was where the producers recreated old Parramatta. They also shot at Colac, in southern Victoria, which proved such a good stand-in for Ireland that at least one reviewer was convinced they'd flown there to shoot. (Hardly possible on a budget of $80,000 per episode.)

Jon made an impact on Wincer from the get-go, when the cast assembled at Old Sydney Town before shooting began. 'He had such great presence. This big character with those dark eyes and straggly hair. He couldn't have been more perfect.'

The initial scene that Jon shot with Wincer proved that he had what was required to be a great actor. It left an indelible impression on the director; 40 years down the line Wincer could still recall it vividly. 'He walked through this hospital room to where Mary was sitting there waiting. This towering figure with those daunting looks walked up to her and said, "You're to come with me." Jon was so perfect; he was just terrific. I think that was his first line in the show.'

'Jon loved the experience,' Wincer added. 'He loved the camaraderie of the crew, of the cast. It was a well-run operation but on the smell of an oily rag. It's so rare when you don't have one drama queen but there were no divas on *Against the Wind*. Good scripts, good people.'

Jon would join the cast and crew whenever they'd have a few beers after a day's shooting. Sometimes at lunch break he'd kick a footy around with the crew.

'Jon also proved to be the world's nicest guy,' said Wincer. 'Everyone on the crew adored him. He was always willing to lend a hand, he was always on time, he'd ask a lot of questions, he knew his lines.'

Not only was *Against the Wind* Jon's TV debut in a leading role, it was also the first major project for Jon and manager Peter Rix, who began representing Jon in May 1977. Jon and Rix had history; Rix, who was the same age as Jon, also played high school basketball, for Narwee Boys High, and would often compete against Jon when he was at Cabramatta High. Jon and Rix would be partners for seventeen years. Rix also managed Marcia Hines, Jon's *Superstar* co-star, as well as singers Billy 'Bad Habits' Field and Mark Holden. He also looked after glam rockers Hush.

Rix understood what Jon required from a manager. 'Jon was already a star. What he needed most was money.' And Rix could sense that this TV miniseries could be huge for Jon. 'He was not well paid for *Against the Wind*, but it didn't matter because you could smell that it would make money.'

———

The original plan regarding the music for *Against the Wind* was to use KPM, a library of existing archival recordings. The plan was for lots of sweeping strings, the kind of music that would give *Against the Wind* a suitably epic feel. There'd be no original music. Jon, however, had other ideas, particularly after checking in one day with Mario Millo at his home studio in Sydney's Seven Hills. Jon and Millo had kept in touch since Jon had co-produced *Four Moments*; for a time, Millo played guitar in Baxter Funt, at Jon's request. Jon had also cut a lot of demos at Millo's home studio.

Jon would spend much of the week shooting, either in Victoria or Old Sydney Town, then return home on the weekend to check in with his family at Surry Hills. He'd also play gigs at the St George Leagues Club — he was performing in yet another *Superstar* resurrection, a ten-week run — and work on new music at Millo's studio. He was constantly in motion. One Sunday Jon caught up with Millo and asked what he'd been working on.

Millo played him a cassette of a piece he'd called 'Midnight'.

'He loved it,' said Millo, 'and asked me if he could take the cassette with him to Melbourne.'

'I think they'd love this,' Jon told Millo. 'It'd be perfect.'

Back in Melbourne, Jon played the piece to Binns and Jones, who agreed that it was a strong piece of music that could work for *Against the Wind*. Director Wincer also agreed. 'It was fantastic the way they put that [music] together. Very simple. Very effective. Very powerful.'

Swiftly, the plan to use library music was dropped and Millo was on a flight to Melbourne to meet with the producers. In short time, 'Midnight' was retitled 'Mary's Theme' and Millo was contracted to work with Jon on music for the entire series.

There was just one hitch — the music budget for each episode was a meagre $600. But Jon and Millo simply took that on as a challenge.

'We were limited to whatever Mario and I could play,' Jon said. 'We'd sometimes splurge on flute or bagpipes. It was fantastic to be able to do that and also a massive advantage for me to be on the set.'

Jon and Millo locked into a working routine; every Sunday, Jon would drop by Mario's studio and listen to the music Millo had been working on during the week and also get started on what they'd need for the following week. Many of Jon's ideas came to him while he was shooting the scenes, like using the traditional Irish piece 'The March of the Kings of Laois'. On Monday, Jon would return to the set in Melbourne, where he'd settle in with music editor Peter Palankay and synch the new music to the footage. It was a perfect match of sound and vision and contributed enormously to the ultimate success of *Against the Wind*.

On one of their Sunday get-togethers, Jon played Millo a piece he'd just completed. He had the lyrics, some chords and a melodic line — basically, the nuts and bolts of the song. Jon titled it 'Six Ribbons', a lilting, melancholy ballad that felt perfect for the show.

Inspired by Tim Rice's advice that some of the best songs are lists, Jon composed his own:

> If I were a minstrel, I'd sing you six love songs
> To tell the whole world of the love that we share
> If I were a merchant, I'd bring you six diamonds
> With six blood red roses for my love to wear
> But I am a simple man, a poor common farmer
> So take my six ribbons to tie back your hair

Millo knew about a Conservatorium-trained flautist named Laura Chislett, who added what would become the haunting signature solo of 'Six Ribbons'. The song was ready — and it was perfect.

———

Jon wasn't part of the first episode of *Against the Wind*, which aired on 12 September 1978, and which he watched from the comfort of his couch at home. He had the sense that it was a hit show and was relieved to learn that the music he and Millo had created fitted in seamlessly. 'I was sitting at home watching and listening to the music and thinking, "This is really very good,"' he later said.

Channel 7 execs felt the same, especially when the ratings came in for that first episode — *Against the Wind* had attracted an audience of more than two million people. These were huge numbers; the only other local show that came close during the entire year was Channel 9's wartime drama *The Sullivans* (which featured Michael Caton, Jon's *Superstar* castmate). *Against the Wind* even out-rated such perennial faves as *Happy Days*, *M*A*S*H* and *The Muppets*.

Channel 7 were so thrilled by the numbers, in fact, that they agreed to screen the series before filming was completed — they'd just shot episode eight, which covered the Battle of Vinegar Hill, when the opening episode screened. This was a huge risk, because if one of the principals had an accident, for instance, the series would be thrown into chaos. Regardless, ratings were king and the production of *Against the Wind* went into overdrive; soon the series became a weekly prime-time obsession for millions of Australians (and, soon enough, a huge international audience). The only show to draw more viewers in Australia during 1978 was the British farce *Are You Being Served?* (Jon would later work with the very camp John Inman, one of that show's stars.)

Clearly, it was now time for Jon to release 'Six Ribbons' as a single and it came out not too long after the series started screening. Jon admitted that 'I wouldn't have that [song] if not for the TV show,' and yet 'Six Ribbons' quickly became his biggest hit to date.

Jon had a simple explanation for the eventual success of 'Six Ribbons'. 'It's from a TV series, so people can add pictures in their head. And it's a simple song: it's a list, lyrically.'

Most of Jon's hits were covers, but not 'Six Ribbons', which, over time, became his best known and most requested song. By the end of the show's run on 31 October 1978, the song was a Top 5 hit in Australia and New Zealand. It was a keeper, a fan favourite, and would remain on Jon's concert set list from 1978 onwards.

'"Six Ribbons" gave him the confidence that he ran with forever,' said Peter Rix.

An added bonus was that Jon and Millo owned the rights to the music, which was unusual; typically it would be owned by the producers of the series. His label PolyGram agreed to distribute the soundtrack to *Against the Wind*, which became a Top 10 hit in Australia.

As the show's popularity skyrocketed, the cast and crew faced a unique problem: fans of the show — long before the days of social media — would learn where shoots were taking place and turn up in droves to cheer on Jon and the cast. Members of the crew were instructed to speak with the crowds and insist they keep the noise down while the cameras were rolling. This wasn't a rock concert, after all.

Critical response to the show was good, although a particularly cheeky scribe in *The Canberra Times* seemed to revel in Jon's character being sentenced to 75 lashes by the whip-happy Reverend Samuel Marsden in an early episode: 'I have often thought, wincing my way through some of English's talentless renditions on *Countdown* that he should receive punishment of some sort, and Reverend Marsden has obviously been of the same mind,' he wrote. 'I look forward to him dishing out similar sentences to Sherbert [*sic*] and to John Paul Young in future episodes of *Against the Wind*. Perhaps he could sentence Ian Meldrum to transportation.'

With Jon's star rising higher than ever — he was starring in a top-rating TV show, he had a song in the Top 10, he was now a household name — he sat down for the obligatory one-on-one with the *Australian Women's Weekly*. Although the *Women's Weekly* was hardly renowned for in-depth analysis, Jon opened up in no small measure.

For a start, he admitted that Peter Rix had asked him to downplay the fact he was a married man with two children. Rix felt that this was not the right stuff for pop stars and sex symbols like Jon; Brian Epstein had taken a similar tack when Beatle John Lennon married young. 'Women always wanted to think that Jon was available,' explained Rix.

'That's his attitude,' Jon shrugged when talking with the *Women's Weekly*, 'and I respect him for it. But I have no such attitude. My wife and I have a very successful marriage. We've been married for 10 years and we've got two nice children.' But there was a caveat, as Jon explained: 'They're all normal people and I don't particularly want to drag them into my publicity.'

Did he want his kids to follow him into the entertainment biz?

'I'd rather they didn't go into rock'n'roll,' Jon admitted. 'I want them to be able to choose a career they would really like and not to have a great deal of trouble getting what they want.'

Jon went on to explain that being on the road — and he continued to fit gigs in around his TV and recording commitments, playing 60 shows in the last quarter of 1978 alone — was the most unpleasant part of his job. While on tour, he said, he found solace in getting out and keeping busy, '[doing things like] fishing and horseriding — anything rather than vegetate in a hotel room'.

The subject of drugs was raised, in a less-than-subtle nod to Stevie Wright. Wright's personal demons, which started at the time of *Superstar*, were now well documented in the dailies and the courts; he had experienced heroin addiction, 'deep sleep' therapy at the notorious Chelmsford Private Hospital, and more. Jon dismissed drugs as 'stupid', and he wasn't being glib: he did avoid marijuana, which didn't sit well with him. Jon liked a drink, though.

'I've seen what happened to someone who was close to me . . . He nearly killed himself [with drugs]. But I object to the overall preconception that rock'n'roll singers are illiterate drug-takers.'

And what about going global — was that on his radar? Not really, according to Jon, even though he mentioned an upcoming US sortie, scheduled for early 1979.

'I like living here,' he said. 'And I'm getting used to Australian audiences.' While he accepted that crowds in the US could be very kind to your ego — 'they'll love anything' — he had a problem with what he called the 'American temperament'.

'It's a bit hysterical,' said Jon. 'And I'm not into hysteria.'

So, what about the future, Jon was asked — where did he see himself in fifteen years?

Jon spoke about a 'recurring nightmare' he had. '[I'm] 45 years old, still trying to wear tight trousers and sing on stage. It's the closest thing I can think of to obscenity, people trying to desperately hang onto their youth.'

'I'm determined it won't happen to me,' Jon said in conclusion, 'and my accountant is trying to figure out ways to make sure that it doesn't.'

Jon had actually started bringing his kids with him on tour. Jessamine, being the oldest child, was the first; she'd go out with Jon and his band, especially if they were playing spots such as the Twin Towns Leagues Club in Tweed Heads. Her sister Josie (also called Jo) would sometimes come along, too. (Later, Josie would spend a lot of time on the road with Jon, working as part of the crew, during his *Gilbert and Sullivan* 'phase'.)

'Jo and I, when we were in primary school, especially during school holidays, would go and spend a couple of days on the road, usually with Greg Henson's kids, Greg and Katie,' said Min. 'It was always very exciting; we'd be in a different place every day, swim in the pool. We'd get a buzz out of getting our breakfast delivered. We'd wake up early, too early for Dad, and switch on the Bugs Bunny cartoons, with the sound really low, so as not to wake him.'

Min loved the quieter moments, like travelling in the car with Jon and visiting tourist haunts like the Big Banana, or looking on as he and his Foster Brothers band set up camp in yet another motel car park and began kicking around a footy.

But attending the actual shows, while exciting for Min at first, gradually became the least appealing part of the adventure. 'It always felt a bit weird going to the gigs,' she said. 'I always felt like I was in a place I shouldn't have been. I was under-age, there were pissed adults everywhere, there were rude jokes being told on stage.'

It was 'weird', she added, to see her dad surrounded by people after his shows, watching his uneasiness. 'I could see his discomfort with that.'

CHAPTER 10

'Whatever happened to Harry Miller?'

Jon's popularity just kept on escalating in the wake of *Against the Wind*. It was a heady time, with 'Six Ribbons' taking up what seemed like permanent residence in the Australian Top 10. In January 1979, Jon embarked on an Australian tour opening for US band Chicago; when they played a huge outdoor show at the Sydney Sports Ground, Jon — along with the Australian World Series Cricket team, no less — joined Chicago on stage for the encore. The band's manager, Jeff Wald, the husband of Australian legend Helen Reddy, became a Jon English convert.

But by tour's end, Jon needed a break. He told Don Groves from *The Sydney Morning Herald* that he was feeling 'really bushed'. 'Touring really is terribly exhausting,' Jon said. 'You're either performing, doing sound checks, travelling or giving press interviews.' His biggest dream was to take a holiday.

A little later in the year, soon after winning the TV Week Logie for Best New Talent for his performance in *Against the Wind*, Jon agreed to the release of a best-of collection, *English History*, which came out in August. Jon had only been recording for five years, but he managed to cram the album with hits — 'Turn the Page', 'Hollywood Seven', 'Words Are Not Enough', 'Six Ribbons' (of course) and 'Get Your Love Right', a Top 30 hit in May 1979, were all included. With Jon's popularity at an all-time high,

English History managed to somehow eclipse *Against the Wind*, reaching number 4 in Australia and number 3 in New Zealand, and becoming the highest selling double album to date in Australia. By the end of 1979, it had sold more than 100,000 copies.

It was manna from heaven for Jon's old friend Peter Plavsic, who was now working in A&R at PolyGram, Jon's label. 'It made my entire budget for the year in two months flat,' he revealed.

Sydney radio station 2SM hosted two special *English History* shows at the Hordern Pavilion in late July, giving out freebies to listeners. It was perfect synergy: the hot radio station hosting an artist at his peak. 'An Australian superstar,' announced the on-air ad for the show, 'making English history. Jon English will explode onto the stage at the Hordern Pavilion . . . We're inviting you to watch history in the making.'

In time, the album would sell roughly a million copies worldwide.

A new single, 'Hot Town', kept Jon's hot streak going; it reached the Top 10 in early 1980, while a following single, 'Carmilla', which Jon had written — inspired by a nineteenth-century story about a lesbian vampire by Irish author Joseph Sheridan Le Fanu — fared almost as well in April 1980. ('Come and kiss me and drink my wine,' Jon sang. 'We'll be together til the end of time.') It was lifted from a new album, *Calm Before the Storm*, which was a Top 20 hit in April and had been recorded at the fabled Alberts studio in Sydney — aka the House of Hits, where AC/DC, John Paul Young and The Angels had worked — between July 1979 and January 1980.

Discussion of 'Carmilla' would frequently provide Jon with a sly chuckle, because a lot of people, especially radio DJs, were convinced it was about Carmen. 'I thought it was blatantly about a nineteenth-century vampire and these guys would ask why I wrote a song about my wife,' he told TV host Clive Robertson, smiling broadly.

A few months earlier, on 4 November, Jon, looking great in denims and a white sleeveless top, his hair billowing in the afternoon breeze, was at the Sydney Opera House forecourt, as part of 2SM's Concert of the Decade. Other acts on the huge line-up included Sherbet, Skyhooks and Dragon, as well as Jon's former *Superstar* peers John Paul Young, Marcia Hines and Stevie Wright. Jon was greeted by an 80,000-strong crowd; the crowd was so big, in fact, that it spilled over into the neighbouring Sydney Botanic Garden.

The screams that greeted Jon as he burst onto the stage, positively exploding with energy, might well have reminded him of that Beatles show at the nearby Sydney Stadium, the concert that changed his life back in 1964.

Jon was on a natural high as he and the guys from Baxter Funt raced through a mini-set of hits, pumping out 'Turn the Page', 'Six Ribbons' and 'Hollywood Seven' in rapid-fire succession, as the crowd went absolutely nuts. It was ample proof of just how far Jon's star had risen, played out before a massive audience. Jon even caught a pair of pink knickers that were flung his way, showing all the skills of a cricket slips fieldsman.

As he tore up 'Superstar', his big closer, Jon grinned as he looked out over the huge crowd and shouted: 'Whatever happened to Harry Miller?'

Jon was king of the world.

———

In the wake of *Against the Wind*, requests began coming in for Jon to tour overseas. The show had been a big hit in South Africa, Germany and much of Scandinavia, especially Sweden, where it was known as *Mot alla Vindar* — it had even been the first major Australian TV production to screen in the US, in March 1979. The *Against the Wind* soundtrack had charted as high as number 4 in Sweden, while 'Six Ribbons' did even better, topping the singles chart. Jon's best-of, *English History*, and the single 'Hollywood Seven' both cracked the Top 20 there, too.

When he agreed to tour Europe in February 1981, Jon didn't have a backing band. But Mario Millo did. And it was a red-hot band: Budapest-born, Sydney-based Jackie Orszaczky played bass, Cos Russo was on keyboards and Nick Lister, who'd worked with jazz great Kerrie Biddell, played drums. Richard Gawned, who, like Orszaczky, had played in Marcia Hines's band, played sax and flute. Jon simply hired Millo's musicians.

The original idea was for Millo to travel ahead to check out the venues, and make sure all was in order. But the demand for Jon was so strong — 'The series hit a nerve,' said Millo — that his tour plans were fast-tracked. Sweden was Jon's biggest market and he was to play shows in Örebro, Gothenburg and Stockholm, as well as Copenhagen in Denmark; the venues were 4000- to 5000-capacity theatres, elegant concert halls. In a neat act of synchronicity, Jon was playing some of the same rooms as recent tourist Bob Seger, whose 'Turn the Page' had been Jon's first hit. Jon rated as highly as Seger in Scandinavia; Bruce Springsteen had also filled many of the same venues. The tour was pulled together by promoter Thomas Johansson, who'd worked closely with ABBA.

This would be very different from doing the rounds of Aussie pubs and clubs. While Jon had frequently toured New Zealand, and had fielded some interest from the US, this was his first major international tour. It was a big moment for him, possibly the start of a whole new phase of his career.

They had enough time for a few rehearsals, including one at Jon's home. Jon settled on a set list that started with a Millo instrumental, which he'd dub 'Stockholm 81' in honour of the tour, and then they'd work their way through the hits: 'Turn the Page', 'Words Are Not Enough', 'Hollywood Seven' and, of course, 'Six Ribbons', which formed part of an *Against the Wind* medley. Some nights, on Jon's encouragement, Millo would play an instrumental passage, his own spin on Bizet's *Carmen*.

Jon and the band, along with Peter Rix, their tour manager and a rep from the Swedish label Frituna, arrived in the midst of a bleak Swedish winter. The temperature outside the comfortable confines of their hotel and their twelve-seater tour bus plummeted well below zero. It was a big shock after another blazing Aussie summer.

'If you didn't continue blinking and moving your jaw,' recalled Millo, 'you froze.'

Prior to opening night in Örebro, a largish city with a population of around 100,000 that was best known for its medieval castle, Jon and the group appeared on a Stockholm TV show, a sort of Scandinavian version of *Countdown*. The host's name was Klaus, a 'typical Viking, tall, blond', said Millo. But this was a more upscale production; the audience was seated cabaret-style, and the band played live. The response was enthusiastic — as Jon's following there had been built on his TV work, the audience was surprised that he could sing and perform so well. There'd been a history of UK performers, popular TV stars, coming to Scandinavia and revealing that they couldn't really sing. That clearly wasn't the case with Jon English, although some confusion remained.

Early in the tour, Jon was asked whether there was possibly another Jon English in Australia, a musician. It just didn't register with the locals that he could excel at more than one craft. (Another, more confused Swedish fan would tell him, 'Yes, Jon England, we saw you in *Gone with the Wind!*')

Audience response for the opening night was euphoric — as were the reviews. This was a slightly different show from the one Oz audiences were familiar with; while Jon still interacted with the audience, the band played a bit harder. It was a balls-out rock show.

'The write-ups that we got stated how refreshing it was to see that someone who they saw as a TV star was an even better stage performer than actor,' said Millo. While in Stockholm, Jon and Millo were presented with gold records for *Against the Wind*. (One now hangs on the wall of Peter Rix's Sydney office.)

The troupe reached Copenhagen, when they were hit with every performer's worst nightmare — a mid-show blackout. The band looked at each other in the darkness, wondering what the hell they should do. But Jon had a brainwave and ducked backstage, returning with an acoustic guitar. What happened next lingered with the memories of the audience long after the show ended.

Jon stood at the edge of the stage and started waving his hands. 'Shut up everyone!' he yelled. 'Shut up!'

A hush descended on the audience and then Jon began singing 'Wonderful Copenhagen', made famous by Danny Kaye in the 1952 film *Hans Christian Andersen*, and the crowd lapped it up. Mario Millo, standing alongside Jon, was stunned.

'I thought: "There you have it. This is why Jon English is who he is. He's amazing. What an amazing performer." A fantastic moment.'

At the end of the tour Jon travelled to London, where he met with English producer Tim Friese-Greene, who'd produce his next album, *InRoads*, which would appear later in 1981. Millo and keyboardist Russo met with Jon in London where they caught a show by Judie Tzuke, an Elton John protégé, who'd been all over the charts in 1979 with her big ballad 'Stay With Me Till Dawn'. Tzuke's father, Sefton Myers, had managed Andrew Lloyd Webber and Tim Rice during the time of *Superstar*.

Millo was surprised by the Tzuke gig — he felt it was insipid by comparison with the shows he and Jon and the band had just played in Sweden.

'Both Cos and I concurred. Our show with Jon' — what Millo referred to as an 'international rock show' — 'was head and shoulders above this. It lacked dynamics; it was pretty lame, really.'

On his return to Australia, Jon and the band swiftly returned to Earth: their first homecoming gig was at the Lithgow Workers Club, 'to about 50 people', recalled Greg Henson. But they were then booked for a lucrative week-long run of dates at the Twin Towns Services Club in Tweed Heads, a 1000-plus capacity venue, a regular gig for Jon. Jon's wife Carmen made the trip north from Sydney too, as did his children. Millo's wife, Liz, also travelled with the English entourage. It was essentially a working holiday, which was the closest thing to an actual holiday that the Englishes had shared to this point.

The Twin Towns shows, however, were different from the European gigs. Jon started telling more jokes, toying with the audience, whereas in Sweden he and the band had clobbered punters with their aggressive style. At the end of each Twin Towns show, Jon and the band would leave the stage, only to race back for an encore after barely 20 seconds had passed. After a couple of nights of this, Millo — whose opinion Jon respected — pulled him aside. He didn't think Jon was properly 'milking' the moment.

'Let them clap. We've played for two hours. Let them clap, build it up. Let them work.'

Jon disagreed.

'Morrie, I know these audiences,' he said to him. 'You don't understand.' With that they once again rushed back on stage.

After one particular gig, Jon was so eager to return to the stage that he left Millo stranded in the backstage toilet. He was forced to zip up and race back to his spot on stage, by which time the band was already halfway through their encore.

The next day Jon, Millo and their wives sat down to breakfast. Jon had an announcement.

'I've been thinking about things, Morrie,' Jon said. 'I need you as much as you need me. We have to do this together.'

'You're absolutely right, mate,' Millo replied. 'You and I can make this an international thing. You are the best frontman in the country.'

Their wives also agreed. 'Whenever you work together, great things happen,' they said. They were right, of course — from Sebastian Hardie to 'Hollywood Seven' and *Against the Wind*, their collaborations had resulted in some of Jon's best and most successful work.

It seemed as though they were on the verge of a big new adventure, seizing on their Swedish success and taking on the world. Yet a couple of weeks later, during a production meeting between Jon, the band and Peter Rix, 'it all fell apart', according to Millo. There was talk about a return to Europe, and Millo had brought up the subject of retaining the instrumental opening to their sets, which helped build anticipation for Jon's onstage arrival. It had worked in Sweden and Millo thought it should be a keeper.

According to Millo, Rix shut it down — he told Millo that it wasn't his show and that he should keep quiet. Jon and Millo never toured together again (although Jon did return to Sweden in late 1981 for more shows).

To Millo, it seemed to be a case of 'the money in the hand at the time versus the larger picture', as he recalled. 'But I always thought he had amazing international potential. We worked together so well.'

There were two sides to this story. Peter Rix said that the idea of 'going back and starting at square one' — which is what Jon would have had to do to make his name outside of Australia and Scandinavia — didn't appeal to his client. 'He had a wife and children,' said Rix. 'To pack up and head off meant that he would have to start from square one, but here [in Australia] he was a star.'

And being a star did have its benefits. On the plane back to Australia from London, Jon had been invited by the captain up to the cockpit — this was even better than travelling first class. While there, the captain turned to Jon with a question.

'Mate,' he said, 'I'm in the Castle Hills Lions Club and we do an annual Christmas Carols at Castle Hill Oval — would you like to come and sing some Christmas carols?'

'I'd love to. Fantastic,' replied Jon, not thinking for a moment that the request was a classic case of quid pro quo. Whenever Marcia Hines found herself in a similar situation, she'd simply hand over Rix's business card and say, 'Best call my manager'. Not Jon.

Peter Rix picked up the story. 'Three months later the captain rings the office to make the final plans and I don't know anything about it. I called Jon and he said, "Get me out of that, for god's sake." I rang the captain and I got this bucketload. He'd obviously told everyone that he had Jon English for the show.'

'Jon didn't want to have an enemy in the world,' said Rix. 'And he'd get into trouble as a result.'

CHAPTER 11

'Tell the teacher to get fucked!'

S tarring in *Against the Wind* had many benefits for Jon — he became an international name, the series rated off the charts, he had his first original hit in 'Six Ribbons' — but there was an additional, unexpected bonus. He needed to learn to ride a horse for the show and underwent training in a semi-rural spot near the Hawkesbury River, 45 kilometres north-west of Sydney.

Jon loved the area and asked his instructor, Peter Roach, who was also the local vet, if there were any properties for sale.

'As a matter of fact, there is,' Roach told him.

The 30-acre spread, on the side of a hill, with a long driveway leading down to the property itself, was in a suburb named Glenorie. The actress Maggie Kirkpatrick — *Prisoner*'s 'The Freak' — and TV talk show host Mike Walsh lived nearby; the Hawkesbury had become a hideaway-of-choice for people in the public eye. It was perfect for Jon, someone who craved privacy just as much as he adored being loved by his fans. And the locals weren't the kind of people who'd fawn over a celebrity.

When Jon bought the property in late 1978, its only residence was a partly built fibro house, which he immediately dubbed the Half House. Carmen's parents, Lembit and Benita — Pop and Granny to the kids — moved in and Carmen's father set to work building a proper farmhouse.

When it was finished, they continued to live, for a time, in the Half House, while Jon, Carmen and the children lived in the main house. Eventually, what was once the Half House became Jon's home studio. (Sadly, Carmen's father contracted cancer and died on 27 December 1984, and her mother moved into an Estonian retirement village. Benita died on 6 January 2002.)

'I loved it at first,' said Carmen. 'We used to go horseriding with the neighbours, Peter Roach and his wife Lyn, who became good friends. They ended up having four children roughly the same age as Jon's and mine, so it was a very close-knit rural area.'

Over time, the Englishes acquired two horses, goats, dogs, lots of chickens and as many as thirteen cats. Jon had a thing for strays. 'The vet made a lot of money out of us,' recalled Carmen.

Jon loved to show off his new home. 'It was fantastic,' said Jon's old Sebastian Hardie bandmate Graham Ford. 'It was on the side of a hill, overlooking the water. That was a beautiful house. Very private. A retreat.'

'It was off the beaten track,' said Foster Brother Peter Deacon. 'You wouldn't know it was there.' Jon would frequently have friends and fellow musos swing by, sometimes without telling Carmen, who was always expected to cater. As Jon's daughter Min observed, 'We didn't really know who was going to show up. There'd often be people sleeping on the floor.'

Simon Gallaher was another colleague of Jon's to visit Glenorie and understand what it meant to him. 'He loved his farm. He was really proud of being out there with his family,' said Gallaher. But Gallaher also recognised the problems that came with the life Jon had chosen, as he'd spend long periods of time away from Glenorie. 'Of course Carmen was really stuck there, with four young children, the youngest [Julian] in nappies. It would have been a really isolating experience for her, when he was on the road.'

Living a semi-rural life came with its complications — bad things tended to happen when Jon was out on tour, as Min recalled. 'There'd be floods, mad storms where the power would go out for days, tank water, so you weren't able to flush the toilet — I don't know how Mum did it.'

As for Carmen, she sometimes craved adult company, especially when the Roaches left Glenorie and moved to Turramurra, in Sydney's northern suburbs, some 30 kilometres away. 'I found myself getting very lonely, because Jon was always on tour. It wasn't easy. But I managed. And I worked bloody hard.'

Like so much of his life, Jon's time as a dad, at home on the farm with Carmen and the kids, was compartmentalised. He could be away for weeks, sometimes months at a stretch. While he accepted it as being part of the world in which he worked, it was also a cause of some great frustration for Jon.

It was a complicated situation. He loved being home; his family and the farm were his retreat. But he knew he had to keep working to support their lifestyle, and that kept him away from home for extended periods of time. And Jon's new life didn't come cheap. 'The farm gobbled up a lot of money,' said Peter Rix.

Over the years, Jon's eldest son, Jonathan, who was born on 15 January 1982, got a sense of his father's mixed feelings about the life he was leading. 'I think about it often from his perspective, when he'd sometimes go into not great places. A lot of it was, "This is my house and I'm a total bloody stranger here." There were five people living as a unit, [we had] everything sorted, and that would have been very weird for him. I feel like the mood could shift very quickly; it'd be equal parts super fun, super excitement, and then, "Oh, Christ, someone's upset someone."'

'I think there was definitely a time of adjustment, for him and us, after a tour,' said Min. 'Dad was a big personality. There were even things such

as the TV being so loud, because he was a bit deaf, stuff like that. Then
there'd be lovely family times.'

Typically, the first few days after Jon's return were the trickiest, as he'd
regroup and decompress. It would take some time before he and Carmen
struck upon the perfect parenting rhythm. 'You could see Mum and
Dad's frustration,' said Josie. '"How do we do this again?" Then they'd
find their groove and it would be great. He'd take off his Jon English suit
and be the real him.

'It made me understand he was often a long way from home and not by
choice. He would have preferred to come home every night.'

'We all had our own routine, and so did Jon,' said Carmen. 'It was difficult because we'd have to be quiet in the mornings, because he was fast
asleep. He'd sleep until lunchtime because he was used to working late
nights. I had to get up and do the school run. I think it was awkward for
all of us. It took a while for Jon to actually relax.'

'He'd come home and fall into a heap for a day or two; we'd have to be
really quiet,' added Min. 'Then he'd climb out of it and get into a groove,
especially if it was out on the farm, which he loved, or if it was footy season. He'd go and slash the paddocks' — running a tractor with a slasher
hooked to it — 'and he'd listen to the footy.'

Jon would keep a spiral notebook in his pocket, in case inspiration
struck. 'She Was Real', a genuinely eerie ghost story set to music, came
to him while he was riding his motorbike around the area late at night. It
was one of his best songs, inspired by his semi-rural hideaway.

Christmas on the farm at Glenorie was always a big event for Jon, Carmen and the kids. On Christmas Eve, as was the Estonian tradition, the
children would open their presents, often with Carmen's family looking

on. Jon was a huge fan of puzzles and riddles, and he and Carmen would sit up on Christmas Eve, writing out a series of clues for the kids to read on Christmas morning, so they could find their second batch of presents. ('As if we were going to go, "No, we don't want two Christmases,"' laughed Josie.) Jon and Carmen would leave the clues all over the farm — both inside the house and outside; they'd be up late, walking around with torches, planting clues. Over time, the process became more and more elaborate; sometimes Jon would rope in the neighbours and get them involved, too.

'We had them running all over the place,' said Carmen. 'They loved it.'

'We'd wake up Christmas morning,' said Min, 'and there'd be a note with a clue on our beds, something quirky, poetic or funny, which would lead us to where we needed to go for our next clue. One year I remember Jo had to dive into our pool to retrieve a clue that was bagged. They'd also be under the eggs in the chook house.

'It'd take maybe an hour, an hour and a half, and would always lead us back to the stockings in our room. It was so fun.'

Boxing Day was often spent with Jon's side of the family, although sometimes they'd hold off until 16 January — 'Sydmas' — which remained a constant for all the Englishes. They usually celebrated with yum cha in Cabramatta. Typically, after settling into their seats, Jon would slyly insert a lolly snake in his nose and wait for someone to notice. Anything to get a laugh, to keep the mood light.

This wasn't Jon's only quirk. There was an exaggerated face that Jon loved to pull, usually accompanied by a silly noise. Soon enough his kids would be copying it. They came up with a name for it: they called it 'graaghing'. If Jon was on stage and knew that the kids were in the crowd, he'd spot them and pull the goofy face that only they recognised — it was their in-joke. 'Nix' was another of the noises Jon liked to make for the kids; he had the word written on all his road cases. This was another in-joke — Nix was Jon's nickname, which began when Mario Millo accidentally called him 'Nick' several times. 'Nick' became 'Nix'.

Everyone had a nickname — Jon called Carmen 'Boo', short for Boo Boo, after the character in *Yogi Bear*. Josie would be Jo-Jams; Jessamine was always Min; and Jonathan was called 'Leg', because, like his father, he had skinny legs, just like a chicken. Jonathan had trouble pronouncing his little brother's name — it always came out as 'Hudian' — so Julian, who was born on 16 October 1984, became 'Hoody'.

Jon had a bunch of favourite phrases. He often related a story about being a student when the family was still in the UK. He recalled the miserable school dinners that were provided; the only relief came when they served dessert.

'He'd tell me that when whoever was in charge asked if anyone wanted more dessert, everyone's hand would go up and they'd say "Ooh, me!"' said Jonathan. 'But one day it was tapioca pudding — the most grim thing imaginable. On that day, when it was asked if anyone wanted seconds, just one kid raised his hand, crying out, "Ooh, me!" So the person in charge, the major-general or whatever, took a look at him and said, "Get out!" It stayed with Dad forever, that phrase — "Get out!"'

'That was the response Jon used all his life when you'd caught him out on something and he didn't have an answer,' added his brother Jeremy: '"Get out!" It's a great punchline. Very Basil Fawlty.'

Jon loved *The Three Stooges* and pie-in-the-face humour. Getting 'pied' was another family tradition. 'Everyone had to get pied on their birthday,' said Jonathan, 'with a paper plate full of shaving cream. It was all about taking them unawares.'

Jon continued this when he was on the road, as his eldest son often witnessed. 'They'd be taking their big bow, with their hands on each other's shoulders, and then — *bam!*'

Jon also loved to cook. Like so much else in his life, he cooked 'big'. Jon had an account at the nearby Campbells Cash & Carry, which enabled him to shop in bulk.

'Everything was job lot with Dad,' said Min. 'Five-kilo bags of potatoes, that kind of thing.'

'You'd wake up and there'd be 85 butterscotch biscuits and twelve Fray Bentos pies in the pantry,' remembered Jonathan.

Jeremy suspected that Jon's need to stock up dated back to their youth — rationing was still in place when Jon and Jeremy were born. World War II was still a very strong memory for their parents. 'I think that might have come from the wartime thing, rationing and that. If you've got stuff in the cupboard and shit happens, you'll be OK. Maybe it got passed on from Mum and Dad.'

One trait Jon definitely acquired from his mother was an inability to shop right. Sheila always had a shopping list, but it was never revised. 'And she'd never check,' said Jon's sister Jan. 'She'd simply write down what she'd written the week before, so we'd end up with 195 cans of tomatoes, that kind of thing.' In that, Sheila and Jon were similar: 'She always bought as though she was feeding twelve.'

As for Jon, he shopped as though he was feeding an army. Dumpling stew, served in a massive pot, was one of Jon's favourite dishes to prepare. He'd spend hours slaving away in the kitchen getting the feast ready.

'He'd put every vegetable he could find into it,' said Min. 'It was this huge thing.'

Jon didn't simply serve the food; even that came with a performance. He'd sometimes absent-mindedly place his hands on the steaming pot, burning himself. 'He'd never use tea towels,' said Min. 'He'd grab the handles and roar.'

Even putting the children to bed was a chance for Jon to entertain the kids. Jonathan and Julian shared a bedroom in the loft of the farmhouse, which was reached by a ladder. It was a small space and a bit tricky to access.

As Jonathan recalled, 'Dad would put us to bed, and — bang! — hit his head on the rafters. Then he'd fall down, ham it up, all the while saying, "Keep quiet, keep quiet." Then he'd grab Julian, throw him onto me, and it turned into a wrestling match — total chaos. There was no way we were going to sleep. We were totally hyped.'

'That's what I miss the most,' said Min. 'The running gags.'

Occasionally, Jon would genuinely lose his cool, such as the time he decided that the kids needed to be taught a lesson about keeping a reasonably clear front doorstep. He took all their shoes, which they left in a heap outside the front door, and threw them into the paddock.

'We had some people coming over and there was no space for them to take their shoes off at the front door,' said Min. But outbursts like this were uncommon; Jon was really just a big kid. 'Mostly it felt like he'd come home and want to have fun with us, once he got over the jet lag, or whatever,' Min added. 'The only time he'd yell is when he couldn't cope anymore, not because he wanted to pull rank.'

When it came to dealing with the children's teachers, Jon was still very much Sheila's son — authority was not to be trusted, or respected. His daughters attended the local Hillside Public School and sometimes there'd be trouble — one of the kids might have been warned about wearing the wrong uniform, or they'd caused some disruption in class. Jon's solution was simple: 'Tell the teacher to get fucked!'

'Seriously, this is what he'd say: "Tell them to get fucked!"' said Min. 'We didn't want Dad to draw any more attention to us, but he'd get very protective.' The kids were savvy enough to not follow through on their dad's advice.

Yet Jon was willing to get involved in some school activities, one of them being the Easter Hat Parade. This was a chance for him to express himself creatively, much to the horror of his children.

One year, 'Jo and I were wigging out about making a hat,' Min recalled. 'I didn't like being the centre of attention, ever. So the Easter Hat Parade was a great cause of anxiety. Dad was home and said he'd help.'

What Jon came up with became the talking point of that year's parade. He turned Jo into Pontius Pilate, complete with pilot goggles and helmet. (The pun may have been lost on the kids' classmates.) Jon transformed Min into The Last Supper.

As she recalled, 'He was quite resourceful with it. I had a basket on my head with a thing tied around it to hold it still. It had a loaf of bread, some fish fingers and a bottle of wine. And he sent me off to school dressed like that.'

One school holiday, Jon decided, on the advice of Carmen's brother, Ivan, to enrol Josie in an Estonian summer camp. It was his attempt to embrace Carmen's ethnic roots — a half-arsed attempt, as it transpired.

When they arrived, while Jon spoke with the other parents, Josie introduced herself to some of the kids at the camp. They did what some young kids do and made the camp out to be a nightmare, in the process scaring the hell out of the 'newbie'. 'Oh, it's really scary here,' they told Josie. 'And look out for that girl,' they said, pointing. 'She'll get you!'

Josie was rattled. She walked back to Jon and said, 'I don't know if I like it here.'

Jon looked at Josie, then looked around, shrugged his shoulders and declared: 'Yeah, fair enough. Let's fuck off then.'

With that they jumped in the car and drove home, never to return. So much for summer camp.

'That's definitely been passed on,' said Jonathan. 'I'm so quick to throw in the towel if something doesn't look like it's going to be a good experience.'

Occasionally, Jon's family were exposed to his celebrity, and the awkwardness he sometimes experienced when dealing with fans. While on a campervan holiday in Tasmania, Jon pulled into a greasy spoon in Queenstown and ordered lunch. The woman behind the counter recognised Jon and started working the phone — 'You'll never guess who's in my shop!' — and soon enough the place started filling up with curious onlookers. Jon, who was quietly waiting on their order, took one look and said to Carmen and the kids, 'Let's get out of here.'

According to Carmen, 'Fans could be quite pushy — and Jon had to be nice to them. They were his bread and butter, the people who'd see the shows and buy the records. I didn't want any part of it.

'We just tried not to go out in public too much as a family. He was always being recognised. People can't help themselves; they would always come over and interrupt us. And I was never very good at hiding how I felt. There was a lot of grimacing going on.'

Once, when Jon was unpacking after yet another long tour, Min caught a glimpse of something Jon had been given by a fan — it was a piece of knitted handiwork, in the shape of a penis and a pair of balls. 'I was maybe eight, and my reaction was "Eww!" I didn't quite know what it was, but I knew it wasn't right.'

In their quieter domestic moments, Jon and Carmen loved nothing better than curling up in front of the TV and watching a VHS tape that the kids had given Jon as a gift. It contained his two favourites: a selection of John Belushi's mad moments on *Saturday Night Live* and the film *Monty Python Live at the Hollywood Bowl*.

'He and Mum would watch it and just howl,' said Jonathan.

During warmer weather Jon and Carmen would slip off their clothes and sunbake nude by the pool. Nudity was commonplace at Glenorie, especially with the boys, Julian and Jonathan. Min and Josie, having spent time living in the inner city, were a bit more circumspect, but sometimes the boys, who only knew life on the farm, would be in the car on the way to the shops before anyone realised they hadn't been dressed.

'Poor Glenorie would be like, "What is it with the Englishes?"' laughed Josie.

Occasionally they went out to a movie. The first film that Jon took the kids to see was the remake of *King Kong*, starring Jessica Lange. Jon and Carmen were mad keen to check out the film adaptation of Stephen King's novel *Carrie*, so they hid the girls in the back of the car (this was before the boys were born) and headed off to the drive-in at Box Hill. The film was R-rated and extremely bloody in parts, and was a lot to take in for very young kids.

'They couldn't get any babysitters,' said Min, 'so they made us hide under the seat and we watched bloody *Carrie* with them. I was traumatised.'

Josie was confused by her parents' act of subterfuge — she thought that they couldn't afford to pay for everyone, which was why they were hidden in the back seat.

'No,' Min whispered. 'I don't think we're allowed here.'

Yet while R-rated horror films were fine for the kids, certain popular TV shows definitely were not. Jon stopped the kids from watching *The Brady Bunch* and *Young Talent Time*, two of the most popular programs of the day.

Finally, the kids had to ask Jon what prompted his decision. Were they missing something?

'Why? Because they're bullshit,' Jon replied. 'It's all bullshit.' He hated the fakeness of both shows, *The Brady Bunch*'s make-believe flawless family. No one was that perfect.

'We were the weirdos at school watching horror films but not *The Brady Bunch* or *Young Talent Time*,' laughed Josie.

Later in life, Jon would hold reality TV in equal disdain. To him, it was nothing but bullshit.

Jon also rejected organised religion and told the school that his kids were not to be involved in any religion classes. 'Dad would write ten-page essays about why his children weren't to be indoctrinated,' said Josie. 'He was very protective.' They were the only students to sit out scripture, which didn't help their efforts to blend in with the crowd. As the only kids at school with a famous dad, they didn't like the scrutiny that came with that — Josie and Min, in particular, had a real disdain for the spotlight. That was their dad's thing; it wasn't for them.

Jon and Carmen were curious parents, in some ways: while they were wary of authority figures, rejected religion and had no problems with nudity, they could also be quite conservative. 'They were so weirdly wholesome,' said Josie, 'but anti-establishment. They would have hated to be called hippies, but they sort of were. Yet Dad loved the Queen, too.' Jon was so upset by the death of Diana, Princess of Wales, in 1997 that he almost had to cancel a gig. 'Dad was in tears,' said Josie. 'He didn't even know if he could perform.'

As the kids grew older and began bringing home partners, that, too, came with its own complications. Nudity was one potential problem; another was the fact that it was never quiet around the English dinner table. Everyone had something to say and needed to be heard. 'We'd talk over each other, be animated,' said Min. 'It was a big adjustment period for partners when we brought them home.'

One night, Josie came home with a girlfriend for a sleepover and discovered Jon and Carmen making love on the lounge room floor. She ran upstairs and woke Min, who was the more prudish of Jon's daughters.

'I've never seen her so angry,' said Josie. 'She must have been fourteen. "How dare you!" she screamed. She was coming on like Mother Superior.'

Jon, without missing a beat, said: 'At least you didn't come home and I was punching her.'

Min didn't speak to her parents for days, while Josie swore her friend to secrecy.

'Dad did have a point,' Josie eventually conceded. 'But they could have gone upstairs.'

In the early 1980s, Jon's band morphed into The Foster Brothers, the pieces falling into place after a final tour of New Zealand with Baxter Funt. The band at that point comprised Trevor White's brother Peter (known as 'Chalky') on keyboards, Mike Wade and Tony Naylor on guitars, John Coker on bass and drummer Greg Henson. White left the band and was replaced by Peter Deacon, who had played with Henson in the *Superstar* band and, like Henson, would become a 'lifer' with Jon. John Dallimore soon joined on guitar.

Eventually, the 'classic' Foster Brothers line-up gelled, with Henson on drums, Deacon on keyboards, John 'JD' Dallimore and Keith 'Stretch' Kerwin playing guitars and Coker on bass. This line-up remained relatively steady for the better part of 30 years.

Apart from the line-up changes, there were musical differences between Baxter Funt and The Foster Brothers, as Henson explained. 'Baxter Funt was a rock'n'roll band but more leaning towards fusion, which was a great way to learn for me. Then [Foster Brothers] was more of a rock'n'roll band.'

But they weren't a regular rock'n'roll band. Over time, The Foster Brothers, with Jon very much at the helm — manager Peter Rix called him the 'head prefect' — would incorporate elements of slapstick and vaudeville into their set. Every night was party night when The Foster Brothers played. Piss-taking was mandatory; even Jon's rock opera *Paris*, which started to take shape during the 1980s and became his number-one obsession, was ripe for mocking. Someone came up with the idea of creating a miniature replica of Troy's wooden horse, which would be wheeled out on stage to much fanfare.

'Rarely did a show pass when we didn't have someone in stitches on stage,' said Deacon. 'Someone would say something and we'd all just crack up. That would come across to the audience: "These guys are having fun!"'

Jon and the Fosters would record a number of studio records together: 1982's *Jokers and Queens*, a collaboration with Marcia Hines, as well as 1983's *Some People*, which was Jon's first — but by no means last — record with producer David Mackay. But it was their live album, April 1982's *Beating the Boards*, that truly captured Jon and the band where they were at their best: live on stage.

The album took choice cuts from shows in various Oz venues — the Sidney Myer Music Bowl in Melbourne, the Civic Theatre in Canberra, the Musicians Club in Sydney and Newcastle's Civic Theatre, one of Jon's favourite rooms — as well as European gigs in Oslo and Copenhagen. Set list–wise, it was essentially the best of Jon English, with such hits as 'Turn the Page', 'Lovin' Arms', 'Get Your Love Right', 'Hot Town' and 'Six Ribbons' complemented by 'The Shining' and 'Beating the Boards', songs that really did the business in concert. The album was only a minor hit, reaching number 24 on the Australian charts, but that hardly mattered. It was a terrific snapshot of one of the country's hottest bands at their peak and one of the best live records produced in Australia. And the cover image said it all: a striking shot of Jon at his moody (and sweaty) best, deep in the moment.

'The best thing Jon liked in life was to get The Foster Brothers together and get on the road,' said Peter Rix. 'They could sell out wherever they played.' During the band's 1980s peak, they'd fill 600- to 1000-capacity rooms six nights a week all across Australia, typically grossing somewhere in the vicinity of $60,000 a week. Most years they'd spend six months on the road.

Playing with the Fosters also satisfied one of Jon's biggest urges: his ferocious need to please an audience. 'It was an essential part of his being,' said Rix. 'He couldn't leave a stage until he had the audience on their feet screaming. He'd throw another song in. He could sell a song better than Gerry Harvey. Jon was always an entertainer.'

Chaos was never too far away whenever the Fosters filled a room. They played a New Year's Eve gig on a barge on the Brisbane River, with the audience looking on from the shore. They plugged in just after the midnight fireworks, but the power cut out in the middle of their opening song.

'It went black. Silence. Nothing,' said Peter Deacon.

They were trapped, stuck on the barge. It happened several times during the night, yet somehow the gig went on. The gig always went on.

There would also be a notorious night in Melbourne, one now etched in Foster Brothers folklore. Jon liked to have an electric fan on stage, which would keep him cool and give him the perfect windswept rock star look. A drunken female punter staggered to the front of the stage, swayed for a minute or two and then vomited straight into Jon's fan, spraying spew all over him. Drummer Henson copped a face-full, too; for a moment he regretted having spent 'twenty years staring at Jon English's arse', as he often joked.

Jon never had any problems taking the piss out of his bandmates: everyone was fair game when The Foster Brothers were on the road. After a show at the Bexley North Hotel, one of many Sydney venues they'd fill on a regular basis, drummer Henson was in the band room, having a drink, when a bouncer approached him.

'Sorry, mate, it's time to leave now.'

Henson replied, 'No, no, I'm in the band, mate,' but the bouncer didn't believe him.

'No, mate,' he said. 'You're out!'

'Look, come with me,' Henson said to the bouncer. 'I'll introduce you to Jon and he'll tell you who I am.'

They marched down to the dressing room and knocked on the door.

'Mr English,' asked the bouncer as they stepped inside, 'this bloke says he's in your band. Do you know him?'

Jon smiled at Henson and slowly said, 'I've never seen him before in my life. Do you want an autograph?'

Women were constantly drawn to the band, especially Jon. 'It was a smorgasbord,' said Rix. 'Jon would never finish a show and close the door and go to bed.' But Jon struggled to come clean with his bandmates about his infidelities on the road, as obvious as they were: attractive women standing by the side of the stage after a show were a common feature of Foster Brothers gigs.

'I didn't dig it at all,' said three-times-married drummer Henson, who by his own admission was 'no saint'. But this was different.

'I did a lot of shit, but Jon lied. I'd say, "Who's that?" And he'd say, "She's just an old friend." He wouldn't say, "I'm boning her," he'd say, "She's an old friend." I'd think, "Come on, mate, I'm an old friend, tell me the truth." He just wanted to be loved by everybody but it was a shallow way to think.'

For all their wildness — keeping in mind this was a band who named themselves after a beer — Jon's work ethic remained very much intact. 'Jon would never miss a gig, even if he was crook,' said Henson. Henson was a similar type of character; he once played while so ill that he threw up into a bucket beside his drum kit between songs.

Jon and the Fosters had the uncanny knack of being able to rapidly shift gears between vaudeville, ballads and balls-out rock'n'roll. One minute they'd be pulling off synchronised guitar moves, complete with high kicks, cancan style; the next they'd play 'Words Are Not Enough', anchored by the Henson/Coker rhythm section and powered by a wonderfully gutsy, soulful vocal from Jon. Yet back in 1978, Jon almost hadn't recorded 'Words Are Not Enough'. Peter Plavsic, in his A&R role at PolyGram, brought 'Words' to Jon; the demo was sung by Renée Geyer. But the song didn't grab Jon.

'As a favour to a mate, just do the vocal,' Plavsic pleaded with Jon. 'If you don't like it, I'll ditch it.' It was a Top 5 hit and became a live staple.

On stage, Jon and the band had a high time laughing their way through 'Words Are Not Enough', undertaking what Jon introduced, with a cheesy flourish, as the 'floor show', with the audience clapping along on his instruction. Jon would usually shut the song down midway, cheekily chastising the audience for not clapping properly: 'You bastards!' Then, with a leer and a wink, he'd announce that it was time to pull out the 'big one' — 'No, not that big one!' — as he and the Fosters linked hands and sang the song's chorus like a drunken men's choir, steadily working the crowd into a lather. Then they'd change the mood and pour themselves into story songs such as 'She Was Real' or 'Hollywood Seven', which allowed Jon to utilise his theatrical skills.

It was a consummate performance, night after night, by both Jon and the band. And Jon looked a million dollars in his leather pants and vest, his chest on full and proud display, a huge smile on his face, sweat pouring off him. He was in rock'n'roll heaven.

CHAPTER 12

'I'm playing the Pirate King, the one that falls over a lot.'

Jon appeared on TV's *The Mike Walsh Show* in October 1983 with some big news: he'd just been cast in an Australian production of Gilbert and Sullivan's *The Pirates of Penzance*, his first major stage role since *Superstar* Mk II back in 1975. Walsh, a Gilbert and Sullivan tragic, asked what prompted his return to the theatre.

'I thought it was time to do something theatrical again rather than trawling around the country in my leather trousers,' Jon said — oddly enough, while he was wearing leather trousers, teamed with lime-green shoes and a bright red jacket. 'I'm playing the Pirate King, the one that falls over a lot. I get to sing a couple of songs. It's great fun.'

Walsh had caught the Broadway production and understood that this was not your typical *Pirates* — this was Gilbert and Sullivan revamped for a modern audience. 'For people who can't stand Gilbert and Sullivan, you'd love it — it's so acrobatic and energetic and fun,' he told his viewers.

Jon agreed, then admitted that the lengthy stretch of *Superstar* had put him off long-running productions. As far as he was concerned, *Pirates* had a short season planned — six weeks in total — and then he would be onto whatever next caught his interest. *The Pirates of Penzance*, however, had other plans for him.

On paper, casting Jon as the Pirate King seemed like madness: what was the dark-eyed rocker doing in a dusty old musical that dated all the way back to 1879? But this was no random act of madness on the part of the producers. The January 1981 Broadway revival of the production had been a massive hit, running for almost two years and some 800 performances, and winning three Tony Awards, including Best Revival, even though the original plan was a six-week run in New York's Central Park. And the success of the Broadway *Pirates* was in the casting: rather than depend entirely on seasoned Broadway performers, the producers — Joseph Papp and the Public Theater of NYC — opted for what was known as 'star casting'.

Actor Kevin Kline, who'd briefly appeared in the long-running soap *Search for Tomorrow*, was cast as the Pirate King, a character who put the 'swash' into 'buckle', while West Coast music great Linda Ronstadt, a Grammy-winning singer better known for such pop/rock standards as 'You're No Good' and 'Blue Bayou', played Mabel, the love interest. It was Ronstadt's first time on Broadway. Actor Rex Smith, who was cast as Frederic, the dutiful apprentice at the centre of the story, had also been a pop singer; in 1979 he reached the US Top 10 with a song called 'You Take My Breath Away'. These weren't your typical Broadway thespians, by any stretch.

When the idea was first pitched to Jon, he was resistant to the idea. Carmen eventually persuaded him to drive to the Roseville Cinema to watch the Kline/Ronstadt film version of *Pirates*. As they sat in the darkness of the cinema, Carmen could see that the role of the Pirate King had Jon's name written all over it.

'This part is made for you,' she said to Jon as they walked to their car. 'Don't be stupid — go and do it!'

Jon agreed — and any lingering doubts he may have had were alleviated by the $8000 weekly pay cheque.

Still, when the co-producers of the Australian production — the Victorian State Opera, the Victorian Arts Centre and the Australian Elizabethan Theatre Trust — revealed their casting, eyebrows were collectively raised in theatre circles.

The Theatre Trust was chaired by silver-haired, ever-droll actor Noel Ferrier, who had appeared with Jon on Channel 10's celebrity game show *Blankety Blanks*. But it was Ken Mackenzie-Forbes, the head of the Victorian Arts Centre, who specifically sought out Jon for the role.

Jon would play the Pirate King; Simon Gallaher, the golden-haired darling of the *Midday Show* set, was cast as Frederic; and nineteen-year-old Marina Prior, who was studying music, was cast as Mabel. Acclaimed soprano June Bronhill took on the role of Ruth; she also took on the role of den mother for the men's chorus, who she'd take out wining and dining between shows, usually returning them back to the theatre a little worse for wear.

At the centre of this was a very odd mix: the blue-rinsers' darling, Gallaher, teaming up with Jon, the shaggy, sweaty rock'n'roller, king of the beer barns. Couples didn't come much more odd. Even physically they were vastly different — Jon towered over Gallaher.

Gallaher, who'd just turned 25, was fully aware of the stir that the casting caused.

'The first reaction from everyone was: "Well, that's Gilbert and Sullivan from the nineteenth century — fancy putting a rock'n'roller like Jon English, a guy like me who appealed more to the ladies on *The Mike Walsh Show*, and June Bronhill, with her legitimate opera and operetta background, in the same show! Surely it's a recipe for disaster." It *was* a very odd mix.'

Yet they did have some shared history: Gallaher had recorded his first album at Mario Millo's home studio in Seven Hills, where Jon often recorded.

'I was very aware of the presence of Jon when I worked with Mario,' said Gallaher. 'I thought: Wow, this is where they did "Six Ribbons"!'

They'd also both been signed to PolyGram by label exec Ross Barlow, while Jon's friend Peter Plavsic became Gallaher's A&R man — his go-to guy at the label.

As for Marina Prior, being cast in *Pirates* was hard for her to digest — when she auditioned for the part of Mabel, she was busking for change in Melbourne's Bourke Street Mall. The first stage show Prior had seen was *Jesus Christ Superstar*, when she was still in primary school. She'd found it hard to take her eyes off Jon's Judas; the idea that she'd one day be working with Jon was beyond her wildest expectations.

'I was totally mesmerised by the whole thing — the show, the music,' Prior recalled. 'I thought his Judas was so dynamic. I turned to my mum and said, "I'm not sure what this is, but that's what I want to do when I grow up." I was a suburban girl who loved music.'

Not surprisingly, Prior was a bundle of nerves when she arrived for the first day of *Pirates* rehearsals in late 1983. The first person she caught sight of when she walked into the theatre was Jon.

'I walked past one of the studios and I saw Jon rehearsing,' she said. 'I had such a start; it was the first time I'd seen a famous person in the flesh. It was an amazing feeling.'

Jon assumed that this young woman must be playing Mabel, so he stopped, smiled and waved to her.

'Hello, luv,' he said.

'I think I blushed and ran away,' said Prior. 'I was so naive, such a novice.' But the ice had been broken.

Jon hadn't met Simon Gallaher, either, before those rehearsals began in advance of the show's January 1984 opening at the Victorian Arts Centre (some 103 years since the first Australian production of *Pirates*, at Sydney's Theatre Royal). It was a big step up for Gallaher, who, while experienced in amateur musicals, had never appeared in such a large-scale production. Like Prior, Gallaher couldn't have been greener; so was Jon, for that matter, at least in a musical such as this, which was far more traditional than something like *Superstar.*

Jon came into rehearsals looking every inch the rocker, something that Gallaher, and the rest of the cast, couldn't miss. Jon was impossible to miss. Perhaps it had something to do with the fact that he had recently been knighted by Prince Leonard of the Hutt River Principality in Western Australia; Jon had written the national anthem for the eccentric farmer's 'kingdom'.

'Jon, in those early days, liked to play the cool rock'n'roller in the rehearsal room,' said Gallaher. 'So there was a little bit of distance, perhaps, when we first met — but we just didn't know each other.'

Yet something magic happened during rehearsals. A side of Jon not yet given full flight on stage — his sense of humour and his flawless comic timing — quickly emerged. The time he'd spent guesting on *Blankety Blanks* had been well spent; he'd learned plenty about comic timing from the master, Graham Kennedy. Watching *Monty Python* and John Belushi on repeat didn't hurt, either.

Pub gigs didn't afford Jon much opportunity to crack wise; crowds were more interested in loud music and booze and sex. Now he could finally utilise his skills as a comic — a high-kicking, hip-swivelling, eyebrow-wiggling comic, no less. It was as though he was finally living out his childhood dream of becoming a stuntman, because the role was incredibly physical.

'The Pirate King was the closest character to Dad,' said his son Jonathan.

'He had it all figured out from day one,' said Marina Prior, who quickly became friends with Jon. 'The Pirate King was Jon, from the swagger to the kind of Goon-y sense of humour, as in *The Goon Show*. The charisma, sex appeal, that unique voice. I remember thinking, "Gosh, this is the level we're working at!" He knew it all.'

And he was accommodating, as Prior remembered. 'No ego whatsoever. That stuck with me — don't bring your ego into the rehearsal room. He was so not what I expected. I thought he would have carried his stardom into the room but he didn't.'

At the end of a very productive first week of rehearsals, producer Mackenzie-Forbes pulled Jon and Gallaher aside.

'Gee, I just never knew you were funny,' he said to Jon. Then he turned to Gallaher: 'And I never knew you could sing!'

Gallaher shot the producer a look. 'I thought, "How the hell did you cast this show?" Boy, he got lucky.'

In spite of its Broadway success, there was no guarantee that the Oz *Pirates* would be a hit. Local theatre was in the doldrums; recent shows such as a revival of *Oliver*, starring Garry McDonald as Fagin, and *Song & Dance*, the first Australian production of a musical from superstar Cameron Mackintosh, had opened and closed in quick succession.

Pirates of Penzance opened at Hamer Hall in the Victorian Arts Centre on 7 January, and early box office was slow. A few theories were thrown around — perhaps the $19 ticket fee was too low (it was upped to $25); maybe people were more interested in the big movies of the moment such as *Silkwood*, *Scarface* and *Terms of Endearment*. Maybe *Oliver* and *Song & Dance* had put them off the theatre.

Jon almost didn't make the first show. With just two days left to opening night, he fell during rehearsals — the mattress that was supposed to cushion his fall had been moved. He badly sprained his wrist and was in hospital until the early hours of the morning of opening day.

An early review of the show, in *The Bulletin*, summed up the initial wariness about the show.

'I went with some trepidation to see *The Pirates of Penzance*,' wrote David McNicoll. 'From all the publicity, it sounded as if the new producers had made the whole thing a bit too "cute".'

Yet McNicoll, who'd praised Jon in *Superstar*, was eventually won over. He declared that the show had 'a verve, an ebullience which transmitted to the audience and brought on an extraordinarily enthusiastic reaction'.

Covering opening night for *The Canberra Times*, W.L. Hoffmann was equally enthused. 'Jon English, with his husky voice and bounding energy, is a vital and commanding King of the Pirates . . . [it's] a rollicking, rumbustious and continually entertaining presentation which shows just what an enduring masterpiece this comic opera really is.' Hoffmann noted the youthfulness of the audience; it was different from the typical theatre crowd. 'There was a high proportion of young people,' he wrote, 'who had obviously been attracted by the stars they knew — English and Gallaher.'

The 'star casting' had done the trick. Ticket sales improved and the show ran in Melbourne for six weeks, breaking box office records. But that was only the beginning.

———

Jon's remarkable metamorphosis, made all the more challenging because he wore two bulky microphone packs while performing, was something Simon Gallaher witnessed at close range. He was floored by Jon, night after night, show after show.

'From the day we opened, and the word of mouth . . . it was Jon, he just exploded onto that stage,' recalled Gallaher. 'But the producer was right — no one knew Jon was funny and clever, like that. Nobody had ever seen his comedy prowess, least of all Jon. But he was just a natural.'

The role was 'absolutely suited' to him, Gallaher said. 'He was Charlie Chaplin, he was Buster Keaton in his comedy skills — a lot like Peter O'Toole in [the 1982 film] *My Favorite Year*, sending up that swashbuckling figure. It takes someone with immense and impeccable timing to do that — and he had it in spades.

'Jon understood the discipline of theatre, that people who see it on the eighth performance of the week want it to be the same as the first. He knew how to lock it down, and for everyone around him to understand what he was going to do, and when. It was a masterclass.'

Marina Prior, too, was blown away by Jon's performances, eight shows a week. Her Mabel didn't have a huge amount of stage time with the Pirate King, so she would often watch him perform from the wings. And Prior made sure she never, ever missed the big musical number, 'With Cat-Like Tread', where Jon was at his irreverent, swashbuckling best. It was simply too good to resist.

'It was electric, you know — how many encores are they going to get tonight? How much are he and Simon going to play up to the audience?'

There was one encounter, however, that Prior regretted. During her brief period on stage with Jon during the show, there was a scene when Mabel had to stand up to the Pirate King. She decided to put her foot down — quite literally.

'In rehearsal, the director told me to stamp on the Pirate King's foot,' Prior recalled. 'Being unaware of stagecraft, I really stamped on his foot.'

Jon pulled her aside afterwards. 'Darling,' he said, wincing in pain, 'just put your foot upstage of mine and pretend. OK?'

'He was so gracious,' laughed Prior.

Jon's work ethic hadn't waned one bit — he'd berate members of the cast for missing a show; to him, a headache or a cold was no reason to not show up for work.

'It's a really obvious fact of life, that they've paid their money and they deserve a show, full stop,' Jon explained. 'The rules have never changed. If you've got a hangover, or a bad leg, or sunburn, fuck it, do it anyway.' At one point, Jon played the Pirate King with heavily strapped broken ribs.

As Prior put it: 'To Jon, unless you were dead, you were on stage.'

Dancer David Atkins only agreed to participate in *Pirates* if he could be understudy to the Pirate King — and he got just the one gig, standing in during a matinee after learning that Jon ('a bit of a petrolhead at the time', said Atkins) had crashed his car. During that show, Atkins was forced to wear Jon's costume and discovered that he could just about squeeze his entire body into one of Jon's pirate boots; he 'had to roll the pants up seventeen times' to fit into them. He was, in his own words, 'the Pirate Dwarf'. Atkins consoled himself with a nightly role as the Sergeant of Police.

Jon shared a dressing room with Atkins and, in the words of Peter Rix, 'two more heterosexual men you'll never meet'. Though it was a rule of the theatre that there was no booze backstage, Jon and Atkins's room was well stocked with cognac, whisky and beer.

One afternoon, Rix received a call from producer Ken Mackenzie-Forbes. 'Peter, I'm wondering if you could come into the theatre — now!' he urged. 'I have a bit of a problem backstage.'

What had happened was that various members of the men's chorus had come down with minor injuries and ailments, and when Jon took the stage, bursting into 'I am a Pirate King!', he had turned to see he only had eight fellow pirates on stage (there were usually ten, all drawn from the men's chorus). Jon came off stage fuming, yelling blue murder. 'Where the fuck are my pirates?'

Then, when David Atkins took the stage as the Sergeant of Police, he was shocked to see there were only five other policemen on stage; again, these roles were drawn from the men's chorus.

When Rix reached the theatre, he found that Jon and Atkins — who'd both had a few drinks — had cornered the men's chorus in their dressing room and were explaining to them the meaning of the term 'work ethic'. Loudly.

'They were terrified [Jon and Atkins] were going to beat them up,' laughed Rix. 'By the time of the evening performance, they were back to the full contingent. The two of them ran roughshod over them for the rest of the season.'

———

As word of mouth helped turn *Pirates* into the hit Oz musical of 1984, and the production shifted from Melbourne to the Regent Theatre in Sydney, Jon began to overwhelm Gallaher, quite unintentionally. Every night Gallaher would step out into the lights — and he was on stage for almost the entire show, singing his heart out — and play the straight man to Jon's swaggering, endlessly hammy Pirate King, who, while he had less stage time, got the biggest audience response. The crowds had come to see Jon; that was undeniable. As Gallaher saw it, the Pirate King 'gets all the laughs, gets all the giggles', while Frederic was essentially a 'wimp'.

American Craig Schaefer, who'd worked on the Broadway *Pirates*, was choreographer for the Australian production, and he sensed that Gallaher felt Jon was stealing the spotlight. After a performance, he sat down with Gallaher.

'The mistake that every Frederic can make is that they want to be the King,' Schaefer explained. 'Frederic cannot be the King, otherwise the show falls apart, because then you've got competition on the stage, and it won't work. What Frederic has to be is loyal, dutiful, earnest; at the same time he has to be the straight man to the funny guy's gags.'

And, like every straight man, Schaefer said, 'You have to feed him the line.'

This registered straightaway with Gallaher.

'I immediately saw it and thought, "Yes, that's what you've got to be — second banana," like Bert Newton used to call himself. That's how the dynamic did change over the first month or so. I saw how we could make Jon even funnier — by playing it absolutely straight against him. It made him look all the more ridiculous. It was really good advice.'

A strong personal bond grew between Jon and Gallaher, one that continued for the rest of Jon's life. In later years, Jon would call Gallaher on every leap year's 29 February and wish 'Frederic' a happy birthday. (Prior, too, would forever be 'Mabel' to Jon. 'He had a sort of paternal attitude towards me, which was really sweet,' she said.)

Jon and Gallaher would joke about their relationship, calling themselves 'the chalk and the cheese', and, as Gallaher readily admitted, 'I was the cheese.' To Gallaher, Jon was the 'Al Jolson of modern day — you'd put the spotlight on him and he just went. He was a performer in every bone of his body'.

Pirates of Penzance had proved to be the perfect outlet for Jon. He'd somehow become an even bigger star.

Away from the stage, especially during the long Sydney season, Jon proved reclusive. Most of the cast would head out for drinks after an evening's performance, but more often than not Jon would say his goodbyes and drive back to the farm, to Carmen — an 'amazing earth mother', according to Gallaher — and his four kids. His son Julian was still in nappies.

Nor did Jon partake of the marijuana smoked by some of the cast; he told Gallaher that dope made him 'go nuts'.

Sometimes, on his way home from the theatre after the evening's show, Jon would call ahead to his favourite Greek restaurant in Dural, about 25 minutes from the farm, and place an order. But this was not your regular takeaway meal.

As his daughter Min recalled, 'He'd stop and pick up this over-the-top platter of food — seafood, salad, dolmades, everything — it probably cost about $300. He'd wake us all up to have this feast with him. He did that several times; he was ostentatious like that.'

Jon did, however, spend some time with Marina 'Mabel' Prior backstage, usually between shows. They'd sit together with guitars and play some of their favourite songs. 'We'd sing Linda Ronstadt stuff, Joni Mitchell stuff,' said Prior, 'just jamming.' It was a rare chance for Jon to simply kick back. Jon asked her to sing the Helen of Troy part on one of the Paris songs he was working on at the time.

'Jon didn't suffer wankers well; he hated pretentious people,' Prior said. 'It would be very easy in that position to dismiss a young kid like me, starting out, but he gave me time and he gave me respect.'

Another retreat for Jon was Comic Kingdom, a Sydney institution that was walking distance from the theatre. A lifelong fan of the form, Jon devoured comics, pretty much everything published by DC and Marvel, and had a separate room at his farm where he stored his collection. During breaks he'd swing by Comic Kingdom and pick up the latest Phantom or Spiderman comic — on his birthday, Jon even treated himself to a Spiderman pinball machine. The sight of long-haired, chain-smoking Jon sitting backstage at the Regent, devouring the works of Stan Lee and co between shows came as a shock to the more urbane 'culture vultures' among the crew and cast. Who was this savage?

But above and beyond everything else, his farm at Glenorie was Jon's safe haven from the madness of *Pirates*. He'd disappear into his home studio where he could work on new music. Somehow, in and among his crazy *Pirates* commitments, Jon managed to squeeze in a tour with Joe Cocker; he also began a ten-week tour with The Foster Brothers in August 1984 — the No Big Deal tour. A new best-of, *Modern English*, which revisited most of his hits — including 'Hot Town', 'Hollywood Seven', 'Six Ribbons' and 'Words Are Not Enough' — had charted strongly earlier in the year.

It was inside his home studio where the rock opera *Paris*, Jon's biggest obsession, was slowly starting to take shape. His family quietly began referring to *Paris* as Jon's 'fifth child'. If only they knew how true that would become.

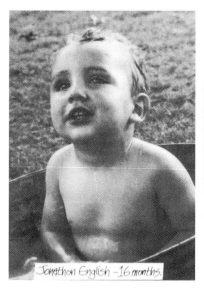

Jon aged sixteen months,
still in the UK, 1950.

Jon, aged three, with his sister Janet
(Jan), in Canterbury, UK.

Jon's mother Sheila, with Jon aged two and Jan aged three,
picking blackberries in Cornwall, UK, 1951.

Jon, far left, with (from left) Jan, Sheila, Jill and Jeremy,
in Cabramatta, Sydney, 1964.

Jon and Jan at the Grove Park Polish
Camp, early 1950s, where the Englishes
were living in this converted bus.

(From left) Jan, Jeremy, their
father Syd, Jon and Sheila.

Ace sportsman Jon (back row, third from left) with
Cabramatta High School's rugby league team, 1964.

Jon, c.1970, on stage with Sebastian Hardie bandmates (from left)
Peter Plavsic, Alex Plavsic and Graham Ford.

Jon as Judas Iscariot, *Jesus Christ Superstar*, Sydney, 1972.

With his *Superstar* co-star
Trevor White.

Jon on stage at the time of *Superstar*.

With baby Jessamine (Min), the first of Jon and
Carmen's children, born in May 1973.

Jon with Julian, his fourth child, born October 1984.

Jon at the time of his debut album, early 1973.

Jon signing a copy of his debut album *Wine Dark Sea*.

Jon with daughters Jessamine (Min) and Josephine (Josie) in the creek on the family property at Glenorie, mid-1980s.

Learning to ride a horse for *Against the Wind* brought Jon to Glenorie.

Jon and guitarist Mario Millo receiving
gold records for *Against the Wind*.

A Swedish record store
display for Jon's album
English History.

In the snow with
Mario Millo, Sweden 1981.

Welcoming better weather
on that first tour of Sweden.

Jon on stage in the mid-1980s, out front
of the Foster Brothers.

On the 1982 Jokers & Queens tour with
Marcia Hines, whom Jon first worked with in
Jesus Christ Superstar.

Pirate King Jon (back row, fifth from right) in smash hit
The Pirates of Penzance, 1994.

With a just-pied Josie,   The Pirate King in action.
The Mikado, 1995.

Jon with his fellow cast members, *All Together Now*, 1991.

Jon in costume as faded rocker Bobby Rivers.

English family gathering at Glenorie, 1992.
From left: Judd in Jeremy's arms, Joel (front), Jane, Jasper, Jan, Jacob (Jay), Jon's son Jonathan, Sheila, Jon and Carmen.

Jon, live in the 1980s, assuming a look
known as 'The Hulk'.

Jon in his home studio at Glenorie working on *Paris*.

On the set of *This Is Your Life*, 1998, with his fellow Englishes, from
left: Jzawo with Josie, Min, Carmen, Jon, Jonathan and Julian.

Jon with his sons Julian (far left) and Jonathan, late 1990s.

Jon with his wife Carmen, who was at his bedside when he died.

Jon with his brother Jeremy and sister Jan, Tamworth, January 2008.

Jon (centre) and Jonathan (far right), Joe Kalou (far left) and members of the band Spearfish, Swedish Rock Festival, June 2013.

Jon (centre) with the cast of *The Rock Show* at Nowra NSW, January 2009.

Jonathan James English, 1949–2016.

CHAPTER 13

'Born in forty-nine / Part of a long, long line of roses and wine / And the war clouds had fled and we buried our dead / The future was mine, or so they said.'

When asked about his album and musical *Paris*, Jon would trace its roots to the song 'Oh Paris', a standout on 1983's *Some People* album. Jon admitted that he and producer David Mackay — an expat Aussie who'd married a British woman and based himself in the UK — wrote the song as a challenge for listeners and DJs. Jon's lyric was very clearly inspired by the story of Paris and Helen of Troy, one of the Greek myths he'd loved since he was a child, but he wanted to see how others reacted to it. Would they get it?

'Sure enough,' Jon said, when in conversation with *Midday* host Ray Martin, 'I was up in Grafton one day, and this DJ began playing it, went out and got a cup of coffee, came back and said, "What made you write a song about France?" From there it snowballed.' (Proving that Jon was still very much his mother's son, the lover of a good yarn, in another version of events it was a DJ from Lismore. Still, the message was the same: some people didn't listen closely.)

There was another song that helped spark the idea of *Paris*, and it was also a classic case of a misunderstood lyric — radio DJs being the culprits yet again. The song was Ultravox's 'Vienna', a huge synth-pop hit in 1981, which, while set in the Austrian capital, was actually about a holiday romance. 'I used to get pissed off,' Jon told Ray Martin, 'because the DJs never knew what it was about.'

Of course there was greater motivation for Jon to pursue his passion project than simply testing people's lyrical awareness. 'He didn't have the credibility that he sought,' said Peter Rix. Jon craved a project that would prove to everybody that he was a true artist, not just a great song interpreter and an onstage larrikin in purple tights. 'There was an obsessiveness to Jon English that was never to be underestimated,' said Rix.

There was yet another factor at work, too: Jon had been raised on Greek mythology and as far as he was concerned, the saga of Helen of Troy and Paris was 'one of the best stories ever written'. It was also one of the most enduring. 'The quotations are still around today,' said Jon. 'Beware Greeks bearing gifts. The face that launched a thousand ships.'

Jon hoped to capture the spirit of that epic story in song. He'd set himself a huge goal — he wanted to create what he described as 'our own large-scale epic musical', an Australian-made production that would rank with the best in the world. It was nothing less than the largest project he'd ever tackled.

'Anyone who knows me knows it's been an obsession for years and years and years,' he told Ray Martin. 'I earbash people and play them stuff and they walk away thinking, "What a nice chap. Why's he going mad?"'

Simon Gallaher, for one, could attest to that. As early as 1984, when he and Jon were starring in *Pirates of Penzance*, Jon would corner him backstage between performances and play him songs under development.

'What do you think, Frederic?' Jon would ask Gallaher. This would happen repeatedly. 'Incessantly,' corrected Gallaher.

But *Paris* pre-dated even that. In October 1983, Jon had raised *Paris*

— or *Oh Paris*, as it was then known — with talk show host Mike Walsh, when he was ostensibly plugging The *Pirates of Penzance*.

'We're getting there; it's worth a try, I reckon,' Jon said. 'We'll make the album — we're trying to do it here. It's about Greeks so I thought we could do it in Melbourne,' Jon added, with a knowing chuckle.

Jon had bonded with David Mackay during the recording of the *Some People* album — which included 'Oh Paris' —and asked him to help bring his dream to life. Mackay 'got' Jon's obsession; he described him as 'a tragic about Greek tragedy'. Mackay felt that between them, he and Jon might just be able to make this work.

'Musically, there's a lot of scope, it's quite a big story with lots of room for an orchestra,' Mackay said during the early stages of a project that bedevilled Jon for the rest of his life. 'The combination of the two types of music Jon and I represent [makes] for a good fusion.'

At this point, late in 1983, Jon had some draft notes and songs in rough demo form. Mackay met with Jon in Sydney and then returned to London to give them a thorough going over.

'I called him after that,' recalled Mackay, 'and said, "Yes, I would be keen to co-write but we would have to start from scratch.'

That's just what they did, said Mackay: 'We started with one song, "Oh Paris", and a blank page.'

Paris wasn't going to come cheap. Jon and Mackay understood that they would need a sizeable recording budget to give full and proper life to the story. Jon was not good with money — his daughter Min believed her father spent unwisely because he 'just got so excited when he had it in his hands' — so he gladly handed over the financial side of *Paris* to his manager, Peter Rix.

Rix tried raising the money they needed to get the record made from various sources but in the end decided that they'd have to do it themselves. Jon contributed $200,000 to the Paris Recording Partnership, while Rix and Peter Roach — Jon's Glenorie neighbour — each contributed $300,000. Philip Walker, Rix's business partner, and a few others, also invested in *Paris*.

Business-wise, it wasn't a smart move for Jon, the artist, to pour money into his own project. As the co-creator, he had enough on his plate in coming up with the music; investing his own money added extra pressure. But they needed a lot of money and it simply wasn't available elsewhere, especially now that Jon wasn't the bankable recording artist he'd been a few years earlier. WEA Records, with whom Rix negotiated a licensing deal for the finished record, advanced $100,000, but that was barely ten per cent of the cash they required to record it. Jon and Mackay envisaged numerous vocalists, an orchestra, actors, the works. It was going to be a costly record, but Jon was consumed: he had to see this through.

There was regular back and forth between Jon and Mackay for several years, right up to the end of the decade, while they both fitted *Paris* in and around their many and varied commitments — Mackay worked on records with English acts Joe Fagin and David Ride, even housewife superstar Dame Edna Everage. Jon, meanwhile, continued to juggle rock'n'roll and theatre work.

Pirates, of course, consumed much of his time and energy in 1984 and 1985, but there were other projects that Jon undertook. One of these was a new record that would reconnect him with his *Against the Wind* collaborator, Mario Millo.

In 1987, Jon had met with renowned producer Charles Fisher — sometimes known as The Song Doctor — with a view to recording his tenth studio LP. Fisher's track record was hard to fault; he'd produced such hit records as Air Supply's *Lost in Love*, Moving Pictures' 'What About Me?' and the Hoodoo Gurus' *Mars Needs Guitars*, and in 1984, he'd worked with Jon and Renée Geyer on a track called 'Every Beat of My Heart', a feature of the *Street Hero* film soundtrack.

But Jon wasn't so sure. After the meeting, he and his wild-haired guitarist John Dallimore dropped into Mario Millo's house in Seven Hills. Jon had kept in touch with Millo over the years. They remained good friends — old mates.

According to Millo, Jon told him: 'I've just had this meeting with Charles Fisher and I can't see myself working with him. I want you and me to produce my new record.'

Millo agreed in a heartbeat and they began recording in his studio. As the sessions evolved, Millo felt that while Jon's songs were good, the record currently lacked the one track that would return Jon to the charts. He hadn't had a charting single since 1983's 'Some People'. While his tours with The Foster Brothers continued to draw big crowds — a good week on the road could still gross upwards of $50,000 — Jon's days as a commercial chart force seemed at an end.

Not that Jon would ever believe that, according to Peter Rix. 'Jon never for a minute thought his recording career was tapering down. He always thought he was one song away from his next hit. And what he was most interested in was writing that song himself.'

That was his intention with this new record — to write the bulk of the material himself.

At the same time, US-born, Aussie-bred songwriter Steve Kipner, who back in the late 1960s had learned his craft with the Bee Gees, was in the midst of a hot streak. He'd co-written a track originally called 'Let's Get

Physical', which he hoped Rod Stewart might record. But with the help of manager Roger Davies, another member of the so-called 'Koala Mafia' — Aussie expats working in the US — the song, renamed 'Physical', was cut by Davies' client Olivia Newton-John and became a worldwide number 1 in October 1981, selling two million copies in the US alone. The video also slotted in perfectly with the new craze of working out in the gym — ideally in lycra, with sweatbands. It was a massive hit.

Millo had a deal with the same music publisher as Kipner, and asked if there were any Kipner songs that might suit Jon. He was offered two; the first was titled 'Love Sick', the other 'Moth to a Flame'. It was the latter that caught Millo's ear.

'I thought it was such a great song, so perfect for Jon. It had the right edge to it,' said Millo.

Yet Millo was surprised by Jon's response. He was so intent on writing the bulk of material for the album — and in the wash-up, Jon either wrote or co-wrote eight of the eleven tracks on the finished album — that he had no interest in cutting the song, potential hit or not.

'He just didn't like it,' said Millo. 'I said to him, "You need a hit, you need to put this on the album." But he didn't agree with me.'

In the end, Jon did write the one standout song on the album, one of the best he'd ever compose, entitled 'Glass Houses'. It also captured one of his best vocals. And unlike songs such as 'Carmilla', with its tale of a lesbian vampire, or the 'list song' 'Six Ribbons', Jon was writing about himself, his own life. The yearning ballad floated on a sea of keyboards and strings, and opened with the candid, autobiographical lines, 'Born in forty-nine / Part of a long, long line of roses and wine / And the war clouds had fled and we buried our dead / The future was mine, or so they said.'

'Glass Houses' had all the atmosphere and candour of Pete Townshend's epic 'Behind Blue Eyes'. While it wasn't an obvious hit single in waiting, it was a fitting, stirring closer to the album, which Jon titled *Dark Horses*.

'I thought it was a really lovely song, a beautiful song,' said Millo. 'If he'd had a big hit up-front it could have been a second or third single.'

Unfortunately, that wasn't to be the case. With no obvious radio hit, *Dark Horses* floated in and out of the Oz charts when it was released in May 1987. It stalled at number 84 and slipped away after less than two months.

Millo, despite his frustrations with Jon, had nothing but fond memories of making the album, despite its chart failure. There was one incident, however, that almost led to a major fallout between him and Jon.

Keith Kerwin was a member of Jon's band, known to all and sundry as 'Stretch'. Millo only knew him by his nickname; he didn't know his real name. Kerwin had contributed a couple of songs to the album: 'Treated Like a Lady', along with 'I Can Do Better Than That', which he'd co-written with Jon. Millo was no big fan of Stretch's songs, however, and made that clear when they were being recorded.

One day Jon came into the studio, a serious look on his face, and pulled Millo aside.

'I want you to look me in the eye,' he said, 'and tell me you don't hate Keith Kerwin, because you've been saying his songs are weak.'

Millo was confused; he had no idea who Jon was talking about. 'Who's Keith Kerwin?' he asked.

'Stretch,' Jon explained. 'Keith Kerwin is Stretch.'

Millo was shocked: 'I felt terrible, because I'd been saying these things about his songs in the studio.'

In a footnote to *Dark Horses*, that Kipner song Jon rejected, 'Moth to a Flame', was recorded by Olivia Newton-John for her album *Soul Kiss* in 1985; the album which hit the US Top 30 and was certified gold. Jon may well have missed out on a comeback hit.

As much as Jon wanted to dedicate himself wholly to *Paris*, there was always other work to undertake; he needed to provide for his family and keep the farm afloat. Jon was cast as 'The Mad Monk' Gregorii Rasputin, in the musical of the same name, in August 1987, alongside fellow rocker Angry Anderson (playing Lenin), which Jon considered a casting masterstroke. 'I wonder how many theatrical directors would have even contemplated that?' he said to a reporter from Channel 9.

Terry Serio and Robbie Krupski were also in the cast, while Jon made sure that Foster Brothers Greg Henson and Peter Deacon got work in the house band. (Henson also played in the *Pirates* band.) A young Danielle Spencer was also in the cast.

Jon, now sporting a beard liberally sprinkled with salt and pepper, believed that the role of Rasputin suited him 'because I look a bit loony'. He was also drawn to a story that had echoes of his own *Paris* — Rasputin, in the words of a *Sydney Morning Herald* writer who met with Jon just prior to opening night, 'is a story of passion, power and politics'. Exactly like the story of Helen and Paris.

'I quite like playing baddies,' Jon said. 'The fun of Rasputin is watching him go bad.'

Rasputin was an all-Australian production that was financed, produced and staged locally. Peter Rix was among the investors; the key financier was a producer named Harry Vogelsanger. The entire production cost around $3.5 million — huge money for 1987. The chorus was 33-strong, while 24 original songs had been written for the show.

But according to Jon's sister Jan, Jon wasn't enthusiastic about *Rasputin*, particularly not with his own musical slowly taking shape. 'Jon was driven into doing *Rasputin*, which he loathed, and was in his opinion a really, really bad musical.'

'I've got a really good musical,' Jon told her, 'and I'm put in this rubbish.'

Jon was almost as blunt when he spoke with the *Herald*. 'I'll look you straight in the eye,' he admitted, 'and tell you honestly it's not as good as *Jesus Christ Superstar* . . . I don't think anything ever has been.'

Reviews of the show were lacklustre — and Jon wasn't above criticism. Writing for *Variety*, Debbie Kruger wondered if Jon's indifferent performance 'may be a casualty of the poor writing', but noted that his portrayal of Rasputin was 'a disappointment'. She went on to say that his Rasputin lacked 'the power and passion of previous performances, and his singing is uninspired'. She did, however, concede that Jon seemed to be the only cast member 'at ease with the dialog, where the humor inherent in Rasputin comes through, and he looks the part — his stature is immense, his eyes are haunting.'

Rasputin closed after just four weeks.

There were other projects for Jon, including a stage show, *Big River*, based upon Mark Twain's classic novel *The Adventures of Huckleberry Finn* — and a recent Broadway hit that ran for more than 1000 performances — in which Jon appeared (as Pap Finn) with Cameron Daddo. The show opened at Her Majesty's in Sydney during January 1989 and also ran at Her Majesty's in Melbourne, the Lyric Theatre in Brisbane and the Festival Theatre in Adelaide. Also in the cast was Jon's *Superstar* peer, Marcia Hines, as well as John Bell, who'd met Jon when they worked together on *The Bacchoi* back in 1974.

Jon left a big impression on Daddo very early in the run. Jon walked into the main dressing room at Her Majesty's and, as Daddo looked on, reached up to the AC vent and ripped down a piece of cardboard.

Without missing a beat Jon turned to Daddo: 'Bloody opera singers.'

Before every show, they'd have a nip of what Daddo called 'Jon English medicine'. Jon also handed along some solid advice to Daddo, as they prepared for a preview of *Big River*. 'Don't worry about tonight, mate,' he said. 'Nobody paid.'

The punters were the people that mattered to Jon, not the critics.

Soon after *Big River*, Jon released a new album, *Busking*, produced in the UK by David Mackay and featuring a song called 'Always the Busker'. The album failed to chart, although it did provide him with the inspiration and impetus for future project *Buskers and Angels*.

Jon decided that it was time to really focus on *Paris*. While in the UK, he and Mackay compared notes and, as Mackay recalled, 'mapped out the story and ideas for songs'. Three months later, Mackay travelled to Australia and spent a few months with Jon and his family, staying on the farm. They had one new song each: Jon had written 'Business'; Mackay had written 'Perfect Stranger'.

'That got us going,' said Mackay.

While Mackay was in Australia, Jon made a connection that would help them enormously. He had a contact named Cameron McDonald-Stuart, who worked at Apple, a company starting to make waves in the tech world with their Macintosh home computer. He and Mackay met with Apple and discussed *Paris*.

'They loved the idea,' said Mackay, 'and were keen to support us.'

Jon and Mackay were both given computers and access to the company's trailblazing 'in-house mail system', this being well before email existed. It was a huge breakthrough, as Mackay revealed. 'It gave us a facility to contact one another and share writings on a daily basis.'

Of course, it could get problematic for Jon, especially in a house full of young children. Jon's kids were fascinated by this new technology and would often play games on the Mac. Jon drilled into them two essential keystrokes — Apple S (for save) and Apple Q (for quit). If his work was still on the screen, they had to save and quit before playing a game.

Sometimes, however, they got the sequence wrong and accidentally deleted Jon's work. It didn't go down well.

'Julian and I just knew Apple Q— quit — then we'd put the computer game in,' remembered Jonathan. 'We quit out and didn't save a couple of things. Dad would tell us: "Please! Apple key S. Apple key Q. Save and quit."'

Jon and Mackay would still meet when it was possible as they chipped away at the story and songs, getting it to a point where, in Mackay's estimation, 'we felt it was really strong'.

The first stage of *Paris*, the writing, was complete. The process had consumed the better part of eight years. Jon's next challenge was how to make it into a record.

———

Jon adopted the *Superstar* principle when it came to recording the *Paris* album — make the record first, release it, then use the finished product to hopefully entice investors and producers to come on board and back a theatrical production. The one risk, of course, was that the album needed to be a hit. What self-respecting producer would finance a show based on a dud record?

Recording of the cast album began in the UK in 1990, at Mackay's base in Surrey, where the rhythm tracks were laid down. The cast of musicians included members of The Foster Brothers, who flew over from Australia, along with numerous UK-based studio players who'd worked with Mackay in the past.

'It was a very involved process to record,' said Mackay, clearly a dab hand at understatement. 'It was a very expensive process and took about eight months.'

He and Jon knew that they'd need an orchestra for the more 'stagey' parts of the record and, by sheer luck, Mackay was working on a TV program in the US with David Cullen, who'd orchestrated many of the hugely popular Andrew Lloyd Webber/Tim Rice musicals, including *Cats* and *The Phantom of the Opera*. Cullen agreed to write scores for the London Symphony Orchestra, who'd signed on to work on *Paris* — but they didn't come cheap.

'The LSO cost a fortune,' said Mackay.

Then the search for the right vocalists began. Mackay had reached out to legendary singer Harry Nilsson, whom he'd worked with in the past (and who had shared the same music publisher with Mackay, Eaton Music). Nilsson was a Grammy winner for the timeless ballads 'Without You' and 'Everybody's Talkin'' and a former member of the notorious 'Hollywood Vampires', hard-partying musos whose numbers included John Lennon, Keith Moon and Alice Cooper. Mackay had sent him some demos and the script and was 'amazed' when Nilsson — who'd recently discovered he'd been embezzled by his financial advisor — called him to say 'I love it. I'm in.'

Nilsson recorded his part in Sydney; he was flown out first class and put up at the Regent Hotel. But he wasn't in great shape. 'The man was a mess,' said Peter Rix, who looked after Nilsson during his stay. 'Barely able to walk.' Nilsson recorded parts for three songs — 'The Beggar', 'A Horse with No Rider' and 'Oh Paris' — but *Paris* would be one of his final recordings. He died in 1994, from heart failure, aged 52.

While in LA for a planned meeting with Rod Stewart, which never eventuated, Mackay heard singer John Parr — of 'St Elmo's Fire' fame — and thought he'd be perfect for the part of Paris. Who needed Rod Stewart? 'I met [Parr] in London and he fell in love with the project,' Mackay said.

Mackay began calling in favours of acts he'd previously worked with, including hirsute Greek singer (and kaftan lover) Demis Roussos ('We needed a Greek,' Jon explained); Francis Rossi of Status Quo; and The

Parker Sisters, Sheila and Sheryl. Barry Humphries, whose alter ego Dame Edna Everage had recorded the *Neighbours* theme with Mackay, also agreed to contribute, as did David Atkins, Jon's buddy from the days of *Pirates*, and Trevor White.

Paris was taking very impressive, if wildly eclectic, shape.

John Parr sang the lead role of Paris, while Sheila Parker was Helen. Doc Neeson, lead singer of Oz rock greats The Angels, sang the role of Achilles; John Waters, who'd trod many of the same boards as Jon since the days of *Superstar*, sang the part of Agamemnon. The very pricey London Philharmonic Choir also contributed to the recording.

It was ironic, really, given the A-list cast assembled by Jon and Mackay, that the best performance on the record was by Jon. He sang 'Love Has Power' like a man possessed — which in some ways he was, at least according to Peter Rix. 'Jon had really taken on *Paris*,' Rix said. 'He'd become *Paris*, the rock opera. It never changed for ages. He was so obsessed with it all.'

To complicate matters further — *much* further — Jon and Sheila Parker, who was 'singing' Helen, had fallen in love. But Parker, a petite, blonde Welsh singer seventeen years younger than Jon, knew that he was married and, as she explained, 'I could not be the woman that stole a man from his wife and children.' She ended the relationship with Jon, although, as she readily admits even today, 'I loved him. And that love was never lost.'

While staying with friends at the time, Sheila met John Dallimore, Jon's guitarist, although she didn't realise that Jon and Dallimore were close. She began a relationship with Dallimore and when Jon found out about it, he was beside himself with rage.

'It was like hell,' said Parker. 'He'd lost me to another man.'

Years later, Jon and Parker talked together about the situation and their relationship. 'We both cried about it,' Parker remembered.

'Jon was away from home far too long,' explained Mackay. 'At times I think he may have made some regrettable decisions, but who are we to judge? It was a fractious time neither of us had experienced before, and the pressure — as we were financing way more than the budget for the project would cover — was pretty severe.'

Despite the challenges, Mackay was still confident in what they had created: 'The final album met both of our expectations and we totally believed it could be a major work, given the chance.'

Perhaps the chaos, however, should have been seen as a warning sign: the future for *Paris*, just like its two star-crossed lovers, was complicated. Very complicated.

———

Jon had befriended droll late-night TV host Clive Robertson and slipped him an advance copy of the record. On 20 August 1990, two weeks before the album's official release, Jon talked about *Paris* with Robertson on his program *The World Tonight*. Jon was dressed down for the event — he wore a grey jacket and blue shirt; there was a smattering of silver in his hair, perhaps the result of his recent testing times.

Jon began by talking about his love of Greek myths, and how he'd known these stories since he was a kid. He also raised his pet hate of radio DJs who didn't grasp the meaning of songs — in this instance Jon said the broadcaster who didn't understand 'Oh Paris' was from Gunnedah. (Close enough.)

Robertson was not the kind of man to falsely flatter, but he praised the record, describing it as 'technically marvellous'. Still, he asked Jon, why did he make the album first — why didn't he try and get *Paris* straight into production?

'I think it's the best way to test the waters,' Jon replied. 'I've always thought if you've got an opera and no one likes the music, you haven't got much of an opera at all.'

Robertson asked Jon to explain the story to the uninitiated.

'*Paris* is an encapsulated version of the Trojan Wars, the love affair between Paris of Troy and Helen, the queen of Sparta,' he offered, 'who fall in love — star-crossed lovers — and run off to Troy, and the holocaust that follows.'

Had he fiddled with the story at all?

'Enough,' Jon admitted, with a laugh. 'Paris was actually killed during the siege, and Helen . . . probably shacked up with his brother. But that doesn't really gel [so] we made her desperately in love with him and him dying at the end.'

'We called Ulysses "Ulysses" as opposed to Odysseus, according to the Greek myth, was simply because it was easier to rhyme . . . I figure if my friend Tim Rice managed to eliminate the Virgin Mary and the resurrection from *Superstar*, we're at least allowed to eliminate a couple of pagan gods.'

Jon estimated that *Paris*'s gestation period was roughly ten years, with much of his other work over the past three years 'on hold while we recorded it'.

This wasn't quite true, of course, but his point was clear: this was his number one priority. And he was shooting for the moon.

'In an ideal world,' Jon stated, 'I'd like to be going to Broadway in five years and watch a production of *Paris* that we made here.'

A few days later Jon appeared on Ray Martin's *Midday Show*, standing alongside David Mackay. They were at the Sydney Opera House, where many of the album's contributors — including Harry Nilsson — had gathered for the media launch. Jon started with a joke — the idea for *Paris* had come to him 'when I was buffalo hunting in the Northern Territory' — but took a more serious turn when it came to trying to get *Paris* on to the stage.

'It's about time we made our own large-scale epic musical here,' he said. 'We want to do it all here, get it working here, and then take that version — the same set, the same choreography, the same everything — over to England.'

Making the record was a huge achievement, perhaps the biggest in Jon's career. But to get *Paris* to the stage would prove to be one of the biggest challenges, and the biggest frustrations, of Jon's life.

CHAPTER 14

'There's a few too many things in my life I can't handle right now ... like the '90s.'

Pino Amenta and Philip Dalkin were Melbourne screenwriters, who, like Bronwyn Binns and Ian Jones, creators of *Against the Wind*, had learned their craft at Crawford Productions. They wrote a TV pilot, which they called *Rhythm & Blues*, initially with John Waters in mind. The concept was straightforward: the lead character, Bobby Rivers, was a faded and slightly drug-fried 1970s rock star whose one big hit, 'Easy Street', was now — like the man — a relic from the past. Forty-year-old Bobby learns that he's the father of fifteen-year-old twins, Anna and Thomas, when his former lover dies in a plane crash. (Bizarrely, Jon's Foster Brothers bandmate, Peter Deacon, had just learned he had a sixteen-year-old daughter, although Jon insisted that it was purely a coincidence.)

It's 1990 and Bobby, who is trapped in a tie-dyed, peace-and-love time warp, sets up house with the kids and their guardian. The show was *Family Ties* meets Sunbury, a G-rated ensemble piece.

Jon was cast in the role of Bobby, which was a world away from *Against the Wind*'s broody convict Jonathan Garrett, his last major TV part. But Jon proved very smart at playing dumb.

'I think he was more comfortable making people laugh than dramatic acting,' observed his sister, Jan. And she was absolutely right: this was the perfect vehicle for Jon's comic skills. He also didn't have to work too hard to play a middle-aged rocker.

According to one of his co-stars, Bruno Lucia, Jon was at the same time 'really adamant about not making Bobby too dumb'. This would prove to be a contentious issue.

Jon's manager Peter Rix could see the benefits of this new project. 'It was a very good vehicle for Jon and I didn't want him to get caught up as just the rock'n'roll singer. There was so much more to him.' The payday was good — Jon would get $7000 per week — even if it meant holding off on a proposed revival of *Pirates of Penzance*, which Simon Gallaher had proposed.

'When [the show] came along, it became a matter of finding time in Jon's schedule,' Gallaher said. Jon said yes to the revival, in principle, 'but not while he was doing TV'.

The sitcom's casting was solid. Working with Jon was Lucia, who'd play Wayne Lovett, Bobby's slick, fast-talking agent. Lucia was a musician and stand-up comic, whose most recent gig had been opening for Stevie Starr, who performed under the stage name the Regurgitator.

'I felt like someone wrote this part for me,' Lucia said after he read for it. 'I know the guy.'

New Zealand–born Rebecca Gibney was cast as Tracy Lawson, the twins' attractive guardian; stand-up comic Garry Who, Jane Hall (ex–*The Henderson Kids*, where she played opposite a very young Kylie Minogue) and Steven Jacobs (future long-time weather presenter on Channel 9's *Today* program) all featured.

The show was to be produced in Melbourne, forcing Jon into yet another long-distance working situation, the latest instance of what Simon Gallaher called Jon's 'double lives'. He found an apartment near the Channel 9 studio, as did Lucia, who'd moved down from Sydney. Jon returned home on the weekends, as did Garry Who, who also shuffled between cities.

Jon's schedule was hectic. On Monday the cast would rehearse with scripts. On Tuesday he'd rehearse for half a day with the others and then do whatever promo work was required: interviews, voiceovers, promos. After a third day of rehearsal the cast and crew would shoot on the set on Thursday. First there'd be a rehearsal, then a final run through; both were shot in front of a live audience (the finished edit usually cut between the two versions).

Before the first shoot, and during breaks, Jon and Lucia, in character, would busk for the studio audience; the money they collected was donated to the homeless. 'The audience got a free gig, in character,' said Lucia. 'It was great.' Shoot day would typically end just before midnight. Only then was Jon's week done.

'And I get Saturday and Sunday with the family,' Jon told a reporter from *The Canberra Times*. What Jon neglected to mention was that he was also responsible for the show's music, which soaked up even more of his time and energy.

The workload was incredibly heavy; Jon's contract with Channel 9 stipulated that he would star in 44 episodes, of 30 minutes each, in its first season. 'It was a sausage-factory contract,' said Lucia. 'I'm amazed the show lasted that long.' In keeping with the rock'n'roll theme, every episode was named after a famous song: 'Are You Lonesome Tonight?', 'I Hate the Music', 'Whiter Shade of Pale', 'Watching the Detectives', 'Paperback Writer', 'The Great Pretender', 'Let It Be' and so on.

'This schedule could kill,' Jon told a reporter.

Everything seemed in place until the producers received a call from Kerry Packer, the gruff head honcho of Channel 9.

'I'm not having a show called *Rhythm & Blues* on prime-time television!' he roared.

To Packer, the term 'rhythm and blues' was wrong for a mainstream audience. He was the boss, so there was no room for debate, and the show was renamed *All Together Now*. (In Germany, its title was even cheesier: it was known as *Rock'n'Roll Daddy*.)

On Monday 14 January 1991, with eleven finished episodes 'in the can', Jon and a band that included regulars Greg Henson and Peter Deacon, as well as sax player Andy Thompson, formerly of Moving Pictures, ex-Sherbet bassist Tony Mitchell and guitarist Peter Grimwood gathered on the GTV-9 studio's sound stage. After a few speeches from Channel 9 execs and a preview of the opening episode, Jon plugged in and played a brief set. A feature, of course, was the show's theme song, which Jon had written — and then quickly rewritten when Packer demanded the name change.

Eight days later, on a Tuesday night, the first episode screened nationally at 7.30 pm, safely sandwiched between *A Current Affair* and *Australia's Funniest Home Video Show*. *All Together Now* quickly became the summer's surprise hit, rating particularly well in New South Wales and Victoria, achieving an audience share of around 24–26 per cent. If, by some outside chance, Jon hadn't been a household name at the start of the show, he definitely would be now.

The opening episode, 'Daddy Cool', directed by Pino Amenta and written by Philip Dalkin, set the tone for the entire show. Bobby drifted haplessly through the episode, a vision in tie-dye and denim, whose go-to word was 'cool'. Exchanges like the following, when Tracy meets Bobby for the first time in years, typified Jon's character:

Tracy: You haven't changed.

Bobby: No, I just got up.

And then, when talk turned to Beth, the children's mother:

Tracy: The children needed a mother. And she was off shooting
             the rapids.

Bobby: [After a beat] Oh, I don't approve of guns.

Or this, when Bobby tried to talk his way out of becoming an accidental father:

Bobby: Look, I'm really sorry, but this is not my trip. There's a few
             too many things in my life I can't handle right now.

Tracy: Like what?

Bobby: Like the '90s.

Cue laughter.

Reviewing the show for *The Canberra Times*, David Vine went straight to the elephant in the room — the often dodgy nature of homegrown productions. He admitted he was wary of simply watching the show, 'for no-one likes to see a locally-made product turned turkey'. He was, however, relieved. '*All Together Now* is no world-beater,' he wrote, 'but it's got a good deal more going for it than those tedious little between-the-overs teasers might have suggested.' (Channel 9 had advance-plugged the show heavily during breaks in the summer cricket.)

While accepting that the show was 'strictly formula sitcom fare' — which it very clearly was — Vine praised the 'promising characters and attractive cast' and felt that there was 'enough fizz in the dialogue to suggest that the writers know what they're about'.

During the first season, the crew would often head out for a late dinner after the Thursday night shoot. One night, Jon pulled Lucia aside. 'Hey, mate, why don't we go out?' As Lucia recalled, 'A few times after a shoot we'd have a drink and chill out and talk about things. But he was always busy; he was always working on something.' One night, Jon took Lucia to see The Foster Brothers play a gig at Ferntree Gully, just outside Melbourne. Jon stepped up and sang a few songs with his brothers from another mother. Lucia couldn't believe how lucky he was — he was working with a true rock'n'roller.

Occasionally, *All Together Now* would feature guest stars. One was from Christopher Truswell, better known as the mouthy 'Nudge' from the Channel 7 sitcom *Hey Dad!*, who had a cameo as Jane's boyfriend. He was stunned when Jon and Lucia occasionally veered off script and started to improvise.

'Man, this show is so cool,' Truswell told the others. 'When we get a script every breath was on the page. No one ever improv'd.'

Wayne Lovett's catchphrases — such as 'Chicky babe!' and 'Wayne Lovett, agent to the stars' — came out of improvs from Lucia.

Being a professional comic himself, Lucia was impressed by Jon's ability to get laughs. 'Jon could tell a joke,' said Lucia, 'and because of his work on *Pirates*, he knew how to work an audience and let the material breathe.'

———

All Together Now viewing night in the English household was, in the words of Jon's son, Jonathan, 'high stress night'. Jon, as music director for the show, would sit with his collaborator, Charlie Hull (who'd go on to become musical director for the Australian stage production of *Priscilla: Queen of the Desert*) and agonise over every second of the show. They'd also spend Sunday in Jon's home studio, working out music for the next episode.

'We'd think, "Cool, we get to see the final product,"' said Jonathan, 'but Dad would be, "Shut up! I have to listen to that cue, make sure I haven't stuffed that up." It could get pretty heavy.' It eventually got to the stage where his family would find reasons to excuse themselves from the room.

Jon's new starring role also created some other unusual problems for his kids. They'd always known their father as a public figure; as Josie explained, 'By the time I came along Dad was famous; you can never undo that. So I never knew any different.' But being a TV star was different to stardom in rock'n'roll or the theatre. *Everybody* watched TV.

Jon had warned them, when he signed on for the role, that they may suddenly have a whole lot of new, fake friends: 'You might get treated differently.' But that wasn't the English kids' problem — it was that their classmates were convinced that his dumbed-down on-screen persona was the real Jon English. This led to some conflict.

'*All Together Now* was the first time Julian and I kind of copped it as kids, in primary school,' Jonathan remembered. 'Prior to that he was just doing rock'n'roll gigs. Suddenly he's on Tuesday night at 7.30. We'd get the classic kid logic: "Your dad's acting stupid, therefore he is stupid, therefore you are stupid."'

Josie recalled that she 'hated Wednesdays' because of the comments she'd cop at school after the Tuesday-night episode.

'I'd get, "Gee, your dad's dick looked big in his jeans." I was a girl in Year 9, an awkward fourteen-year-old, and I didn't want to hear that. And it was always done with an audience. You know, "Oh, your Dad's dumb."'

Not all the comments were hurtful, though. 'One kid said to me so innocently, "Does your mum get upset having all those people come over on Tuesday night?" I had to tell her: "That's not our house. It's fake."'

Bruno Lucia, too, was receiving some unwanted attention. He'd leave his house and immediately hear calls of 'Chicky babe!'

'I lapped it up for the first six months, but then I started to hate it. I

couldn't go out anywhere without some drunk idiot coming up to me,'
said Lucia. 'That was a bit tough to handle. You saw the ugly side of fans.
I got six months of joy and bliss then six months of the universe slapping
me in the face. The yin and yang. It did change my life forever, and I
wasn't ready for it. Jon was OK; he had already been there.'

Some concessions were made for Jon and the cast by the time of the
second season. While still required to generate 44 episodes, their shooting season was split into two parts, with a short break in between. But
some stiff competition was emerging in the form of *The Simpsons*, and
the show's ratings started to slip. There were also some rifts emerging
within what had been a tight cast in season one.

'I could smell that something wasn't right, because there was division
between the troops,' said Lucia. 'Rebecca and the kids were on one side,
and Jon and the boys on the other. I tried to unify everyone, but it didn't
work. It wasn't affecting the show to the point where they couldn't work
together, but sometimes there'd be little things.

'We were very unified at the beginning, and it was an ensemble piece.
But it's like a band: before you know it someone's put out a solo album
and everyone's getting pissed off.'

During that second season, singer Jack Jones, whom Gibney would
marry, began turning up on set to watch the show being filmed. Then
Gibney announced that she was leaving; she was replaced for the third
season by Kerry Armstrong, a move that didn't really work. 'It was on its
last legs,' said Lucia, 'and Jon and [Kerry] just didn't click.'

Lucia knew the gig was up when Bruce Gyngell, the head of Channel
9, turned up on the set one day. 'We knew the show was going to be axed.
The undertaker was here!'

Production on the show was shut down in September 1993, some thirteen episodes into the third season, 101 episodes down the line. This left
a gaping hole in Jon's work schedule; he'd blocked out the rest of the year

for another 44-episode season. Jon eventually sued Channel 9 for not fulfilling his contract for the third season, and a settlement was reached.

If there was one episode of *All Together Now* of which Jon was particularly proud, where he got to do more than play dumb, it came late in the show's life, during an episode entitled 'Only Women Bleed'. In it, Armstrong's character Beth Sumner has a cancer scare, and in a rare moment of 'straight' drama, Bobby walks into her empty room, his heart heavy. That's where things started to go off script — as Jon's sister, Jan, remembered.

'At the end of the episode, he goes into her room and looks at a photo, and without meaning to, destroys her entire room. He bumps into something, knocks something over — it was complete slapstick. It was supposed to be serious. He destroyed the room in five minutes. The idea was completely his.'

In a curious case of a sitcom imitating life, in the same episode a producer tries to entice Bobby to appear in a rock opera. Off screen, it was another rock opera that consumed Jon's time and energy.

Even while *All Together Now* was still in production, Jon's passion project, *Paris*, remained his priority. Yet another successful local revival of *Jesus Christ Superstar*, this time starring John Farnham, Kate Ceberano and Jon Stevens, had been launched in 1992, and Jon looked on with interest. He was using it as a barometer for *Paris*, to see if there was an audience, and potential backers, awaiting him; he figured he needed something like $5 million to stage *Paris* properly.

'I'm glad to see *Superstar* selling well because it augurs well for *Paris*,' he said at the time. 'It's the same genre. When we came out with [the concept of] *Paris*, people said that style of musical was old-fashioned.'

Jon was so consumed by *Paris* that it seemed like every interview he gave — even when he was plugging *All Together Now* or shows with The Foster Brothers — inevitably turned towards his rock opera. He hinted at US interest in staging *Paris*; he was also speaking with 'the Canadians'. When not shooting, he would fly out to meetings with potential producers and investors in London, explaining that 'it would seem a bit cheeky if I asked them to come here because I have this sitcom in Australia'.

'Jon was consumed,' said David Mackay, still working shoulder to shoulder with Jon on their odyssey. 'It was a passion he had fostered for so many years. We invested ten years of our lives, and the cost of us flying to work with each other, taking months each year with no income and having continuing expenses. We were both continually having to scramble to make ends meet.' Mackay estimated that he and Jon had spent 'hundreds of thousands' of dollars of their own money before they even released the record. That tally would continue to mount.

The possibility of *Paris* being 'old-fashioned' wasn't Jon's biggest problem. Simply getting the record released in Australia had been a struggle. When Jon delivered the finished album to record label Warner (WEA) in 1990, he didn't get the response he anticipated.

'Warner got this huge, extraordinary record and said, "We can't release this; it's too big,"' said Peter Rix. 'Things had to be cut for the release. It broke Jon's heart. He never forgave anybody for cutting the record.'

Philip Mortlock, then at WEA, recalled the difficulties. 'The reality was that no matter how impressive the work, the cast, the package and presentation' — and WEA's art director Ken Smith had produced a striking design for the 'premier album package' version of *Paris* — 'we didn't have a show. And no song from this album was going to get radio airplay . . . Jon had based his concept on what happened to *Jesus Christ Superstar*, a rock opera/musical with an impressive cast for the original cast recording. The project was grand, but out of time.'

Jon hadn't had a Top 40 single since 'Carmilla', which had reached number 27 in April 1980. It had been a long dry streak — 'selling' new music from Jon English was a much harder task in 1990 than it had been during his peak in the 1970s. Neither *Dark Horses* nor *Busking*, his most recent albums, had sold particularly well. While the *Paris* album did go on to win the 1991 ARIA Award for Best Original Soundtrack/Cast/Show Recording, it, too, wasn't a chart hit. It didn't come 'close to recouping costs or realising its potential', said WEA's Philip Mortlock. And still Jon struggled to get *Paris* staged.

British theatre veteran Paul Elliott, who'd staged the hugely successful Buddy Holly musical *Buddy* on Broadway and in the West End, did express interest in producing *Paris*, to the extent that he prepared a budget. He told Jon and Peter Rix that $6 million would be needed to get it up and running, but neither had the money to invest; they'd already sunk $500,000 of their own money into the album. And, as Peter Rix recalled, no Australian producer was willing to get on board: 'They all saw it was way too ambitious.'

Then followed a troubled exchange with Cameron Mackintosh, the wizard of the West End, who'd struck gold with such productions as *Cats*, *Les Misérables* and *The Phantom of the Opera*. Mackintosh knew Jon's work through his association with *Superstar* and was willing to at least field an enquiry about staging *Paris*.

Peter Roach, the third key investor in *Paris*, was in the UK, with the finished recording tucked under his arm, which he left at Mackintosh's office. Within hours there was a message from Mackintosh, asking to speak with Roach, who was lunching with Jon, Mackay and Barry Humphries.

According to Roach, Mackintosh said he wasn't interested as it needed a couple of potential hit tracks and was too similar to other rock musicals of the time.

Not surprisingly, Jon's mood darkened. Production meetings, where possible reworks of *Paris* were discussed — such as giving the story a happy ending — became prolonged battles between Jon and his manager, as Jon dug in.

'Jon would not change a thing,' said Rix. 'Not a thing. It needed to be workshopped and Jon didn't want to know about it. We'd have these production meetings and he'd storm out. I couldn't give him what he wanted.

'There'd be late-night meetings where Jon and his angst would emerge. He was still *Paris*. I always forgave him because he was so consumed by it. But I wasn't. It was a business proposition. Jon had this incredible unhappiness that it hadn't had the acceptance — and who's to blame for that? Your manager. We were friends, we were mates, but I needed him to look at the future.'

When it became apparent that *Paris* wouldn't be staged — certainly not with the size and scope that Jon envisaged — Rix opted to sell his share, for $1. It was not a great return on his $300,000 investment.

Rix continued to suggest to Jon that it was time to move on and think about what he should do next, but then made what he later realised was a 'terrible mistake'.

He sat down one day with Jon. 'Can you have a look at Rod Stewart performing?' he asked.

Englishman Stewart, who was just a few years older than Jon and had gone through his own share of career shifts and fluctuations, was undergoing a rebirth with his triple-platinum *Unplugged ... and Seated* album. He would soon turn his gaze to the Great American Songbook; Rod the Mod was morphing into a crooner and taking it all the way to the bank.

'We need to get you out of the leather trousers,' Rix added. 'Cut your hair a bit. Think about repertoire.' But Jon wasn't interested. 'The only repertoire he wanted to think about was his own: his own songs.'

Jon and Rix went their separate ways in December 1994, ending what

Rix described as 'seriously interesting and successful times' for the pair. Rix and his business partner, Philip Walker, had previously organised for the rights to Jon's master recordings and publishing rights to revert to Jon. However, the rights to the *Paris* recording and its songs were owned by Paris Music, of which Jon was only a minor shareholder. And still no stage production was forthcoming.

Jon, his spirit flattened by the problems of *Paris*, not to mention his huge financial loss, realised it was time to give Simon Gallaher a call.

CHAPTER 15

'We haven't finished yet! There's some very important dialogue to do!'

Behind the scenes, much had changed since the first production of *The Pirates of Penzance*. While waiting for Jon to complete his work with *All Together Now*, Simon Gallaher approached virtually every impresario of note in the country, searching for backers for the second coming of *Pirates*. The 1984–86 version of the show had been a huge hit, running successfully in Melbourne, Sydney, Perth and Adelaide, before returning to Melbourne in 1985 and then playing Brisbane for the first time. There were some 750 full-house performances in all, and every night the cast got a standing ovation. Surely a revival would be an easy sell; wherever Gallaher went, people on the street asked him, 'When are you going to do *Pirates* again?'

Gallaher, however, was in for a rude awakening.

'I was given a total turn back on every corner,' he remembered. Everyone said: 'No, no — been there, done that. It's old hat, it won't work.'

Gallaher had formed a company called Essgee, and he decided to stage the show himself. It was then he had a brief rethink. He was also a huge fan of Gilbert and Sullivan's *The Mikado* — he'd written his own adaptation when he was fifteen, re-imagining it as a rock opera, with Nanki-Poo as a guitarist — and began to wonder if that might be the best vehicle to re-introduce him and Jon. That could be followed, perhaps, by a restaging of *Pirates*.

'But then it turned around again,' said Gallaher, 'and I thought about it commercially — it was all my own money at this point — and I thought that it was just too risky to do *Mikado* on the back of a show we'd done ten years ago. I thought it was better to say, "The Pirates Are Back."' *The Mikado* would have to wait.

Apart from Jon and Gallaher, the principal cast for the new *Pirates of Penzance* were Toni Lamond, a stage veteran and half-sister of singing great Helen Reddy, as Ruth, and newcomer Helen Donaldson as Mabel. American Craig Schaefer, the man who gave Gallaher priceless advice about the relationship between Frederic and the Pirate King, would again direct.

Gallaher's next challenge was dealing with the producers of the Broadway version of *Pirates*, as he needed permission to stage the show. When they proved, in his words, 'difficult to deal with, and too expensive', he decided to re-interpret the show himself.

'I thought, "Why am I doing this with a property that Gilbert and Sullivan created, which is in the public domain?" I was skilled in knowing the work very well and knowing that the re-orchestrations weren't that different. It wasn't reinventing the wheel, in my mind, so I decided: let's do our own. I had lots of ideas that I wanted to put into it, so off we went.'

Some of the new ideas for *Pirates* Mk II included a closing 'Mega Mix', which comprised encore versions of many of the show's musical highlights; and, instead of using a full female chorus, Gallaher brought in a three-piece female trio, styled like a 1960s girl group. The staging would be different, too; when the show began its Sydney run, it was decided to use what was known as a Victorian toy theatre, which looked 'like a picture book pop-up', said Gallaher. 'That was designed to put the emphasis on the performers, down front.'

With this all in place, Gallaher 'sold' a season of the new *Pirates* to the Lyric Opera of Queensland (now Opera Queensland) and also to the Burswood Casino in Perth. He used that money to underwrite the pre-production and was also helped out by a 'mystery investor' — entrepreneur and adventurer Dick Smith, it was later revealed — who helped back the Sydney season. As it turned out, despite the ten years that had passed since the last time they had shared a stage, Jon and Gallaher each slipped into their old role like a second skin. Three weeks had been set aside for rehearsals, but that hardly seemed necessary. On the first day of rehearsals, Jon and Gallaher breezed through their roles; it was if the show had never ended.

Jon looked at Gallaher, smiled, and asked, 'Well, what the fuck do we do for the next three weeks?'

Yet there was one more hurdle to overcome before the show opened in May 1994 at the Queensland Performing Arts Centre in Brisbane. Just prior to the last dress rehearsal, the head of the Lyric Opera sat down with Gallaher and told him that the Mega Mix had to be cut. Gallaher was shocked.

'Excuse me? Why?' he asked.

'Our subscribers will hate it,' he was told.

'I thought you were trying to appeal to a wider audience,' replied Gallaher.

But she was adamant. It had to be cut. Gallaher went away and checked his contract and was reassured to read that he'd been given artistic control of the production. He set up another meeting and insisted that the Mega Mix would stay, with a caveat: 'Unless the audience tells me otherwise. If it doesn't work, I'll be the first one to cut it.'

Gallaher admitted that his heart was in his mouth when Jon and the rest of the cast gathered at the end of opening night, in front of a very full and appreciative house, to take part in the Mega Mix.

'I thought, "Oh god, here we go" — and at the end the place exploded. The roof lifted off the place. I suddenly felt vilified. The head of the Lyric Opera never spoke to me again.'

'These people in their ivory towers didn't have their finger on the pulse,' Gallaher said. 'It was poetic justice that when *Pirates* did come back, the audiences flocked to it.'

As for Jon, a reporter asked him how it felt to be back in the spotlight; did his head ever get a bit swollen? 'I have very good friends around me,' he replied, 'who'll pull me aside and say, "Jon, you look bloody ridiculous." But then again [I'm] doing Gilbert and Sullivan, wearing purple tights at eleven in the morning . . . *That* is ridiculous!'

———

Jon again underwent a remarkable transformation as the Pirate King; he embraced the role even more energetically than he had in 1984. He was a vision in snug purple tights, knee-high boots and cutlass, as he bounded about the stage reminding all and sundry that it truly was a glorious thing to be a Pirate King. To which he'd sometimes add: 'A-ring-a-ding-ding,' channelling his inner Dean Martin.

Jon had undeniable presence as the Pirate King — he'd break down the 'fourth wall' between performers and the audience, reminding punters with a nudge and a wink that it was all a bit of fun. Sometimes he'd banter with the conductor, Kevin Hocking, stage a mock striptease, or swing into the audience on a rope — he once spotted his mother in the audience and casually called out 'Hello, Mum,' as he sailed through the air. And he'd help turn such *Pirates* standards as 'With Cat-Like Tread' into rollicking, swashbuckling knees-ups, usually ending in him falling flat on his back, exhausted. A standing ovation would almost always ensue, which would force him to shoosh the crowd and tell them, feigning indignation: 'Wait a minute. This is very important. We haven't finished yet! There's some very important dialogue to do!'

The audience would roar with laughter, and clap until their hands ached.

'Dad never liked a gag that left the audience out,' said his son Jonathan. 'He always made sure that a gag was inclusive. If someone on stage was about to be tripped up, he had to make sure the audience was aware. Dad was really good at that.'

This new production of *Pirates* was a very 'hot show', due to extra-bright lighting. This presented a big problem for Jon, who was possibly the sweatiest man in Oz. Gallaher, like so many of Jon's band members, usually copped the lot.

'With Jon nearby you tried to keep your mouth closed as much as possible,' Gallaher said. 'You tried to keep out of the firing line.' Jon tackled the problem by donning a headband. 'It was a little more Bon Jovi.'

Jon's secret, according to Gallaher, was his discipline. 'Jon wasn't a loose cannon on stage — it enabled him to take more licence. As much as Jon would appear to run riot, it was very choreographed and disciplined on Jon's side.

'The importance for me was to maintain the straight man, to make him look sillier and funnier. I was now older and had learned my craft a little more, and we could play with that a little more.'

There was another layer to *Pirates* Mk II: the public knowledge that this was Gallaher's baby. Jon may have been in charge on stage, but Simon was the producer. Those in the know quietly chuckled about his and Jon's roles, which were reversed off stage.

'It was funnier in a way,' said Gallaher. 'Frederic was so straight and pure and innocent, but behind the scenes I was Jon's boss.'

Pirates was once again a smash. A production that was screened on TV drew an audience of more than two million. A video also sold strongly.

Jon celebrated by taking his family on holidays — and for the first time, these weren't working holidays. There were no gigs to play, no interviews to give. The Englishes went to Fiji, the Cook Islands, the US — 'the whole Griswold family holiday', said his daughter, Min. Carmen said that it was during these holidays that she finally saw Jon unwind properly; his life up to then had been consumed with work. Things had changed. 'Jon learned to relax, for the first time ever. He did lots of reading, lots of lying on the beach, swimming.'

There was always a lively rivalry between Jon and Gallaher — Peter Rix said that Gallaher 'was the businessman Jon wasn't'. Jon called Rix one day, shouting down the phone.

'Simon's got a convertible Mercedes!' he said. 'I have to have a convertible.'

Jon was then driving a sedan that had seen much better days, when he wasn't riding his motorbike to the theatre.

Rix explained that it was a budget buster — 'and Simon's leasing it, anyway'.

'What's that?' asked Jon. The world of finance was not his strongest suit; he didn't actually know what a lease was.

Two days later, Jon arrived at the theatre in a convertible Saab. He called Rix.

'I've learned about leasing,' he said. 'The papers are on their way.'

The Pirates of Penzance continued to pull huge, enthusiastic crowds, as the show moved from Brisbane to Sydney and then to Perth. Jon was doing very well from it, too, pocketing about $10,000 per week. By the end of 1994 the show had played to 500,000 patrons.

Producer Gallaher's biggest challenge was what to stage next. He could see the obvious demand for Gilbert and Sullivan, and he was a huge fan. He also wanted to keep the winning team — he and Jon, the chalk and the cheese — together on stage. Now, clearly, was the right time to stage *The Mikado*. But Jon, at least initially, wasn't keen on the idea when Gallaher pitched it to him.

'Jon was originally hesitant to do another one,' said Gallaher. 'I think he was scared of his own — of our — success. He was still obsessed with getting *Paris* on, trying to convince me constantly [to stage it]. I'd had chats about doing it, but it was so expensive.'

Gallaher had suggested to Jon that he stage *Paris* as an oratorio: a dramatised work performed on a concert stage with a sizeable orchestra, choir and soloists, but without the big set and all the trappings. Jon could approach one of the larger festivals and have them back the show, just as the Adelaide Festival did back in 1972 with *Superstar*.

'Do it like you did the first *Superstar*, which was a huge success,' Gallaher said to Jon. 'The likes of Lloyd Webber crawled before they walked.'

But Jon wasn't interested. 'He still saw it as a fully fledged *Phantom of the Opera/Les Misérables* sort of thing,' said Gallaher.

He remained undecided about doing *The Mikado* but changed his mind after a woman spoke with him and Jon one night towards the end of *Pirates'* lengthy run, as they waited at the stage door about to take the stage.

'Wouldn't it be great if you could do a sequel!' she said.

It was apparent that the audience demand was there. Gallaher offered Jon $12,000 a week to sign on. He also told Jon that they could get the show up and running quickly and Jon finally agreed.

The Victorian toy theatre set that had been a feature of *Pirates* was re-used; all the crew needed to do was add *Mikado* fascias. Jon was cast as Pooh-Bah, Gallaher was to play Nanki-Poo and Helen Donaldson would also return, as Yum-Yum. Drew Forsythe, a 35-year-old Sydneysider who'd won an AFI Award for the film *Caddie*, joined the cast as Ko-Ko, Lord High Executioner of Titipu. The Fabulous Singlettes, the vocal trio that had appeared in *Pirates*, were also back.

'Jon always loved to work with family,' said Gallaher. 'That's why he loved to work with his own band all the time, his own crew — suddenly the Essgee crew became his own family.'

It also helped, of course, that the Essgee crew usually included members of Jon's road buddies The Foster Brothers, who found steady work playing in the house band. Others, including director/choreographer Craig Schaefer and orchestrator/conductor Kevin Hocking, were now also Essgee regulars. Jon was surrounded by familiar faces.

Jon didn't just have his 'road family' with him; he wanted to have his own family as well. He decided to get his daughter Josie a job with the *Mikado* crew. She was eighteen and had recently finished her HSC but had deferred uni. She was living by herself for the first time and, by her own admission, was 'really fucking around. I was working in insurance and hated it. I was majoring at drinking beer at the pub and talking shit.'

Jon offered to find Josie a job and in return he'd pay her rent. One day, Jon gave Josie an address in The Rocks and told her to introduce herself to a man named Jimmy Paine, the technical director for Gallaher's company, who did the hiring and firing. When she tracked him down, Josie was startled to learn that he wore an eye patch — one-eyed Jimmy looked like a modern-day pirate.

As Josie recalled, she received 'the lecture' about what was required: 'There's no women [currently] working backstage, blah blah blah. If I'm happy with you, you might get a permanent job.'

While Jon may have called in a favour to get her the job, Josie would have to prove her worth on the road. And Jon would have wanted nothing less.

'It was vintage Dad,' Josie said. '"Surprise! You've got a career." But it was great.'

Josie proved to be a good hire; over the next three years she'd work as assistant stage manager and she also ran the props department. 'My job was to make people on the stage look really good. That was the magic.'

But something wasn't right. Jon wasn't focused during rehearsals, which was unusual; something was clearly distracting him. It transpired that he was involved in a relationship with the estranged wife of a bandmate. Jon was so distracted that the director was forced to have a quiet word with him.

'Jon,' he said, 'you need to go home and learn your lines.'

As Gallaher recalled, 'Finally, he got his act together, but it was very difficult. Jon never liked drama [but] he liked excitement, he loved having this affair, but I think he wanted it to be lovely and romantic. The volatility that came with it was mind boggling.'

By the time the show opened in Brisbane's Lyric Theatre on 1 June 1995, Jon had sorted himself out in order to perform. But he was in for quite a shock a few weeks into the tour. One night, after a show, he was in Josie's room and he found a box of condoms. Jon was stunned. Not knowing quite what to do — he wasn't the type of father who discussed sex with his daughter — he decided to speak with the wardrobe manager, Ray Godden.

'What do you think this means?' he asked, showing him the offending box.

He gave Jon a look that pretty much said, 'What do you *think* she's doing?'

'She's probably fucking someone, Jon.'

Still in a flap, Jon called Carmen, who calmed him down and then spoke with Josie. She talked with her father soon after.

'Dad,' Josie explained, 'wouldn't it be worse if I *didn't* have them?'

Jon insisted that she tell him who she was sleeping with, but Josie refused. 'Dad was so old-fashioned about Min and I,' she said.

Over time, they settled into a comfortable post-show routine. Josie was a pot smoker, and she'd join her dad in his room, spark up a joint — Jon would relax his no-pot stance and take a few tokes — and together they'd watch late-night infomercials, doubled up with laughter at the hammy acting and bizarre gadgets that were being flogged. But sometimes the offers — 'Wait! There's more!' — were just too tempting. Back home at Glenorie, a weird assortment of products would turn up in the post, prompting phone calls from Carmen.

'Jon,' she'd sigh, 'what did you buy this time? Have you two been smoking weed again?'

Jon and Josie were always close, but the experience was making them even tighter. Jon particularly admired her ability to deal with difficult situations; she had an uncanny ability to call a spade a fucking spade.

'Where the fuck did that come from?' Jon once asked her. That was one trait Jon didn't possess; he was so focused on trying to make everyone happy that it sometimes resulted in chaos.

'You've been the best teacher, Dad,' she told him. 'You've got to stop putting yourself in uncomfortable positions just to make people happy. Because at the end of the day, you're the one with your head in your hands going, "Fuck!"'

'I saw that in myself,' said Josie, 'which made me work really hard at not doing it.'

Josie was occasionally worried about her safety when Jon's fans got too close. 'Fans would be very excited; it was hard to understand if they were happy or angry, and I found that quite frightening.' Even when she was young, Josie said, she could see Jon's discomfort. 'Especially with these drunk, grabby women. He'd whisper, "Get me the fuck out of here." I could tell from a young age that it was sexual. I could just tell.'

Josie would sometimes sit in the dressing room, reading. One night, on the road, she was engrossed in a book when Jon's tour manager, who was nicknamed Scooby, appeared in the dressing room with three young women.

'It was pretty obvious what they were,' recalled Josie. They were groupies.

'Jon, where are you staying?' the women asked excitedly,

'Oh, we're all staying in town,' mumbled Jon awkwardly. He grabbed Josie by the arm: 'And this is my daughter Josie and she's staying with me in town.'

Josie came to learn that her father was unfaithful while on tour. She asked him, 'If you love Mum, what's that about?'

'I'm lonely and it's five minutes and another warm body and it means nothing. I don't even remember them,' Jon told her, point blank.

Josie thought this through for a minute before replying. 'I appreciate your honesty,' she told him.

She came to understand, if not condone, Jon's moments of weakness. 'I went away and *I* was lonely,' she said. 'That "five minutes of a warm body" shit he said made sense. I kind of got that. I just didn't have a wife and kids at home.

'But how can you go from being on stage and everyone saying, "Wow, you're amazing," then you go back to your room alone?'

For Carmen, however, Jon's infidelities were inexcusable, and led to their eventual separation. 'To him it meant nothing, but it devastated me,' she said. 'I knew he was in contact with certain women. I became very cold towards him. I just thought, "How could you do this?" It was like he could separate that side of him from what he had at home.'

———

183

Reviews for *The Mikado* were favourable — *The Sydney Morning Herald* called it 'an unfolding caravan of delights', while *The Australian* declared 'no praise could be too excessive' — but on stage, Jon, according to Simon Gallaher, 'felt a bit like a fish out of water'. The role of Pooh-Bah didn't demand the same sort of physicality as the Pirate King, nor did it give Jon quite the same opportunity to be a commanding presence on stage.

Gallaher came up with an easy fix; why not add a dash of Pirate King swagger to the role?

'Come on, let's have a rope, just like the pirates,' he told Jon. 'You can swing on the rope and do all those sort of gags.'

It worked a treat, because the show was yet another big hit. Jon and Gallaher were a highly bankable pairing, box office gold — the show ran and ran, finally closing fifteen months later in Perth after seasons in Brisbane, Sydney, Melbourne, Adelaide and Canberra.

Gallaher now set his sights on expanding his company into New Zealand, using a simple philosophy: dating back to the colonial era, Gilbert and Sullivan shows usually worked well wherever the people played cricket. In 1996 Jon trod the boards across the Tasman as Pooh-Bah and the production was a hit all over again.

Some critics, however, could be a bit unkind to Jon. One morning, Jon was in his dressing room when a cast member began reading out a review of the show that had been posted on the company noticeboard. The reviewer mentioned that Jon had sprouted a bit of a waistline and his backside wasn't quite as pert as it once was. Upon hearing this, Jon's voice boomed out of his dressing room: 'Yeah, but I've got a massive cock.' He'd delivered the line with perfect comic timing.

Jon liked to remind anyone within earshot that *The Mikado* was merely an entrée. '*Mikado*'s OK,' he'd tell people, 'but wait until you see *Pirates*. It's fantastic.' Oddly, when Jon and Gallaher staged *Pirates* in New Zealand, the reaction, while enthusiastic, was not quite what Jon expected. The feedback he received was that *Pirates* was OK 'but it's not as good as *The Mikado*'.

'To me it was poetic justice,' said Gallaher, 'but to Jon it was a big shock that his big role didn't quite have the same impact.'

By now, Jon was living and breathing Gilbert and Sullivan. His recording career was effectively over — his last studio LP, *Busking*, had been released in 1989 — and although staging *Paris* remained a major obsession, it was taking second place to his commitments with Gallaher.

As Gallaher admitted, 'Jon had gotten bored with recording — and he was so busy. Things like *Pirates*, where you're doing eight shows a week, you're absolutely fucked. You can't think of anything else. He was also being paid a lot of money.'

Pirates and *The Mikado* also toured New Zealand in 1996, which gave the Australian audiences a 'breather' and built expectation about what was to come next from the Jon and Simon Show. They duly returned to Oz and toured *The Mikado* once more, this time taking it back to Adelaide and Perth. The show was a hit all over again.

***

H.M.S. Pinafore was the third part of Gilbert and Sullivan's 'big three', their best known and most popular works, and Gallaher decided to stage it next.

Jon wasn't sold on *Pinafore*, even though his ensemble castmates Helen Donaldson, Drew Forsythe and Gallaher were all good to go. Gallaher had Jon cast, at least in theory, as Dick Deadeye, figuring that he was ideal for the role. 'Dick Deadeye was a bit sinister,' said Gallaher. 'He had black circles under his eyes. Perfect.'

But Jon remained unconvinced, at least until Gallaher went in with a big pitch.

'We did a sell job to Jon,' said Gallaher. 'We went to him with costume designs, which were designed around his look, so he was looking at himself in these costume sketches. He could immediately imagine himself in these outfits.'

At the same time, Gallaher had not fully dismissed the possibility of staging *Paris*, which was another incentive for Jon to continue working with him. But, as Gallaher admitted, 'There was a lot of baggage, both personal and financial, and it seemed it was all a bit of a minefield to wade through. The scale of the project was also off-putting, so it ended up in the too-hard basket.'

Jon's payday was increased, yet again. Now he was pocketing $14,000 a week. On 2 January 1997, *Pinafore* opened at Melbourne's State Theatre and fast became the third straight hit for Jon and the company. It closed in Perth in October 1997 after a highly successful run across Australia and New Zealand.

A key part of the show was the revolving set, its feature being a three-dimensional ship's deck, designed by Graham Maclean. This was built early on and used in the rehearsal room, which was uncommon; typically a cast has just a few days to become acclimatised to a set on the stage where they are to perform. This was a godsend; by the time of opening night, according to Gallaher, 'we knew that set backwards. On opening night it looked as though we'd been doing the show forever. It flowed so beautifully.'

During the obligatory show-ending Mega Mix, Jon, Gallaher and the rest of the cast combined songs from *Pinafore* with tunes from *Pirates* and *The Mikado*. It was the Mega Mega Mix. Jon and Gallaher, dressed as the Pirate King and Frederic, magically 'flew' down to the stage, to the gasps of the audience.

On the back of their trio of big hits, Jon could now envisage a steady flow of future work — and knowing that there was work on the books was always important to Jon. Surely there was no reason that he and Gallaher couldn't keep working for as long as audiences kept flocking to the theatre. If only it proved to be that easy.

CHAPTER 16

'Drinking is such a part of the culture, but then you go, "Oh god, I haven't had a dry day for a year." Then you realise you might have a problem.'

A Funny Thing Happened on the Way to the Forum was a bawdy Stephen Sondheim musical farce, set in ancient Rome, that had debuted on Broadway way back in 1962, starring the rubbery-faced Zero Mostel. A 1996 revival, starring Nathan Lane in the lead role and then, later on, Whoopi Goldberg, was a massive hit, running for more than 700 performances. Lane won the 1996 Tony Award for Best Lead Actor in a Musical.

Simon Gallaher checked out the Broadway production and was sufficiently inspired to produce an Australian version under his Essgee company banner. In the wake of their huge success with *Pirates*, *The Mikado* and *HMS Pinafore*, Gallaher immediately cast Jon in the lead, playing the slave Pseudolus, whose goal was to gain his freedom by aiding his young master in winning over the girl of his dreams. Craig Schaefer was rehired to direct *Forum*, which would launch at Her Majesty's Theatre in Adelaide in December 1998. Also in the cast were Jonathan Biggins and Drew Forsythe.

During rehearsals for *Forum*, Jon was in for a shock. Mike Munro, the host of Channel 7's *This is Your Life*, walked into the rehearsal space, carrying in his hands the hefty folder that contained all of Jon's life achievements.

Munro announced: 'Jon English, this is your life.'

'You're joking,' Jon exclaimed, looking at the rest of the cast. 'You're kidding. You bastards — you sucked me in.'

Jon was a good actor but the truth was that he was feigning surprise; he had accidentally found out a few days earlier, when someone let it slip.

This was the second time Jon had been approached to appear on the high-rating show. First time around, Carmen had put the kibosh on it — and she very reluctantly agreed when the show was re-pitched. Centrestage held no interest for her, but she knew that Jon would be chuffed by the accolade. And it gave Jon the chance to show off his first grandchild, Jzawo — yet another J. English — who wasn't quite a year old. ('He was the most enthusiastic grandparent,' Josie said of Jon.) Jzawo's father was Marcus Pointon, a dancer from the Gilbert and Sullivan productions.

If Jon looked awkward sitting on the *This is Your Life* couch, Carmen, who was seated alongside him, was even more uncomfortable. Their relationship wasn't in good shape — after almost 30 years together they were drifting apart as his infidelities mounted — and as proud as she was of Jon, she preferred to be on the sidelines. Carmen said very little during the entire episode.

All the likely people were wheeled out over the course of the show. There was family: his four children and his grandson; Jon's mother, Sheila — who related the story of Jon's birth and the numerous sports events that coincided with it, and how Jon 'was very good at sports'; and Jon's siblings, Janet, Jill and Jeremy — who recalled how they got the day of the *Superstar* audition wrong and Jon almost missed out. There were peers, such as *Superstar* co-stars John Paul Young, Trevor White and Michele Fawdon, who discussed the Melbourne farting incident.

Simon Gallaher and David Atkins — Jon's Pirate King understudy and backstage drinking buddy — made guest appearances. There was also actress Tina Bursill, who'd been with Jon on the set of TV show *The Flying Doctors*, in early August 1990, when Jon got a call from his brother telling him that their much-loved father Syd had died at the age of 74. She recalled how when Jon ended the call, he put the phone down, stepped away from the camera, downed a large glass of Scotch, and did his scene in a single take.

'I didn't want to make a fuss,' Jon said at the time. 'No one really knew so I just wanted to get on with it. I just did it.'

Also invited to the *This is Your Life* set were Parramatta Eels legends Ray Price — 'Ray Price was a rock star to Dad,' said Josie — as well as Price's former teammates Mick Cronin, Brett Kenny, Steve Edge and Eric Grothe (who'd one day help Jon record the Parramatta team song). Edge told the story of the night that Jon trained with the Eels, which revealed that a lot had changed since his days as a gun schoolboy footballer. 'We did four laps and he did one,' laughed Edge. 'At the end of one lap he decided to remain a frustrated footballer.' All those late nights and cigarettes had taken their toll.

Elsewhere during the show, Cameron Daddo, who'd starred alongside Jon in *Big River*, appeared in a filmed cameo, as did Marina Prior, along with Jon's *All Together Now* castmates, plus *Paris* co-creator David Mackay, impresario Harry M. Miller and Mary Larkin, who was Jon's leading lady in *Against the Wind*. The night ended, of course, with an all-in rendition of 'Superstar', Mario Millo sharing guitar duties with Jon's son Jonathan, and backing vocalists who included Jon's nephews Jacob ('Jay') and Jasper.

The Australian production of *A Funny Thing Happened on the Way to the Forum* didn't replicate the success of the Broadway production, even though Jon seemed perfect for the role of Pseudolus. It was a huge flop, despite seasons in Adelaide, Perth, Canberra, Newcastle and Brisbane during the first five months of 1999.

It seemed that nothing could rescue *Forum*. 'People didn't come,' producer Gallaher said, quite simply. 'The old showbiz rule — there's no business like no business.' Gallaher even tried to use the pitch 'The Pirates Are Back', but the show just didn't connect with the public. Their hot streak was over.

'We fell into the trap of believing we were bulletproof,' said Gallaher.

And, for the first time, Jon wasn't performing with Gallaher, who wasn't in the show. Gallaher was absorbed with other work; he had a production of *The Merry Widow* on the road, as well as a play called *Masterclass*, featuring Amanda Muggleton, who'd performed in *Pinafore*. The success of these two shows was keeping *Forum* afloat, but even then the *S.S. Forum* was listing badly. Its failure, and Gallaher's absence, weighed heavily on Jon. The planned one-year run was quickly shortened. Jon was dismayed.

'I think he felt abandoned, wounded that I'd deserted him,' said Gallaher, 'that I wasn't there for him every day, and I wasn't there saying, "This is what we're going to do next." It was a very different and lonelier road for him. I'd become his safety blanket and supporter; I was always there for Jon. This was coming to an end but I didn't have the heart to close it.'

As the man taking the biggest bath financially, Gallaher was confronted with every producer's nightmare: should he pull the show altogether? In strictly financial terms, he knew that was the right decision, but he also felt a loyalty to Jon. He was conflicted. Jon had gone through some hard times trying to bring *Paris* to the stage — and now he was starring in a flop. How would he handle this latest blow?

'We limped along, but it was extremely expensive,' said Gallaher. 'I didn't want to pull it early — I should have — because I didn't want the humiliation of that to be wedded to Jon. That would have been a big blow to him, as well, to get cancelled months into a one-year run. A lot of egg on his face.'

By the time Gallaher accepted the inevitable and pulled the show in May 1999, he'd lost a fortune. 'Millions of dollars,' he said. 'It placed my company in a position that we weren't able to look at anything in the foreseeable future, and certainly not an original Australian work.'

This had enormous repercussions for Jon. He'd been writing new songs for a musical that he was going to call *Buskers and Angels*, inspired, in part, by his 1989 LP *Busking*. The plot was not too far removed from the *A Star is Born* formula, involving a busker and a young female singer, an ingénue, who becomes a huge star.

Jon, when asked about *Buskers and Angels*, said that the show also addressed the hot-button topic of misogyny in the entertainment business. To him, the industry was 'probably the most misogynistic industry left'. He was constantly inspired by the strong female role models in his life: Carmen; his mother, Sheila; and his grandmother, Katie, known to the family as KD. According to Jon, *Buskers and Angels*, just like *Paris*, shone a light on 'forthright, strong women trapped by circumstances but not by their own sex. And I sort of miss that badly in a lot of musicals.'

Simon Gallaher really liked the songs and had expressed interest in backing the show, which would have required an investment of two million dollars, perhaps more. But after the failure of *Forum* he was simply not in a position to do so. Jon was forced to search elsewhere in the industry for financing, and when that wasn't forthcoming, opted to finance it himself, along with theatrical agent Chris Rix (Peter Rix's brother) and tour manager Lindsay Hall. It was the wrong decision for Jon — especially so soon after sinking a lot of his own money into the still-unproduced *Paris*, which had, to date, returned very little on his six-figure investment.

Jon should have sensed that the show was doomed. He'd tried writing with David Mackay, hoping to stir up a little of their *Paris* magic, but Mackay could see that it wasn't working. '*Buskers and Angels* was a disaster,' Mackay admitted. 'We started writing it together but Jon went off at a tangent and I distanced myself from it in the interests of *Paris*, and our friendship.'

Even his family wasn't mad about *Buskers and Angels*.

As Carmen recalled, 'I hated that show, hated everything to do with it. He wasn't himself at the time, he really wasn't. He was disappointed that *Paris* didn't take off. I think he was depressed; he was living in some fantasy land. It was a very difficult time for us. He didn't want to listen to reason.

'*Paris* had some worth to it. *Buskers and Angels*, to me, was trite, it was crap. It was like a poor version of *A Star is Born*.'

'*Buskers* was a really strange time,' Jonathan remembered; he eventually went on the tour of the show with his father. 'In our household we were never that supportive of the show. He was so determined because *Paris* never got staged, and that really knocked him for six. I think he probably had a nervous breakdown but didn't address it. Instead he did the typical Dad thing and went, "Fuck it, I'll write another one."'

Looking back, Jonathan felt there was a simple problem — the storyline was too obvious.

'But he never took it past that treatment stage where it's very straightforward. I was sixteen and didn't know to say these things, especially to Dad, but I'd been learning these things and watching them rehearse it and was thinking, "Mate, your main character, the Busker, is a very generous picture of you — it's you with no faults, this sage with all the answers." And the girl gets caught up in the rise and fall of stardom. But it was all so straightforward.

'At that stage,' continued Jonathan, 'he'd done the Gilbert and Sullivan stuff and he was top dog of stage, and he knew *everything*. He was horrified when we — Mum especially, who was really at the end of her tether with him about a lot of things — said that we really didn't think it was very good. And then I was going out on the road with him and he said, "Mate, we'll make it work."'

When Jon told Simon Gallaher that he intended to back it himself, Gallaher knew it was a mistake; to him, the show simply wasn't ready. Gallaher also felt that Jon was wrong for the lead role of the Busker. At 50, he was too old, and the relationship with the young female lead named Angel — played by Belgian-born, Gold Coast–based Martine Monroe, who'd starred in the ABC concert series *A Toast to Piaf*— didn't sit comfortably. At one point, Jon's *Big River* co-star Cameron Daddo was mentioned as a possible male lead — 'The age difference would have been much better,' said Gallaher — but Jon stubbornly went ahead and cast himself.

Interestingly, Martine Monroe, who'd been a backing singer for Jon prior to *Buskers and Angels*, wasn't fazed by the age difference. 'I wasn't really surprised Jon played the Busker,' she said, 'as he was always a great drawcard for musical theatre shows . . . I don't think his age was that important.'

However, even years after the event, Simon Gallaher still disagreed with Jon's decision. 'It just didn't sit for a guy of Jon's age, and style, to play opposite an ingénue.'

———

Jon wrote about the genesis and the inspiration for *Buskers and Angels* in the program for the show:

I've always been fascinated by Buskers. In a way, they're the purest form of what we do. They don't have light shows, sets, stages, managers, nothing . . . They just go out and do it, and if we (the punters) like it, we give them money, not even any specific amount, no booking fee or anything. It's so damned simple it's beautiful. It also takes a lot of guts . . .

Now in my time I've signed recording contracts that are as thick as the Yellow Pages and nowhere near as interesting, I've been in stage shows where they seriously considered cancelling because of faulty air-conditioning, I've seen entire TV variety specials taken off the air because the hairdresser wasn't in a union, and I once heard a well-known manager complaining to an equally well-known booking agent that, 'The trouble with the music business is all those bloody musicians!'

So you take all this on board, and one day you walk past a busker, and he's playing a song you wrote and you ask yourself the obvious question: 'How did it all get so complicated?' . . .

So Buskers and Angels was born ... The story is not without humour, pathos, and all the necessary ingredients to help with the telling, and I'm secretly very proud of the music, but the thing that makes it special to me is that it's basically true ... I haven't really embellished the events that transpire that much at all. So no one can question its authenticity can they? ...

We can only sit back and hope for success, but I think we've already got that . . . After all, 'Success is a state of mind!!'

Before it opened, *Buskers and Angels* was workshopped at the Hills Centre in Castle Hill, Sydney, a venue run by Chris Rix, for three days in February 2000. *Buskers and Angels* premiered at the Civic Theatre in Newcastle in September that year — prematurely, in the mind of Simon Gallaher: 'Jon was a bull at a gate with it.'

In 1987 Jon had told a reporter that he'd never produce his own show. 'It's a bloody nightmare,' he'd said. But his situation had dramatically changed since then. Here he now was, taking on several roles — creator, star, producer — *and* spending his own money. It was too much.

'He was determined to make *Buskers and Angels* a reality, but with no experience and acumen to be a producer,' said Gallaher. 'He went off — half-cocked, I'd say — but to do an original work it takes a lot of work-shopping and some very clever creative people behind the scenes. He'd seen me put on these shows, back them myself, and to a large extent successfully, and he didn't appreciate the risks involved and the losses incurred.'

Reviewing the show for *The Age*, Fiona Scott-Norman praised Jon, who was 'pretty much as he always is — amiable and self-deprecating, a big shaggy dog with a love of bad jokes, and a penchant for ignoring the fourth wall and addressing the audience' — as he'd done so successfully with *Pirates* — but she thought *Buskers and Angels* had fatal flaws. 'The mystery,' she wrote, 'given English's credentials and the sincere love and care that has gone into the show, is that it lacks realism or awareness. The story and characters are simple and obvious.' Those suspicions his son Jonathan had — that the story was too straightforward and needed development — proved to be correct.

The original director, Jonathan Biggins, quit after a month when Jon made it very clear that he wasn't going to change the show. Box office was slow, a simple fact that couldn't be missed from the stage. 'The audiences were not that large,' admitted Martine Monroe, 'but I didn't know any details about production costs versus ticket sales; that side of things was always a bit vague to me.'

The show briefly toured Newcastle and Canberra and closed in Melbourne during November 2000.

'It was crazy,' said Jonathan. 'We had these six- to eight-week seasons in places, but after three weeks it was done. I had a month to spare in Melbourne at the end.'

'It would have been nice for the show to get a longer run,' said Monroe, 'so it was a bit sad when it ended so soon. I think we had a pretty good rapport on stage and Jon always gave his all when performing. He was a natural.'

But Jon's natural talent alone couldn't save *Buskers and Angels*. The show was a commercial disaster. Early on, Jon's then-management team, Multi J Enterprises, arranged the drafting of a partnership agreement for Jon's investment in these shows, which would have freed him from any debts the show might incur. But he forgot to sign the agreement, which was a huge and very costly oversight. That meant that when the show closed, Jon and Lindsay Hall were saddled with $200,000 worth of debts. (Chris Rix had died in the interim, leaving the other two partners with the full debt.) With Hall's help, Jon paid off his debt, thereby preventing a sheriff from taking his possessions as payment, which had been threatened.

Jon may have been hugely frustrated by his failure to mount a large-scale production of *Paris*, but this was worse, a total disaster. It had a huge impact on his state of mind; he later said that 'my doldrums came around 2000. Things weren't going great. Carmen had had enough of me and my moods'.

When Carmen learned about Jon's latest tryst — he had moved into an apartment near the Gold Coast, Queensland, with the estranged wife of a bandmate — she realised it was time for her to get on with her own life. Along with Jonathan and Julian, she moved from the farm to the Sydney suburb of Rozelle, with the idea of living apart from Jon for a time; they even drew up a property settlement. Carmen found a job and started living an independent life.

'They were always very close but it just became impossible for them to live in the same house because Mum could see how destructive Dad had become,' said Jonathan.

Yet Jon had other plans and, quite bizarrely, moved back in with Carmen in the new house when his latest affair ended. 'It was my fault, too,' Carmen accepted. 'I wasn't quite ready to let him go. But he never liked living in that house in Rozelle. We still had the farm and he quite often stayed there on his own and would come down now and then.'

When the local paper revealed that Jon English had just moved into the Rozelle neighbourhood, a tagger sprayed 'Village Idiot' on the gate of their house. It seemed as though some people still mistook Jon for Bobby Rivers.

As far as Simon Gallaher was concerned — and Gallaher knew Jon as well as most people — the failure of *Buskers and Angels* was the beginning of a gradual decline for Jon English, household name, legendary entertainer.

'It brought him undone. The wheels started to come off. He put it all on himself and lost a fortune and I think that's what sent him over the edge,' said Gallaher. 'Not only was it an artistic disappointment and humiliation, but a financially ruining one.

'You know, [this was] a man that had had lots of assets and money — but never really understood money — and suddenly it wasn't there. He was very determined that he was going to put this show on, no matter what, and he became very myopic about it. It really came a cropper.

'His life was crumbling: the prospect of big live shows was no longer there, he'd lost his fortune, and his marriage was in tatters. Jon was in denial about all of that. I think that was the turning point.'

While Jon continued working, he'd never again release any new music, or create another new, original project. And without telling Carmen, he sold the family farm in Glenorie.

'Jon was forever selling property and not telling me,' she said. 'He called me and said, "You better come up to the farm and help me pack up. I've sold it." I think we had about three weeks to pack up the entire farm. He was terrible like that.'

Jon always liked a drink — Mario Millo once believed that Jon's band was named The Foster Brothers because they had a beer sponsorship: 'They always drank so much.'

Jon struggled to recall a single day when he hadn't had a drink; it was simply part of the world in which he worked, the life he lived. But he'd now started to binge-drink, in an effort to blot out the double blow of *Forum* and *Buskers and Angels*, and his ongoing frustrations with *Paris*. He'd disappear with a few bottles and sometimes wouldn't surface for days. Aside from some stints on the wagon, this bingeing continued for the rest of Jon's life, even though he would discuss it in interviews as if he'd moved on.

Jon talked about his battle with the bottle during an interview with a reporter from Channel 10. 'It's almost a cliché in this business,' Jon said. 'Drinking is such a part of the culture, but then you go, "Oh god, I haven't had a dry day for a year." Then you realise you might have a problem. But depression comes first. It seems to go hand in hand with the character we [all] are. You have black spots. You have so many highs, there has to be a proportionate number of lows, even if they're in your own head.

'I thought I'd lost it,' Jon continued. 'I thought, "I don't know how to do it anymore." That's the terrifying thing for any performer: you don't know how you do it. You get out there and wait for the thing to take over — and then you do it. The fear of that thing not taking over one day is terrifying.'

'His star was dimming,' said Jonathan, 'and he was in denial about a lot of stuff and was self-medicating. I remember when he was really falling down, thinking, "Well done, mate, you've gone and ticked all the boxes of rock clichés. You were so anti all that. You didn't touch drugs. You didn't do this."'

Jon's transition from social drinker to serious boozer happened gradually. Carmen recalled that there was never hard liquor in the house during their many years together. 'Jon would have a beer now and then, I was a wine person, but spirits hardly ever. When he was doing shows he might have a nip of brandy because it soothes the throat, but the vodka thing — I don't know where that started. Maybe it was loneliness on the road — that also led to him having women. His drinking got extremely bad.'

Jonathan once felt compelled to say to Jon, 'The younger you would have hated you now.' It was a tough thing for a teenager to say to anyone, let alone his father.

'He got pretty hostile about that. I was really around for the bad times and that was pretty much from the time I started working with him. It stopped me from wanting to be on the road with him. It was awful.'

And Jonathan, like Josie before him, had enjoyed going on tour with his father; it wasn't something he wanted to walk away from. 'I loved it because I didn't get to have much family time with him unless we were on the road,' he said. 'We used to have these long drives and just talk: history, mythology, anything but music. He was really great to talk with.'

'The bottle was a symptom of depression,' Jon once wrote in a 2007 blog, reflecting on this dark phase of his life. 'I was self-medicating. I wasn't a born alcoholic . . . I just wanted oblivion, I guess. It's not chronic depression, I have to say. I'm normally a very up guy, so when you start feeling down about things, or whatever, then there's something wrong.'

Without a doubt, something was now terribly wrong with Jon. His career and his personal life were in freefall.

CHAPTER 17

'I did wonder when I saw [Troy] whether or not they had heard Paris.*'*

I n 2002, after much persuading from those around him and 'nagging' by David Spicer, a writer, performer and community theatre advocate, Jon finally swallowed his pride and released the amateur rights to *Paris*. This allowed smaller, non-profit companies — 'am-drams', as they are known in the trade — to stage the rock opera, although it did little to recoup Jon's sizeable investment in *Paris*. Still, he was pragmatic. 'I thought, "Shit, hang on, I've seen a few amateur productions and they're fucking good,"' Jon told a journalist from *The Age*. 'And you get a free workshop, essentially.'

David Spicer met with Jon at his home to work on the production, while the handwritten scores were retrieved from David Mackay's attic. Kevin Hocking, who, in his usual role as conductor, had sparred with Jon during his Gilbert and Sullivan days, converted the handwritten score into a published music score. This in itself was 'a huge job', according to Spicer. Two companies quickly took up the challenge to stage *Paris*, both in October 2003: Sydney's Regals Musical Society, and the Laycock Street Theatre on the New South Wales Central Coast.

Stuart Smith, not long out of university, was the Laycock Street

Theatre's production designer. He was pleasantly surprised to get a call from Patrick Corrigan, the theatre company's manager.

'Do you want to stage the world premiere of *Paris*?'

Smith couldn't believe his luck. He'd bought the *Paris* CD when it was released, having tracked it down at Ava and Susan's, a specialist store in Sydney. Smith was a big fan; to him, *Paris* was 'a massive album; it sounded incredible. All the musical theatre people loved it.'

He agreed to the job in a heartbeat. But Smith knew he had a challenge: how could he stage *Paris* with next to no money in the production budget? So he set out to create something that was more rock opera than Greek tragedy. 'I was geeking out on it,' he said. 'I loved it.'

The company was deep in rehearsals, about a month in, when Jon turned up at the theatre. He could sense almost immediately that this was more than some earnest amateur production — much more. Jon wanted to get involved. 'He got really excited by it,' Smith recalled.

Jon also found a kindred spirit in Smith. To him, Smith was a rock-theatre guy, someone he could relate to easily. And he loved Smith's love of *Paris*.

'When I first met Jon, I found him really easy to get along with, because he was excited and passionate,' said Smith. I didn't find him to be at all a control freak; he was a collaborator. And that shocked me because it was his baby, his passion project.'

Having clearly connected, Smith decided to run one of his ideas by Jon. 'I want to put people in military jackets, make it a bit more rock. What do you think?'

'Great,' Jon replied in a heartbeat. 'Do it.'

According to Smith, 'Jon wanted to be more avant-garde in the staging. He wasn't interested in the sandals-and-toga look.'

Jon was sufficiently taken by Smith to talk him up when he spoke with a reporter: 'He's really very talented and has some great ideas.'

It was apparent to Smith, though, that Jon had mixed feelings about the venture. Jon still held out hopes of staging *Paris* on a big stage, with a budget to match. 'It was something he didn't want to die,' said Smith, 'and he'd work stupidly hard to try and make it work. He was probably learning to deal with the fact that he was Jon English and he was having to put his show on in an amateur way,' said Smith. 'That was probably a big blow for him.'

Still, with a little prodding from Smith, Jon agreed to appear in their production, unbilled, as The Fisherman. The audience on opening night, on 10 October 2003 — the first of three performances — couldn't believe their luck.

'It was a bit of a stir on the night,' said Smith. 'He didn't want to steal anyone's thunder and play a bigger role. He wanted something simple and fun. He was genuinely thankful that we were putting it on, he really, really was. He could sense that people were getting interested in it again.'

Over time, Jon and Smith discussed many possible variations of *Paris* — they thought about an all-male version (with the exception of Helen, of course); they also discussed the possibility of taking cues from the ancient Greeks, with the actors playing a variety of roles. Jon was gradually opening up to the possibilities of *Paris* — maybe there were other ways to stage it.

'He was trying to find ways to logistically stage the show,' said Smith.

Another amateur production of *Paris* followed in Melbourne, on 29 January 2004, backed by Mark Featherby, a lawyer and amateur theatre buff, who invested $180,000 of his own money into staging *Paris* (he owned the production company Stella Entertainment). It wasn't the big-budget, large-scale, Cameron Mackintosh-type production that Jon had pushed so hard for — none of the Melbourne cast were paid — but again he took solace in seeing *Paris* finally come to life in some form.

According to Jon, 'The best thing about it is, you can look at it and go,

"Aaah, oh, there's not enough of Paris there, in the Second Act." Stuff that you don't really realise before.'

'I have to say,' he continued, 'it makes me a little sad sometimes to see how enthusiastically amateur casts throw themselves into their roles when they do *Paris*, and how much they love the show, and yet professionals are just too scared to take it on because of the sheer scope of the thing.'

It had been a long, hard road to *Paris*. In one of his later website blogs, Jon wrote that 'You can usually trust that any angst I have with "the people in charge" relates to poor old *Paris*.' He spoke about 'turgid business meetings that seem to go on forever and get nowhere'. Twenty years had passed since the concept had first come to Jon while he was recording the *Some People* album with David Mackay.

On the upside, Jon knew that a Hollywood version of *Troy*, starring Brad Pitt, Orlando Bloom and Aussie Eric Bana, was about to hit the big screen, so perhaps his quest wasn't over just yet. 'It's not going to hurt us at all,' Jon said. 'It means loads more people will know the story.'

Jon, however, wasn't especially thrilled by the film version when he did see it. 'It was just a multi-million dollar vehicle for Brad Pitt and they took terrible liberties with *The Iliad*. I was most disappointed.' Curiously, during the movie they mentioned the character of the Fisherman, who was completely Jon's invention. That left Jon scratching his head. 'I did wonder when I saw it whether or not they had heard *Paris*.'

In mid-2007, Jon participated in a piece called *Birds and Beasts* with the Canberra Pops Orchestra. Afterwards, Jon dropped what he described as 'large and unsubtle hints' about a concert version of *Paris* with the head of the Pops, Ian McLean. 'Hey, he didn't outright tell me to piss off,' Jon reported, 'so fingers crossed.'

As Jon noted in 2008, *Paris* wasn't dead yet by any means. The Laycock Street Theatre had recently staged *Paris* for the second time, with Jon in the role of Menelaus. He wrote a new song, 'Menelaus's Lament', specifically for the production.

'The interest from America is still alive and out there in the form of a movie musical now, so you just never know,' Jon wrote. 'Everything has a time, and maybe *Paris*'s time is now. We shall see.'

Jon continued reworking the story with David Mackay. In an attempt to reduce staging costs, thereby making it more cost-effective for potential producers, they sequenced all the orchestral music onto software called Radar.

There was a translated German version in the works, too, which, according to David Spicer, was a dead ringer for the Laycock Street production, right down to the Trojan horse made out of fence palings. (Spicer had sent them a video.) Jon checked in with the producers in Berlin during the northern summer of 2008; his son Jonathan came along for the journey.

Berlin was one stage of a hit-and-run world trip that included more time with David Mackay in the UK and a visit to Florida — 'the Gold Coast on steroids' — and Las Vegas, where Jon checked out the hit Cirque du Soleil show *Ka*, primarily because 'it has a pretty spectacular set' that he wanted to take a look at. Everything was for the benefit of *Paris*.

'One of the quandaries with *Paris* in our final version is just how much of the gods in Greek mythology to leave in or take out,' Jon admitted. 'It's a quandary that I'm sure many tellers of the tale, both in movies and in books, before me have faced.

'To me, if you take the role of the gods out of this most famous of tales from Greek mythology, Paris and Helen turn into randy, rutting, irresponsible royals who managed to cause a ten-year war and destroy an entire nation (or even two, or three). Hard to have any sympathy for either of them on those grounds, isn't it?'

Another conundrum for Jon was whether such a powerful and layered tale deserved to be simplified for a mainstream audience.

'Basically the problem is just how far do you have to "dumb down" a story for the masses to appreciate it,' Jon figured. 'I don't want to dumb down Greek mythology for the sake of entertainment – I'll leave that to the makers of movies like *Troy*.

'I'd rather bring the audience up to a level of understanding of what it is that they are watching. I realise you can't turn a musical into a lesson in Greek mythology, but there's no point to *Paris* if you don't tell his whole story.'

In the end, Jon decided, even if *Paris* never got to receive the large-scale production it deserved, he hadn't compromised, and that was surely worth something. 'If *Paris* never becomes a worldwide success, well so be it. But at least I'll know I will have been true to myself, my vision, and my artistic integrity.'

When not pondering the wild world of Greek mythology, Jon wrote occasional blogs for his website and played live shows. In July 2006, he blogged about a major life change — he'd relocated from Sydney to Raleigh, near Coffs Harbour in northern New South Wales, to live with his new partner, Coralea Cameron, 'who also happens to be my highly efficient and organised PA and the one who keeps my life running on well-oiled wheels'. Jon at the time, was still in deep debt, owing $100,000, including debts to Lindsay Hall, the Australian Tax Office, the bank and his accountant.

Jon wrote that he'd swapped the 'concrete jungle' for 'a green, peaceful valley and mountain view . . . a wonderful oasis to come home to'. He'd sit at the kitchen table and drink in the view; he found the valley especially stunning after rain. It was just the sanctuary he needed after the turbulent past decade. Hollywood star and fellow NRL obsessive

Russell Crowe was a near neighbour, although, as Jon pointed out, 'Up here a neighbour could be anywhere within a hundred kilometre radius.'

Jon had reconnected with singer Peter Cupples in 2007. They'd first met backstage at the opening of the Sydney Entertainment Centre in 1984, a night that Jon's former manager Peter Rix remembered as one of his star client's finest. 'Peter Faiman, the director, put him up in a spaceship and lowered it down from the roof to the overture of *Superstar*. It was hair-raising, amazing.' Jon and Cupples had also played gigs together in the 1990s.

Cupples was the fair-haired former singer of Stylus, who in the 1970s were the first 'all-white' band to be signed to legendary US label Motown. The 'marriage', as Cupples described it, didn't work out so well, but he retained serious bragging rights; after all, Motown was home to everyone from Diana Ross to The Jackson 5 and The Temptations.

'There I was with my Italian designer leather pants, and there you were with your leather pants,' Cupples wrote of their first encounter at the 'Ent Cent' in 1984. 'As I took my $250 belt from my clothes cover to keep my pants up, you took out a roll of gaffer tape to keep yours up. I realised at this point I was in the presence of rock'n'roll royalty.'

Jon and Cupples — whom Jon dubbed 'Captain' — put together a show they christened Uncorked, which they took up and down the country for several years from 2007. The approach was very straightforward: the two of them sat centrestage, cradling acoustic guitars, swapping songs and jokes in equal proportions.

Many of their shows were staged at wineries, a new lifeline for the live music industry, although a curious choice for Jon given his battles with the bottle. (The pair were often given boxes of wine as part-payment.)

In May 2007, they played a fundraiser at Sawtell for lifeguards and lifesavers, in the wake of the drowning of a local bodyboarder. 'I'm proud to say,' Jon reported, 'the show raised over ten grand and earned the Coffs Coast a whole swag of new waterproof radios to help patrol their beaches.' Cast members of TV's *Bondi Rescue* looked on from the audience.

In what might have been an unfortunate omen, Cupples worked his way through an early Uncorked gig with a strained hamstring. This wasn't the last time one of them took to the stage with an injury. 'But, like the true Aussie, battling idiot that he is,' Jon reported, 'Cupps managed to bluff his way through. I swear he sings better [when] in pain.'

There was strong chemistry between the pair.

Jon had also recently resurrected The Foster Brothers, bringing together their best-known line-up — John 'JD' Dallimore on guitar, Keith 'Stretch' Kerwin on bass, Greg Henson and keyboardist Peter Deacon — to play shows for the first time in almost 20 years. Things had toned down considerably since their 1980s heyday, which Peter Rix had once likened to a footy team on a season's end trip to Bali.

But there were some problems on the road. Jon and The Foster Brothers, along with Lindsay Hall, were driving across the Nullarbor, returning from a show in Western Australia, when Jon had what drummer Henson described as 'a fit' in the back of the car. They pulled over to the side of the road in the middle of nowhere, pulled Jon out of the vehicle and laid him by the side of the road, only to find that they'd laid him on top of an ants' nest. When he appeared to be movable, they drove to the nearest roadhouse, in Kalgoorlie, and a call was made to the Royal Flying Doctor Service. As they waited, a woman who was tending to Jon walked over to the others and asked, 'Which one of you is Jon's mate?'

'I am,' said Greg Henson.

'He needs to go to the toilet and he needs your help.'

Henson immediately regretted stepping up, because he was required to get Jon to the bathroom, unzip him and lend a hand while Jon peed.

Jon was flown to hospital where he was diagnosed with serious liver and kidney problems and didn't work for months.

———

When Jon recovered, The Foster Brothers played such gigs as 2007's A Day for Newcastle, staged on the local racetrack, alongside other 'heritage rock' acts like The Radiators, John 'Swanee' Swan, Diesel and Noiseworks. 'Sun shining, smiling faces, great fun,' Jon wrote of the day. By the end of that tour, they had pulled 600 punters to a mid-week show in Newcastle.

'[We] rocked the roof off,' Jon revealed. 'Standing ovations and rowdy encore calls for "more" – ah, gratifying stuff.' It was almost like the heady 1980s all over again.

Tragically, not long after the tour, Newcastle was hit by floods, as Jon mentioned in a following blog: 'Buried by the Hunter River in the space of 24 hours.' (In fact, Jon and the Fosters had just played Gippsland, which had also flooded. 'Now, I don't want any of you prospective promoters to get paranoid,' Jon noted.)

Jon was back in 'Newie' soon after, in October 2007, performing for two weeks as the Narrator, among a variety of minor roles, in a production of Willy Russell's *Blood Brothers*. It was his first live theatre since a stint as Sergeant Wilson in *Dad's Army* during 2004, a show that toured both Australia and New Zealand in May and June of that year.

Of his *Blood Brothers* role, Jon noted, 'The Narrator is a weird combination of non-acting and being invisible to all the other actors, as well as basically saying — singing — the same bloody thing (in rhyme) a dozen slightly different ways throughout the show. Very taxing on this 58 year old memory!

'And because I'm invisible, NOT reacting when a real gun goes off three inches from your nose is par for the course. Not the easiest thing to do, particularly as we didn't actually use and fire the real gun at rehearsals because of firearms licensing laws, so I can tell you it was a bit of a challenge the first few shots!'

Jon also toured with *Blood Brothers,* playing numerous New South Wales regionals — Orange, Taree, Lismore and a gig in his new hometown of Coffs Harbour — in the winter of 2008, as well as Canberra. 'I think I got close to getting it right,' Jon said of his role.

Jon's lively working schedule sometimes left him stretched very thin. Following a late October matinee performance of *Blood Brothers* in Newcastle, he drove to the airport and hopped on a plane to Melbourne to take part in Concert for Max, a benefit show for singer-songwriter Max Merritt, who'd suffered kidney failure and was laid up in hospital. The show was staged at the Palais, which had been the Melbourne home of the original *Superstar.* Jon was hit by a powerful wave of deja vu as he stood on the stage, getting ready to sing 'Turn the Page'.

'It's the feel of the place and the smell that brings it back,' Jon said. 'Even weirder was JPY' — John Paul Young, who had played Annas to Jon's Judas — 'standing right behind me, no doubt experiencing the same vibes.'

The show, which also featured Renée Geyer, Russell Morris, Daryl Braithwaite, Ross Wilson, Swanee and Vanessa Amorosi, raised $200,000 for Merritt. Jon was particularly impressed by Amorosi, who he thought would be perfect for *Paris.* 'I asked her to think about singing Cassandra — she'd be great.' *Paris* was never too far from his thoughts.

Jon appeared at many fundraisers such as this, and sometimes found himself keeping unlikely company for a shaggy-haired rocker of a certain age. In November 2007, he compered a Cystic Fibrosis Foundation fundraiser, held at the Royal Military College in Duntroon. Jon couldn't have been any further from the country's sweaty beer barns. He glanced out at the audience and saw, seated at the head of various tables, morning TV's golden girl Kerri-Anne Kennerley, Peter Cosgrove (a Duntroon grad who'd led the peacekeeping force in East Timor), Paralympics legend Louise Sauvage and former tennis ace John Alexander. This was an all-star event.

Jon continued juggling a variety of projects — one was called *Symphony of Australia*, the brainchild of composer Gavin Lockley — as well as a new TV series called *Time Trackers*, a futuristic work aimed at older kids that was being produced in New Zealand.

'The scripts are really top notch, funny and, believe it or not, educational,' Jon noted.

Jon did, however, find himself stumbling over certain tricky lines of dialogue in his role as Old Troy, a likeable but chaotic hologram. During his first day on set, Jon was asked to recite this tongue twister: 'What do you think would happen if we harvested the substrate molecules and created swarm intelligent alpharithms in their pulsed field magnets?'

'Well what do you think would happen?' Jon said afterwards. 'I'd screw it up. Not once, but several times. Everyone was very sympathetic I must say and put it down to jet lag.'

Jon experienced another wave of deja vu as he looked around the site where the show was being filmed, Avalon Studios in Wellington. Jon realised that more than 30 years back he'd been at the opening of the studio. Not much had changed.

'I swear to god,' he said, 'the doorman is still the same.'

At his peak, Jon had been every bit as big in New Zealand as he'd been at home — 'Six Ribbons' had reached number 3 in the local charts back in 1978, as had 'Get Your Love Right' the following year.

On his way back to Australia, he was stopped by an eager fan at the airport.

'Hey, aren't you that bloke who sang that song, "Tie a Yellow Ribbon"?'

'Close enough,' Jon whispered, as he signed an autograph.

After a fair bit of not-so-subtle nudging on his part, Jon was given the green light to write a theme song for *Time Trackers*. He'd recently shared some bills (and would continue to do so over the next few years) with country-rock band Jonah's Road, whose members included two of Jon's nephews, Jay and Jasper Collie — sons of Jon's sister Jan. As well as winning various awards, Jonah's Road had released two albums: 2004's *Hold On* and 2007's *Counting Down the Days*. The Collies had written music for the kids' show *New MacDonald's Farm*, so Jon made the smart move to collaborate on the *Time Trackers* theme with them. (Jasper Collie passed away on 8 April 2017, aged just 40, from pancreatic cancer.)

Time Trackers comprised thirteen half-hour episodes and screened on Channel 7 in Australia and TV2 in New Zealand during 2008. Jon's grandchildren were instant converts.

Despite the geographical distance that now separated Jon from his family, they remained a vital part of his life, even though he didn't see them as much as he would have liked. He'd host his grandchildren — Lucy, Holly and Jzawo — at Christmas and spoil them with gifts. As for Carmen, they were still close. They remained married, although she'd told Jon that if he intended to remarry, he would have to be the one to file for divorce and pay the fee. But neither Jon nor Carmen had plans of remarrying, so why bother? Ultimately, Jon never asked her for a divorce.

'Carmen took the whole journey with me,' Jon told a journalist from *The Sun-Herald*, 'and although we aren't together anymore, we remain good friends.'

Sydmas was still a constant on the English family calendar, even though Syd had passed away in 1990. Sydmas 2008 brought together thirteen

J. Englishes, along with numerous other family members. 'I'd forgotten what a large and formidable clan we are when we get together nowadays,' Jon pondered. 'There were four generations of us crowded into my sister's house, all talking over the top of each other and creating happy chaos.'

A few days later Jon was at the Tamworth Country Music Festival for the first time. He'd never before attended the annual bash because, for one thing, 'I don't own a cowboy hat.' But in 2008 he was on a mission — first, to see his nephews in Jonah's Road play to an appreciative crowd of 10,000, but also to jump on stage at the end of their set and wish his sister Jan a happy, and very public, 60th birthday. (So public that footage of the moment was screened on TV that night, much to Jan's horror.)

In typical English fashion, rather than opt for what Jon felt was the 'soppy' version of 'Happy Birthday', he channelled his inner Beatle and rocked their song 'Birthday'. But there was a quid pro quo: the organisers of the event, from Tamworth Council, insisted that Jon stay on stage and sing 'Six Ribbons', and he readily concurred. Later on, Jon stood outside the Tamworth Town Hall, in the wet, busking with guitar great and close friend Phil Emmanuel. 'It was pissing with rain so we didn't pull the biggest of crowds, but we still managed to make the papers!'

Early 2008, however, did provide Jon with a heavy reminder about mortality. Jackie Orszaczky, who'd played bass in Jon's crack 1981 band, died on 3 February 2008 after a two-year battle with Hodgkin's lymphoma. He was 59. Jon was among the 500 who attended a memorial afternoon for Orszaczky in Sydney. 'You will be missed, Jackie,' Jon wrote.

Orszaczky's well-attended wake was held at the Harold Park Hotel in Sydney's inner west. Jon spotted Mario Millo in the queue at the bar and whispered in his ear, 'Hey Morrie, when I go, can you do something like this for me?'

CHAPTER 18

'I'll probably only make it to 70, so let's have a fun ten years.'

During his time with Stuart Smith, Jon had discussed the possibility of a 'rockumentary-style' live show, in which he'd sing and talk about the songs that had inspired him. It was an idea that connected deeply with him. Purely by chance, in 2009 Smith received a call from Patrick Corrigan, who was now managing the soon-to-be-opened Shoalhaven Entertainment Centre in Nowra, on the New South Wales south coast. He asked Smith if he'd be interested in staging *Cinderella* for the holidays. Smith, who'd just been to England with Jon and met David Mackay, had a much better idea than a 'panto'.

He called Jon and asked if he'd be interested in exploring the 'rockumentary' idea further. Jon agreed, and so *The Rock Show* was born. Smith, who became the show's director, put together a band of his friends, a mix of formally trained musicians and instinctive 'genius players', in his words. All were multi-instrumentalists. The youngest was sixteen years old; Smith, who was nearing 30, was the oldest. Among them was virtuoso Isaac Hayward, who could play cello, keyboards, lead guitar and more, 'like nothing I'd seen before', said Smith. (Hayward has gone on to receive numerous acclaimed musical director awards for various stage productions.) Most of the players had been involved with the

Laycock Street Theatre's production of *Paris*, so they had history with Smith and Jon.

Smith arranged a first rehearsal with Jon — at Smith's parents' house, no less — and skyped in Patrick Corrigan. The first sound he heard was Jon and the band playing Led Zeppelin's 'Stairway to Heaven'.

'I'm sold,' Corrigan said in a flash.

The concept gradually fell into place, as did Jon's role as the ringmaster of this young and vibrant band of players. They wouldn't just play the 'classics' — this was more than some rock'n'roll jukebox musical. It was more like a 'musical memoir', with Jon subtly revealing much about his life through the songs.

'We knew that Jon would be the perfect mix of rock and theatre that we wanted. We knew he could sing it all,' said Smith. 'I wanted a front-person that was well known and beloved. The stories about the songs would be more, "I was doing this when I first heard this song, I picked up my first guitar and heard this happen." It was Jon's version of rock'n'roll history — how that song came along, how he first heard the Beatles, the Stones.'

The show's debut was set in place for early 2009; there'd be three performances in all. No one involved was quite sure how the public would respond to the idea of Jon English performing classic rock songs alongside such a young and untried ensemble, but 3000 tickets were sold in a hurry. Each night was a sell-out. Jon may not have quite known what he was getting himself involved with, but Smith had a very clear game plan.

He wanted an audience to 'see Jon again as Jon, that inspirational character on stage. I was also trying to find a project for my friends, these musicians, who were world class.'

The Rock Show was an immediate hit. 'The audience went crazy for it,' said Smith. The band had the time of their lives, bouncing around the stage, swapping instruments, showing off their stellar chops. The significant age difference between the band and Jon turned out to be a feature of the show.

'We'd do generational jokes with Jon all the way through it,' said Smith. 'That was the dynamic: he'd found this troupe of musicians, and he was going to show them all off, while performing this history of music.'

On stage, Jon and the band worked their way through the classics, everything from the Kinks' 'Lola' to a Beatles medley, songs from The Who, Elton John ('Rocket Man'), the Stones ('You Can't Always Get What You Want') and a swag of his own hits, including 'Hollywood Seven' and 'Six Ribbons'. Jon also provided dialogue and commentary. It was a true team effort; when he wasn't singing, Jon would play guitar, urging on the youngsters. It might well have been the easiest $5000 he had ever made.

'It's very energetic,' he said, 'and it's done, I think, with the same energy and aggression that the original stuff was done, by people who were about the same age.'

Jon described *The Rock Show* as 'my version of Young Multi-Talent Time playing '60s and '70s rock music . . . Baby Boomer heaven.'

The Newcastle Herald, in their review, captured the spirit of *The Rock Show*. 'Fantastic value for money musically, and a lot of fun, with the rock history stories and the banter between the "old man" and his young crew keeping the crowd laughing as well as rocking on.'

Jon turned 60 on 26 March 2009 and was thrown a surprise birthday party at Sydney's Taronga Zoo, which was attended by a lot of his friends and peers — producer Richard Lush, Peter Plavsic, Mario Millo, Tony Mitchell from Sherbet, John Waters, Trevor White and many others. Millo was surprised when he saw Jon; he seemed somehow different physically from the last time he had seen him at Jackie Orszaczky's wake.

'The thing that struck me was that Jon always towered over me; he was so tall,' recalled Millo. 'I always felt so minute next to him. But at his 60th he was almost on eye level with me. I thought, "I've either gotten taller, or he's shrunk." It was odd.'

John Waters read out a message from Peter Cupples, who wasn't able to attend the bash. 'Jon, of all the people I've met in the music industry over the past 40 years, I've never met a more unpretentious, giving, generous, and dedicated performer. It's been a pleasure and an honour to have worked with you. You love what you do, and you love the people who allow you to do it. We can all learn a lot from you — particularly the way you can down a schooner of port and not fall off your stool; bloody marvellous!'

Further *Rock Show* concerts were booked, in Canberra and elsewhere, in the wake of their well-received debut. But it almost came undone early on, when they were scheduled to play two shows at the Illawarra Performing Arts Centre in Wollongong. Jon had been drinking, and 'just wasn't on his game' during one of the shows, said Smith. He was so drunk, in fact, that the band feared they might be booed off the stage. It was an incredibly stressful situation, given the age of the *Rock Show* band, and their lack of professional experience. What could they do? They decided to stage their own intervention, which was a gutsy move.

As Smith recalled, 'We confronted him afterwards and said, "You can't do that anymore."'

It did the trick. The next day Jon apologised to everyone in the band and their intervention proved to be a turning point in the life of *The Rock Show*.

'By that stage we all loved Jon. He was our friend, and we could see him falling,' said Smith. 'But now he was different; he was open. It was interesting to watch — before that point he was distant from us, because he was hiding something, but we knew, and he knew that we knew, about his depression and drinking, and he took positive steps to make that stop.

Then he got actively involved with making up new parts for the show —
and that's when it got super tight.'

Jon began speaking openly with Smith about his troubles with depression and the bottle. Before each show, Jon would give Smith whatever
booze he had with him and ask him to hide it. 'He was great in that time,'
said Smith. 'We saw Jon English again. I was so honoured to be on the
stage with him in a show with my friends. This was next level.'

In a quiet moment, Jon made a confession to Smith. 'I'll probably only
make it to 70,' he said, 'so let's have a fun ten years.'

Just as he'd done with *The Pirates of Penzance*, Jon loved nothing more
during *The Rock Show* than to smash down the 'fourth wall' that separated performer from audience. As Smith recalled, 'He told everyone
in that band to live in the moment. If they made a mistake, don't hide
it, own it and let the audience in on the mistake. They enjoyed it much
more that way.'

Sometimes, Jon would stop the band mid-song for a photo; the band
would pose for the camera, the shot would be taken, and then they'd
get back to work. Yet the show wasn't chaos; it was choreographed, to a
certain extent.

'Jon was this ringmaster out the front,' said Smith. 'We knew all the
cues, when the jokes were going to happen. It felt to me like we were
doing a theatre show.'

Bookings rolled in for *The Rock Show*. For the next three years, Jon
and the band would typically play three shows a week — almost always
on weekends. They toured the entire country twice. After a few performances, Jonathan agreed to get back on the road with his dad, helping
out as stage manager. But his role wasn't strictly confined to behind the
scenes. Jon would sometimes stop a song and announce that his guitar
was out of tune. 'Jonno,' he'd call out, 'get us another guitar, will ya?' It
seemed that Jon wanted to share the spotlight with his son.

Jon's children were never spoiled on the road and Jonathan was expected to muck in just like Josie had done before him. 'Dad was a real solid graft kind of guy,' said Jonathan, 'so he told me I had to do the road crew first. I spent about a year lugging things.

'He was all about solidarity. He really impressed upon me that your job is not above anyone else's. He told me, "We do really fun stuff and it's going to be great. As long as you're having fun up there the crowd will too. For god's sake, don't pull a sour face if you stuff a chord or break a string." I did once and he said, "Never do that again."'

In *The Rock Show*, Jonathan also had an onstage role; during their rendition of David Bowie's 'Space Oddity', he'd casually stroll across the stage, pick up a guitar and start playing with the band. (Jonathan was, and is, an accomplished guitarist.)

As the band gelled, Jon began testing them out. Sometimes, while playing 'Six Ribbons', he'd turn to the group and say, 'Now, the Nordic rock version', or 'Let's do it reggae style'. The band, as well schooled as they were, had no idea what Nordic rock was.

'It was crazy but so fun,' said Stuart Smith. 'That was who he was.'

Jon began getting right into the autobiographical nature of *The Rock Show*. During the Beatles medley, he transformed the lyrics of 'When I'm 64' into a description of his own close encounter with the Fab Four back in 1964. 'My sister took me down to Rushcutters Bay / We saw the Beatles / Oh what a show / When I got back / Woke up my mum / Got up to my usual tricks / Trouble and strife / But the time of my life / Even though I'm 66.'

As Jon's enthusiasm grew, he encouraged Smith to work more on the staging. They'd been talking about building some kind of structure for Pink Floyd's 'Another Brick in the Wall'. After a while Jon said, 'Stu, why don't you build that wall?' What eventuated was a very theatrical number, in which Jonathan, who was at the front of the stage at the time, would slowly find himself trapped by the emerging 'wall'.

'It was kind of chaos like that,' said Smith. 'The audience never knew what they were going to get, but they knew every song. It was trying to take the piss out of jukebox musicals, and Jon, with his dry humour, was the perfect guy to do that.'

Jon definitely hadn't lost his sense of humour, and the darker the better. Once, while he, Jonathan and Smith were on a small plane travelling to a show, they hit severe turbulence. Jon and his son started re-enacting the death spiral scene from the film *Almost Famous*, then Jon grabbed his guitar and began playing Buddy Holly songs. (Holly had died in a plane crash in 1959.) Smith, meanwhile, gripped his chair and hoped for the best.

A CD and DVD of *The Rock Show* were released during 2012, and the album was nominated for an ARIA Award. *The Rock Show* went on to win two Mo Awards.

When Jon took *The Rock Show* to the Adelaide Arts Festival — where he'd debuted in *Superstar* back in 1972 — he bumped into Marina Prior. They'd stayed in touch for the past 30 years and as far as Prior was concerned, Jon remained one of her biggest mentors. 'We just chatted and chatted about what we were doing,' she recalled. 'It was the same as ever, full of affection. We must have talked for an hour.'

Prior would never see Jon again.

The Rock Show was too good to let die, so after a hugely successful three-year run, it was reborn as *The Rock Show More* in 2012. Again, the concept was the same, although some of the songs were changed. Rather than play Led Zeppelin's 'Kashmir', for instance, they'd rock 'The Immigrant Song'. Then the ensemble would gather at the front of the stage for a Rolling Stones medley. For Jon, it was money for jam. He knew the material inside out and could sing these songs in his sleep.

The Rock Show More was just as successful as *The Rock Show*; they were now filling such venues as the 3000-seat Palais Theatre in Melbourne, and Sydney's State Theatre. Punters who'd seen the original show returned with their friends and its following grew. A show that had originally drawn mainly Jon English fans was now pulling a broader, bigger audience. Oz acting great Jack Thompson was so won over by *The Rock Show* that he saw it three times at his local, the Sawtell RSL, and then invited the ensemble to be the house band at his 70th birthday bash at Sydney venue The Basement. His guests included such luminaries as Peter Garrett, Leo Sayer and promoter Michael Gudinski. The kids in the *Rock Show* band were rubbing shoulders with some of music's A-listers.

'It was a cruisy, fun gig for Jon,' said Smith, 'and that was what we were trying to make. His popularity was rising again, he was getting fitter and fitter, he was jumping around again on stage, screaming.'

But then something happened that changed the creative relationship between Jon and Smith, and many of the others who'd been there from the beginning. When a third show, *Rock Revolution*, was announced, Smith got the sense that it had morphed from its original concept of 'musical memoir' into the type of show they'd been sending up — a tribute show. 'And that's not what it was to me.'

Smith politely bowed out, as did some other players who'd been with Jon since that first gig in Nowra in 2009.

Although he'd created the concept, Smith had never given thought to his legal rights to the show, so he lost control of *The Rock Show*, which, over time, evolved into *Rock Revolution* and *Trilogy of Rock*. Jon starred in both.

Jon had no stomach for confrontation, and Smith liked Jon too much to confront him about losing the show, so they never talked about the unfortunate end to their creative relationship. 'I don't think he wanted anyone to be disappointed and by doing that he disappointed more people,' Smith said. 'He's a really good man but he was not a businessman.'

Smith did, however, remain good friends with Jon. Occasionally he would receive a text: 'Hi mate. I've got this idea about *Paris* . . .'

CHAPTER 19

'I think I'd go mad, really. I'm terrified of retirement.'

n the winter of 2010, in and around Uncorked, *The Rock Show* and Foster Brothers gigs, Jon continued his work in 'straight theatre', taking on a lead role in a production of David Williamson's *The Removalists* for the Perth Theatre Company. 'I haven't done a lot of live theatre without music,' he told Sharon Verghis from *The Australian*, 'but I wanted to challenge myself, to move in a new direction . . . It's a confidence thing, you can't kind of think, "Oh never mind, let's chuck a song in here, they'll all dance to that, it will be all right." You've got to keep on your toes with this play. It's all entrances and exits, split second timing.'

There remained one area of the theatre that Jon knew remained beyond his range: Shakespeare. When he had first met John Bell in 1974, during the days of *Bacchoi*, Jon impressed Bell by revealing that he'd read Euripides' *Bacchae* — and Bell was regularly in his ear about The Bard. 'John Bell's always urging me to do it,' Jon admitted, 'but god, no. You have to know your limits.'

In a broad-ranging conversation with *The Australian*, Jon reflected on *Superstar* — he admitted that he'd had 'zero expectations' when he and Jeremy rolled up to the audition — and his numerous career highs, though he was probably being a tad disingenuous when he said he was 'simply very lucky' to have done so well over the past four decades. As for his breakout role as the Pirate King, especially in the second coming of *Penzance*, Jon explained his success this way: 'We took it back to probably what it was designed to be in the first place — a living cartoon, and it captured this audience that we had no idea we were going to get — boys between the ages of six and twelve. We weren't going to be The Wiggles, but we turned out to be.'

As for *All Together Now*'s Bobby Rivers, Jon had mixed feelings. He resented the scriptwriters' insistence on force-feeding his character 'dumb things to say'. 'I never thought he was [stupid]. I thought he was a bit acid-fried, and quite deaf, and actually, if you're clever writing this, it could be quite good. But no.' (In another interview, Jon told a journalist, 'What you really want to know is the old, "Did you have anything in common with Bobby Rivers?" The short answer is no.')

And what about retirement, now that Jon was 61; was that on his radar? Clearly not. 'I don't know what I'd do. I think I'd go mad, really. I'm terrified of retirement.'

Talk, inevitably, turned to Jon's recent public statements (on his blog) about what he called his 'BA' — 'bottle abuse'. 'I wasn't a born alcoholic,' he said, 'didn't start [drinking] at age thirteen, like in all those classic stories.' A few years back, in order to save himself and his relationship, Jon had decided to confront his demons and gone into therapy, where he learned how boozing and depression were joined at the hip.

'[I was] very gently told I had a disposition towards the Black Dog, not unlike many other high profile performers,' Jon wrote in a blog, 'and I was self-medicating to make myself feel better. Unfortunately alcohol is in itself a depressant and thus begins the long spiral down . . . Thankfully I am pleased to be able to say I'm winning the battle and feeling much, MUCH, better as a result.'

It would still be a few years, however, before Jon committed himself to a rehab facility, and it came about due to circumstances that led many people close to Jon to deeply fear for his wellbeing. Among those was Simon Gallaher. 'I was one of the ones who was very worried and tried to help him along,' Gallaher said. 'I did say to him, "I don't want to wake up in the morning and find that you're dead."'

———

In early June 2013, Jon finally returned to Scandinavia to play the Sweden Rock Festival, backed by a local band named Spearfish. Also playing the four-day-long event were Asia, Europe, The Sweet, and expat Aussie Rick Springfield, who'd grown up just a few suburbs away from Jon.

Jon's return to Sweden had been a long time coming, some 30 years. Johannes Lindström was a Swedish music promoter and a champion of Jon's music; the 1981 album *InRoads* was a particular favourite of Lindström's. (It was a hard-to-find record in Sweden; Lindström resorted to stealing it from a former girlfriend.) For many years Lindström had been trying to convince his partners to bring Jon over for the festival, but the expense was prohibitive. That's when Lindström came up with the idea of connecting Jon with Spearfish. 'As the guys in Spearfish are close friends and fantastic musicians it was an easy choice,' said Lindström. He'd also host Jon, and they'd use Lindström's basement as a rehearsal space.

Jon travelled from Australia with his son Jonathan, who'd play guitar and take on the role of musical director, and with musical all-rounder Joe Kalou, who'd played in *The Rock Show*. Jon's youngest son, Julian, also made the journey.

Jon and Lindström hit it off immediately. Jon reminded Lindström of Phil Lynott from Thin Lizzy, his favourite rock band, and when Jon told him he'd once toured with Lynott, their bond was set in stone.

'We talked a lot about them. Jon was just a natural star when he entered a room or walked onto a stage. We became really good friends.' Jon grew close to Lindström's 80-year-old mother, who also stayed in Lindström's crowded house during the festival.

'My whole family loved him,' said Lindström. 'Everyone loved Jon.'

On the day of the festival, in a post-set interview, Jon, reclining in the sun on a beanbag, talked about everything from his role as an ambassador for Save the Tasmanian Devil, to *All Together Now* ('I had to work very hard to prove I wasn't that stupid') and *Paris*, of course ('which I'd really like to see on the international stage'), all the while insisting that he was now 'semi-retired — I'm 64. *Jesus*.' He had gained some weight but seemed relaxed, at ease.

By late September 2013, Jon was in Brisbane. First stop was the 60th birthday party for Peter Cupples, his Uncorked sparring partner, followed by a photo shoot for his next project, *Spamalot*, with the Harvest Rain Theatre Company, which was to stage a three-week run in October 2014. Simon Gallaher was to co-star with Jon in the production, the first time they'd worked together since another *Pirates* revival in 2001. Frank Woodley was also in the cast, as was Julie Anthony.

Spamalot was a career dream-come-true for lifelong Monty Python devotee Jon. Written by Python Eric Idle and adapted in part from the film *Monty Python and the Holy Grail*, it had been a monster Broadway hit, winning three Tony Awards including Best Musical, and generating a handy $US175 million-plus at the box office.

Jon was cast in the role of King Arthur, while Gallaher was to play his sidekick Patsy (the king's coconut-clomper). Once again Gallaher was playing second banana to Jon, but he'd long ago learned how to cope with that.

Jon had always maintained an impeccable work ethic — as far as he was concerned, you only missed a gig if you were dead — but drinking was now starting to undermine this. When he and The Foster Brothers played a daytime gig at a street fair in Toowoomba, Queensland, Jon was stumbling drunk. 'It was the first time I'd ever seen him blind on stage,' said drummer Greg Henson.

'Wasn't that great, mate?' Jon said to Henson after the show.

'It wasn't,' said Henson.

Jon's mother Sheila, who'd had such a close and complicated relationship with her son, died on 19 December 2013. She was 90. Rather than fading gently into her twilight years, Sheila, even well into her eighties, spent a lot of time on the road, in her Kombi, visiting friends. She sometimes slept in the van. 'Trust me,' Jon said, 'when my mother makes up her mind to do something, well, good luck trying to stop her.' On one occasion during 2008, she helped transport some of Jon's band's gear from Sydney to Brisbane, and back, in her Kombi, with a five-day spell in between while Jon and Jonah's Road played some dates. No problem.

Sheila would be sorely missed, even by those who weren't necessarily her greatest admirers, including her daughter-in-law. 'I cried heaps at her funeral even though I didn't like her much,' Carmen admitted. 'She left a deep impression on people.'

Jon stayed on the wagon between February and August 2014, a period that included a three-week stint at the Northside Clinic, a rehab clinic in the Sydney suburb of Greenwich, in early May. He also attended AA meetings. But his cravings for the bottle never went away.

In August 2014, Jon travelled to Brisbane to begin rehearsals for *Spamalot*. The three-week season was to begin in October at the Concert Hall at the Queensland Performing Arts Centre. Simon Gallaher hadn't seen a lot of Jon since a successful 2001/2002 *Pirates* revival but had been hearing worrying reports about his boozing. In 2005, Jon had been cast as Alfred Doolittle in a Melbourne production of *My Fair Lady*. He'd gotten through rehearsals well enough, but then went AWOL when they moved into the theatre a few days before opening.

'Jon went on a bender and disappeared,' said Gallaher. 'They discovered several empty bottles of vodka in his dressing room. He wasn't cutting it, even though it wasn't really a difficult role, but they had to sack him. That was very publicly humiliating for him.'

Jon was fired and replaced at the eleventh hour by Marty Fields, the son of Oz comedy and vaudeville veterans Maurie Fields and Val Jellay. It was a terrible fall from grace for someone with such a strong work ethic.

When Gallaher heard about Jon's firing, he reached out to a *Pirates* cast member who he knew had been through their own issues with addiction. It was someone Jon respected, someone he would be likely to listen to.

'He needs help,' said Gallaher, who had no experience with this type of situation. 'I'm terribly, terribly worried about him. Can you help him?'

The cast member, however, said no. Gallaher suspected it may have stirred up too many memories for them.

By the time Jon and Gallaher reconnected for *Spamalot*, Jon's physical decline was obvious, although he maintained a typically upbeat frame of mind.

When Gallaher asked how he was, Jon replied: 'Great, mate, great. Everything's terrific.' He hadn't had a drink for three months, he told Gallaher proudly. 'See, I told you I'm not an alcoholic.'

'Mate, it probably means you *are* an alcoholic,' replied Gallaher. 'Alcoholics can't just have that one drink. But it's fantastic; you have to stay on that road.'

During the time of *Spamalot*, Jon had a regular companion, a sort of minder — sometime-Foster Brother Keith 'Stretch' Kerwin. They'd known each other for years and Jon tended to stay sober when he had both company and distractions. It was only when he was alone in a hotel room that the drunken chaos began. Jon was a 'closet' drinker, who typically binged in private.

There was one free weekend during rehearsals, and Jon was accidentally left alone in the apartment in Brisbane — no one thought to check that he had someone with him. Gallaher was halfway to his home in Tamborine Mountain when it dawned on him that Jon was alone and at a loose end. And he knew how dangerous that could be.

'I rang him that night and couldn't raise him. I called the following morning and got him on the phone, but he sounded like no one I'd ever spoken to in my life. He was absolutely comatose.'

'Jon,' Gallaher asked, 'how about you come up to the mountain for the weekend?

'Yeah, that'd be great,' Jon slurred down the line.

Gallaher put down the phone, knowing that something was very wrong with Jon. He called Peter Cupples, who was on his way to a gig on the Gold Coast and agreed to check in with Jon. He said he'd take Jon with him to his show — Gallaher would collect him afterwards and they'd return to Brisbane together.

'He sounds really, really weird,' Gallaher warned him.

At first Cupples couldn't raise Jon, so he continued ringing the doorbell of his apartment until he finally emerged after about half an hour. Cupples quickly called Gallaher.

'He's absolutely maggoted,' Cupples told Gallaher. 'I told him to go back to bed and sleep it off.'

Jon's problems continued during the production. He and Gallaher shared a dressing room, and every time Gallaher stepped out, he'd return to find Jon gargling at the sink.

'I was suddenly seeing a Jon I'd never seen before — a person who was sneaking the booze,' Gallaher recalled. 'I twigged to it and said, "You're fucking drinking every time I leave the room."'

Jon didn't deny the accusation. How could he?

'I tried to keep him on the straight and narrow but I felt like I was trapped in my own dressing room,' said Gallaher, whose heart was breaking. 'If I went outside, he'd take a swig . . . It was tragic.'

The drama continued on stage; Gallaher would, at times, guide Jon, making sure he hit the right spots and made his cues. As Gallaher recalled, 'Jon would become very boisterous and voluble on the stage and I realised, "I'm working with a drunk."'

During one show, while Jon was on stage, Gallaher did what he later admitted was 'a terrible thing'. He went back to their shared dressing room and went through Jon's bag. Inside were two half-empty bottles of vodka.

As Gallaher recalled, 'I thought, "What the fuck do I do?"'

Gallaher would drive Jon and fellow cast member Julie Anthony back to their Brisbane apartments at the end of each day. On one occasion, Jon settled into his usual spot in the back seat of the car and a bottle of vodka fell out of his bag. It was an awful situation.

Remarkably, despite his boozing, Jon still won over the crowds. He'd done his homework; he'd learned his lines and embraced the role of King Arthur. Notices for *Spamalot* were good — at least one critic noted how Jon and Gallaher 'bounced off each other with the same familiar laid-back banter as they did 30 years ago in The *Pirates of Penzance*'.

Yet the problems continued throughout the three-week season. One morning Jon missed a call. When he got to the theatre, he explained that he'd dropped his false teeth, which broke. He'd also broken his phone, clearly during a drunken fall.

According to Gallaher, 'He fronts up with Araldite-d teeth. It was just terrible.'

Yet *Spamalot* was such a success that the producers from the Harvest Rain company wanted to take it on the road. Up to now, Gallaher had done his best to keep Jon's problems concealed — he'd not spoken about it with anyone involved with *Spamalot* — but the idea of touring again with Jon, in his current condition, was too much. He sat down with the producers and spilled his guts.

'You've got a problem,' Gallaher said. 'I cannot go on tour and be Jon English's minder. I'm very worried that we'll end up somewhere and Jon won't be able to go on. What the hell do we all do then? If you do it, you have to employ someone else to be his constant minder and assistant. I ain't doing it.'

The producers had no idea just how bad Jon's situation had become.

'They were wide-eyed and shocked,' said Gallaher. 'It was a terrible situation to be in. Jon had become his own biggest liability. I had to expose it.' Any plans for touring *Spamalot* were quickly shut down.

'We had a wonderful time on stage,' said Gallaher, 'but I could see that he was sort of out of control. I washed my hands of working with him again until he'd sorted himself out.'

The dynamic and highly bankable duo of Jon and Gallaher — the chalk and the cheese, the Pirate King and Frederic, who'd been brothers-in-arms for 30 years — was put on hold indefinitely. Despite all the turmoil, Gallaher still had a lot of love for Jon, and huge respect for his talent. 'He never lost the knack of making it look spontaneous. That's what he brought to the stage, along with his giant stage presence. It was a hell of a skill.'

At the end of *Spamalot*'s run, Jon and Coralea Cameron took a nine-day working holiday as part of *Rock the Boat*, a floating rock'n'roll tour. Jon then returned to Northside Clinic for further treatment.

Jon took solace in June 2015 with a return trip to play the Sweden Rock Festival on the invitation of his friend, the promoter Johannes Lindström.

Initially, Jon was only coming over for a visit, but Lindström persuaded him to once again take the stage with local group Spearfish. Fellow Aussies The Angels were also on the festival bill and they, along with Jon, boarded with Lindström. There were 22 people in Lindström's house: 'Crazy, but something I will always remember.'

After the festival, Jon stayed on for a few days and discussed the idea of making a new record with Lindström. It would be Jon's first collection of original recordings since 2000. 'He was absolutely in good spirits when I drove him to the airport,' recalled Lindström, who'd visited Jon in Australia the previous year. 'He really felt happy about recording again and was eager to come back to Sweden.'

On his return to Oz, Jon sent Lindström two demos, for new songs 'Never Happen to Me' and 'Rhythm of a Heartbeat', as well as some lyrics for possible songs. They discussed plans for Jon to return to Sweden to record an album and agreed on a date: 14 March 2016. It seemed that Jon's muse had finally returned.

CHAPTER 20

'If it goes tits up, I nominate Josephine to kill me, because she's got the balls.'

Jon and Peter Cupples played another of their Uncorked shows at the Flying Saucer Club in Melbourne on 19 February 2016. Two days later Jon visited the Warragul Theatre Company, who were preparing a production of *Paris*. Jon signed posters and spent time with starstruck members of the amateur company.

Then Jon flew to Adelaide for two more Uncorked shows at the Governor Hindmarsh Hotel on 23 and 24 February. Somehow, before the second of the two Adelaide shows, Jon had badly damaged his ribs. Jon gave various accounts of how it had happened, but the actual cause remained unclear; sometimes he put it down to having had a fall, at other times to walking into a door. On the morning of the 24th, Cupples knocked on Jon's hotel room door; they had a radio interview to do that morning. Jon took a long time to answer the door and when he let Cupples in, he showed him his damaged ribs.

'I've had a bit of a fall, Captain,' Jon said.

Cupples left Jon to recover and cancelled the interview. Jon, meanwhile, called his daughter Josie, who could hear him struggling to breathe through the phone line.

'I've hurt myself real bad,' Jon managed to say. 'It hurts when I breathe.'

'You've got to get to a doctor, Dad.'

Jon said that he would do that when he got home, but for the time being he needed a painkiller that he could buy over the counter. Josie gave him the name of a drug she thought would help. She didn't hear from her father for a few days.

Foster Brother Peter Deacon was in town for the show, and he got a call from Cupples. Jon's drinking had again been causing problems with his performances.

'Look,' Cupples said, 'bring the Scotch to the show tonight, but can you hide it behind the sound desk?'

When Jon arrived for the gig, he was clearly in bad shape. Jon had gotten hold of some painkillers, but when Deacon popped backstage, Jon was standing upright, with his arms stretched above his head, leaning against a wall, groaning.

'He was in obvious pain,' said Deacon.

Plans to hide the booze were shelved; Jon clearly needed whatever was at hand to get him through the gig. He groaned every time he moved on stage.

Jon flew back home to Coffs Harbour, but his back hurt whenever he coughed. He was driven by Coralea Cameron to Coffs Harbour hospital, where he was admitted. Jon was diagnosed with four broken ribs, a collapsed lung and — most worryingly of all — an abdominal aortic aneurysm (AAA), which would require surgery. Jon was also diagnosed with high blood pressure and cirrhosis of the liver. His ASA physical status classification was 3; that is, a person with severe systemic disease. (The maximum on the ASA scale is 6, which means brain death.)

Trevor White heard about Jon's hospitalisation on the radio. White immediately texted Jon, wishing him the best.

'I've just hurt my ribs,' Jon replied within minutes. 'Nothing to worry about.'

A message was posted on Jon's Facebook page. 'Jon is currently hospitalised and waiting to undergo a small operation, but is expected to make a full recovery over the coming weeks.'

A new tour, *The Rock Show Oz Edition*, was scheduled to launch in May, beginning in Perth.

Back in Sydney, Josie got a call from her sister, Min. 'Dad's in Coffs Harbour hospital. One of us needs to get up there.' Then Josie got a text from her father. 'I'm in emergency. I'm safe.'

It was decided by the medics treating Jon at Coffs Harbour hospital that Newcastle Private Hospital was better suited to treat Jon's aneurysm; unlike Coffs Harbour, the hospital in Newcastle had a thoracic and a vascular surgeon on staff. He was admitted to Newcastle Private on 29 February, and named Josephine and Jessamine as his next of kin. Realising it was the birthday of Simon Gallaher's *Pirates'* character, Jon called his friend: 'Happy birthday, Frederic,' he said when Gallaher answered. Jon got a call from Alex Plavsic, his old Cabramatta High schoolfriend and Sebastian Hardie bandmate, who had learned he was in the hospital. 'I'm here for a good time, but not a long time,' Jon told him, which, understandably, disturbed Plavsic.

Jon sent many texts to friends from hospital, one being to his friend Johannes Lindström; he still had every intention of returning to Sweden to work on a new album, but suggested pushing back the start date by a few weeks. Lindström already had the band Spearfish in the studio working on backing tracks. When Lindström asked about his operation, Jon told him it was just a 'standard procedure' and that they'd get together again soon. But then Lindström received another, more worrying text from Jon.

'I just want to thank you for everything you've done for me,' Jon wrote. 'You are a real friend. I am scared and a lot of other things but hope to see you soon.'

'I didn't really see that text message as a goodbye until afterwards,' said Lindström.

Jon told the hospital staff that his daughter Josie was on the way and that she should be allowed into his room, regardless of the time. He wanted only family with him. 'We'll be really quiet,' Jon said. 'Just let her in.' Josie joined him there early the next morning and they both burst into tears. Gradually, other members of Jon's family joined them. 'The troops were assembling,' remembered Josie.

'I didn't know how bad it was,' said Carmen. 'Not until we went to the hospital. He opened up a bit but didn't tell us everything. He just said, "I have an aneurysm." But he was a mess.' Over the next few days, Carmen cooked a few of Jon's favourite meals and served them to him while he was bedridden. 'I don't need anything,' he'd tell the staff delivering lunches. 'My wife's bringing something in.'

Jon's doctors had warned him that his condition was very serious but, as Josie recalled, 'Dad was doing his usual deflection-with-humour thing.' In fact, Jon joked about his AAA diagnosis.

'I've just swallowed a battery,' he'd tell everyone. 'I don't know what the fuss is all about.' It became his joke of the moment.

'But in the quietest moments, when it was just the two of us, he was honest about his fear,' said Josie. 'He was really scared, but only one time did he mention being afraid of dying — the actual act of death. He surmised that he'd be unconscious, so he really wouldn't feel it, but what pained him was all of us navigating life without him. That was the most afraid I'd seen him. Ever.'

Jon, always the heavy smoker, had been told that a single cigarette could cause his aneurysm to erupt, so he spent the next few days in bed — apart from an occasional trip out to the garden and a daily scan. He was also told by the doctor that his rib injury meant he would have reduced lung capacity and be unable to sing with the same force again. Jon knew that some big decisions needed to be made, and he spoke bluntly with his kids. 'Listen,' Jon said, 'if it goes tits up, I nominate Josephine to kill me, because she's got the balls.'

'No worries,' Josie replied, 'but can I finish my coffee first?'

It helped that Josie had worked in a mortuary, and that she knew her father better than most. Later that night, in a quiet moment, Josie said to Jon, 'I know you were serious.'

Jon's aneurysm worsened while surgeons waited for his ribs to begin healing, and he grew impatient. 'Let's just fucking do it,' Jon would say to his doctors, but then he would change his mind and ask for a few more weeks. Clearly, he was scared, yet at the same time, as Josie explained, 'in a weird way he was happy. He had no work, he was in this room, his children were there.'

His doctors told him that he'd need a six-month recuperation period, and Jon began talking with Josie and her partner Mark about having a granny flat built in their backyard, where he'd recover. Jon also told his children that he wanted to spend more time with them; he began planning family holidays, something he hadn't done since moving to Coffs Harbour. 'We asked where he'd like to go,' said Josie, 'and more than once, Dad said he'd like to take Mum and us kids back to Aitutaki in the Cook Islands.'

'Jon wanted to get closer again to his family,' said Carmen. 'He wanted quality time again with [them].' Carmen, however, rejected any idea of Jon moving back in with her. 'Personally, I couldn't live with him again.'

'There was a lot of one-on-one with each of us, a lot of honesty,' Josie said of the days prior to his surgery, 'and then there were times when all of us sat around laughing, even on the morning of his operation.'

On 5 March, his doctor noted on his report: 'I think Jon is as good as he is going to get for surgery.' Jon's operation — actually, multiple operations — was scheduled for 9 March, just before 8 am. His last exchange with his family was about the surgical cap and booties he had to wear to surgery. Typically, he made a gag.

'Wherever am I going to find the shoes to match?' Jon laughed.

Then he was wheeled into surgery, with his children, his grandson Jzawo and Carmen walking all the way with him. Everyone hugged him, and Josie said, 'Dad, it's OK, I'm going to be on the other side.'

Jon's eyes grew wide; he was horrified. 'Don't say that! It sounds like I'm about to die.'

Josie was mortified, and made it clear that she meant the other side of the operating theatre doors, where she'd be waiting for him. 'Fuck no,' she said. 'I mean *these* doors, these actual doors.'

Then the theatre doors closed.

The first order of business in the operating room was to repair Jon's collapsed lung; when this was successfully done, Jon was placed on his back so the surgeon could operate on his aneurysm. Access was difficult due to Jon's liver cirrhosis and, during the repair, Jon bled extensively. He was given blood transfusions and inotropic drugs, and cell savers were used to collect and return the blood he was losing, but they were not working as the medical team hoped. An ICU specialist was brought into the theatre, also a cardiologist, but Jon's whole body was going into shock. He'd spent nine hours in surgery. The doctors believed they had done everything they could for him.

Jon's sons, as well as Min and Carmen, had left the hospital to have a meal and freshen up, so Josie and Jzawo were the only family members in the post-op area. Josie noticed that there was a room that was separate to the rest of the post-op space. A box of tissues had been placed discreetly on a table.

'That's the bad-news room,' she said to Jzawo. 'We don't want to go in there.'

A couple of minutes later, a woman emerged from the theatre.

'Josephine,' she said, 'can I talk to you in this room?' She led her directly to the bad-news room.

'Oh fuck me,' Josie whispered under her breath.

'He's still in surgery, we almost lost him,' Josie was told. 'I'm not sure if he can come out. You need to call your mum and your siblings. We're trying to stabilise him and if he can come out of theatre, you're the first person he'll see.'

Josie quickly called the others and told them they needed to get back to the hospital quickly. 'I don't think Dad's going to make it.' As she spoke, a woman walked up to her with a box of tissues; Josie had no idea that she'd been crying.

Jon was wheeled into post-op at around 5.30. At first, Josie didn't recognise him.

'He'd retained a lot of fluid, but I knew it was him. I knew he hated being alone, so I wasn't going to leave him.'

Just before 8 pm, while still in post-op, Jon's blood pressure dropped to a dangerously low level and he was placed on a ventilator. His abdomen was swollen, possibly from an internal haemorrhage. Blood was coming from the drains that were attached to his lungs and chest. He'd suffered massive blood loss; his body was shutting down. His doctors decided that further surgery would not control the bleeding.

By 9 pm, it was clear that Jon wasn't going to pull through. By 10.30, as Josie recalled, 'We knew it was time.' But then she had a panic attack. 'I can't live without my Dad, I'm not doing this. It's not happening,' she cried. However, Jon's family knew that he had no intention of being a burden on them; even if, by some miracle, the staff could prolong his life, it wouldn't be the type of life he would have wanted to live. Everyone knew that it was time for him to go, and they each shared a private moment with Jon.

'It was terrible, absolutely terrible,' said Carmen. 'The registrar came in and said they couldn't do any more. He had internal bleeding. Jon had said to us that he didn't want to end up a vegetable. Josephine asked all of us and we knew it was hopeless. Most of us left the room while they unplugged everything, came back into the room and watched him die.'

Jon English died from multiple organ failure and shock experienced during the surgery to repair his abdominal aortic aneurysm. His life ended on 9 March 2016, just a few minutes before midnight, which was fitting, in a way — 'Minutes to Midnight' was the title of a song, and an album, he'd once recorded. He was seventeen days short of his 67th birthday.

All of his family were deeply in shock. Min and Josie didn't leave each other's side throughout the night and well into the morning. As Josie admitted, 'we held hands and wailed for hours'.

To try to escape the madness, back at their hotel the next morning they turned on the TV, only to be greeted by news reports of their father's death. It was everywhere, unavoidable.

'Min and I looked at each other and knew it was real. It had actually happened. I was on the carpet, wailing. Just seeing it on the TV . . . For a minute, I forgot that my dad was famous and wondered, "Why is he on the TV?"'

Then she walked out into the hotel hallway and leaned against the wall, sobbing hysterically. 'I thought I was going to die.'

———————

The day after Jon's death, the obituaries began rolling out. *The Sydney Morning Herald* remembered Jon as 'the man with the magnetic eyes' and 'a man of many talents'. Jon would have appreciated the newspaper's main headline, in which he was simply described as 'singer songwriter Jon English'. *The Guardian* eulogised him as 'an English-born Australian rock legend'. Sir Tim Rice, *Superstar* co-creator, tweeted about the loss of 'Jon English, superb Aussie Judas'.

Jon's many peers and fans were in shock when the news broke of his death.

Jon's long-time drummer and friend Greg Henson got the call from Josie. 'Dad's dead,' she told him. He called the other Foster Brothers with the terrible news. Even today, Henson still has trouble believing that Jon is gone. 'I'm kind of waiting for him to call me and tell me there are some gigs coming up. I'm still waiting for the call.'

Peter Deacon summed it up best when he said, 'Jon was one of those guys who would never die — you wouldn't even think about it. Never. He was going to live forever.'

Trevor White was having breakfast with his son when he heard about Jon. He struggled to digest the news; White was, by his own description, 'stunned'. He turned to his son and said, simply, 'My friend died.'

'It hit me so much harder than I could have imagined,' White admitted. 'He was such a huge part of my life.'

Simon Gallaher got the call that he'd feared for so long — that Jon was actually dead. 'Jon's death was something I always feared, because of his demise, personal demise, towards the latter time.'

David Mackay, Jon's collaborator on *Paris*, who'd been to hell and back with Jon during the creation of the rock opera, was on a ferry with his wife, travelling from Seattle to Vashon Island, when he got a text telling him that Jon had died. 'My wife and I were in a state of disbelief,' he said. 'I was devastated. I had been so close to the family for so long.'

Mario Millo saw a Facebook post about Jon's death but refused to believe it. 'That's ridiculous,' he thought. 'Someone's just posted some bullshit. That can't be right.' His wife made a call and learned that Jon had indeed died. Like everyone else who heard the tragic news, Millo was in shock: 'I couldn't believe it.' Millo travelled into the city where he met Alex Plavsic, his bandmate from Sebastian Hardie days, who was working with the Sydney Theatre Company.

'How could this happen with Jon?' Millo said in despair. 'It was devastating. He was bulletproof, invincible.'

In Sweden, Johannes Lindström was in his car when he got a call from Australia informing him of Jon's death. He was distraught, and pulled over to the side of the road. 'It was devastating. It was not supposed to happen. For me personally it was a tough blow. When you get older, it's harder and harder to get new friends. Jon was a friend.'

A few days later, Julian English called Lindström and told him that Jon had always spoken highly of him. 'Julian was happy that his dad had gotten a new friend late in life. I still cherish that phone call a lot.'

Lindström now found himself with a dilemma: should he try to finish the recordings he and Jon had discussed, as a tribute to his friend? Spearfish had more than a dozen tracks ready for vocals. Over time, Lindström, with the help of such people as Jon's nephew Jay Collie, Dave Gleeson from The Screaming Jets and Rick Brewster from The Angels, completed the two songs that Jon had sent to Sweden as demos. A limited-edition vinyl-only album entitled *The English Project* was released in 2018, featuring 'Rhythm of a Heartbeat' and 'Never Happen to Me', along with, among other writers' songs, covers of Jon's 'Six Ribbons' and 'The Shining'. Unfortunately, the record was not deemed of a suitable quality for release in Australia, a decision that Lindström didn't agree with.

No one heard his last two songs in Australia, he said. 'That makes me sad.'

When Marina Prior learned of Jon's death, she burst into tears. His performance in *Superstar* had been a huge inspiration, her first big moment in the theatre. She also flashed back to her first day of rehearsal for *Pirates*, when Jon had spotted her, smiled and greeted her with a friendly, 'Hello, luv' — and her nerves had faded away.

'This was a man who was such a really big part of my formative years in the industry. So much of me embarking on my own journey is entangled with my memories of Jon,' said Prior. 'I felt so devastated, especially knowing how much he loved his kids. It was just awful. I really thought he'd be kicking on forever; I thought he was unkillable.

'I always think of him as the Pirate King. Purple tights. The headband. *The swagger.*'

Prior to the public memorial at Sydney's Capitol Theatre, Jon's family held a service which, although intended strictly as a private gathering, was attended by more than 120 people from the many areas of Jon's life: there were footballers, rock'n'rollers, theatre folk, the lot. In his coffin, Jon English was dressed in what his family called his 'day-off attire' — a pair of trackie dacks and his Parramatta Eels jersey. Jon was now truly, finally, at rest.

CODA

In the wake of the public memorial for Jon at the Capitol Theatre on 4 April 2016, his son, Jonathan, began thinking about staging *Paris* as a tribute to his father. It was Jon's passion project, his greatest achievement and his biggest disappointment, so it seemed fitting that the rock opera should be staged in Jon's honour.

Mark Featherby, the director of Music Theatre Melbourne, had previously staged *Paris* — using his own money — at the National Theatre in Melbourne in 2004. When Jonathan reached out to him, he quickly agreed to help stage it again.

In fact Jon, just before he died, had discussed staging *Paris* with Featherby, one of dozens of conversations they'd had about the show. 'We had meetings with him around midnight after his pub gigs; we had meetings with him at 7.30 am for breakfast,' Featherby told a reporter. 'As for the script, he welcomed suggestions, tweaks and radical production ideas more readily than any writer I have ever worked with.'

Now Featherby had a chance to pay his respects to Jon. A four-night run of *Paris* was set in place at the Melbourne Recital Centre for July 2017.

An impressive cast was assembled: John Waters, who'd sung on the original album, was cast as Ulysses, while Ben Mingay, who'd starred in Australian productions of *An Officer and a Gentleman* and *The Phantom of the Opera*, was cast as Achilles. Matthew Manahan would play Paris and Madeleine Featherby was Helen. *The Rock Show*'s Isaac Hayward and Stuart Smith were among the team that helped return *Paris* to the stage. The Whitlams' Tim Freedman also performed.

Smith got a call from Jonathan. He had a plan for *Paris*: to 'turn it back into the CD'. 'It had gone through so many changes,' Jonathan said. Smith knew right away that this was a smart move: 'We wanted to turn it back into what we loved, and what the audience did, too.'

An intense few months ensued, as Smith, Jonathan and Isaac Hayward worked on *Paris* and, in Smith's words, 'turned it back into what it was'. 'We chucked out heaps,' said Jonathan. 'We went back to the record, to the demos.'

It was an emotional experience for Smith, and having Jonathan — 'Jonno' — on board was special. 'We loved working on *Paris*,' Smith said. 'Jon had become a sort of theatrical dad to me, and he was Jonno's dad. And Jonno was there to tie it all together. I think, musically speaking, it was the best structure of the show. I think it was more passion project or a letting-go for fans. And it was for people who loved *Paris*.'

The four shows were well attended, and each night would close with a heartfelt tribute to Jon. Playing guitar, Jonathan led the band into 'Love Has Power', the standout song from *Paris*, an emphatic statement from Jon about the redeeming nature of love. Jon's image appeared on a huge screen behind the stage, singing the opening verse of the song — you could almost see the hair rise on the back of the neck of every single person in the Recital Centre. John Waters then entered from stage right, singing 'Love Has Power,' one of the songs he'd sung so emphatically at Jon's public memorial, but now performed in the shadow of Jon's imposing visage. Soon Waters was joined by the rest of the cast and the choir. As Jonathan eased himself into an aching, soulful guitar solo, and the voices on stage blended and soared in unison, 'Love Has Power' reached for the heavens. The emotional impact was enormous, the applause deafening. It was a perfect moment, the best possible final farewell for Jon English.

'People were standing around crying,' said Smith. 'We all cried. I was devastated when he was gone, but lucky enough to have had that moment to get to know him.'

'It was done out of passion,' said Jonathan, who had no bigger goal than simply having *Paris* staged well in memory of his late father. 'At some point,' he said, 'we just had to let it be.'

BIBLIOGRAPHY

Adams, Cameron. 'Jon English dead: Molly Meldrum pays tribute to legendary entertainer'. *News.com.au*, 10 March 2016.

Anon. 'Superstar: What the cast thinks'. *Tharunka*, 8 August 1972.

— 'Jesus Christ Superstar: A survey by our staff survey writer'. *Go-Set*, 18 March 1972.

— 'Ned Kelly musical'. *Canberra Times*, 30 May 1974.

— 'Paddington's hall of rock'. *Sydney Morning Herald*, 13 January 1975.

— 'The story of *Against the Wind*'. *Canberra Times*, 29 October 1978.

— 'The other side of Jon English,' *Australian Women's Weekly*, 19 December 1979.

— 'Jon's Trojan Horse comes good'. *Age*, 26 January 2004.

Apter, Jeff. *Johnny O'Keefe. Rocker. Legend. Wild One*. Sydney: Hachette, 2013.

Barnes, Jim & Stephen Scanes. *The Book: Top 40 research 1956–2010*. Gorokan, NSW: Scanes Music Research, 2010.

Chlopicki, Kirstie. 'Students pay special tribute'. *Fairfield City Champion*, 21 March 2016.

Connolly, Paul. 'Jon English: I am what I am'. *Sun-Herald*, 5 February 2012.

Dionysius, Bobbi-Lea. 'Monty Python's *Spamalot*'. *AussieTheatre.com*, 5 October 2014.

Hoffmann, W.L. 'An unforgettable premiere'. *Canberra Times*, 17 March 1972.

— 'Pirates of Penzance as a modern musical'. *Canberra Times*, 30 December 1983.

— 'Rollicking Pirates'. *Canberra Times*, 11 January 1984.

Kemp, Kevon. '*Superstar* a stage triumph'. *National Times*, 8–13 May 1972.

Kent, David (ed). *Australian Chart Book 1970–1992*. Sydney: Australian Chart Book, 1993.

Kruger, Debbie. '*Rasputin* review'. *Variety*, 2 September 1987.

Jon English Fansite of Norway, '*Buskers and Angels* (2000–)', n.d., www.angelfire.com/rock3/jonenglish/buskers.html

Lunden, Jeff. 'Rice, Lloyd Webber double down on Broadway'. *NPR.org*, 5 April 2012.

McFarlane, Ian. *The Encyclopedia of Australian Rock and Pop*. Sydney: Allen & Unwin, 1999.

McNicoll, David D. 'Judas scene-stealer of the Festival Superstar Show'. *Sydney Morning Herald*, 19 March 1972.

— (Untitled column). *Bulletin*, 6 March 1984.

Meldrum, Ian. 'Meldrum'. *Go-Set*, 14 April 1973.

Mengel, Noel. 'Jon English rockin' in new show'. *Courier-Mail*, 17 August 2011.

Miller, Harry M. *Confessions of a Not-So-Secret Agent*. Sydney: Hachette, 2009.

Neutze, Ben. 'Jon English in *Pirates of Penzance*: The purest expression of Australia's theatrical spirit'. *Daily Review*, 10 March 2016.

Nugent, Darel. '*Superstar*'s last Sydney show . . . Wow!' *Go-Set*, 31 March 1973.

Nuttall, Lyn. 'Where did they get that song? Jon English: Hollywood Seven'. *Pop Archives*, n.d., poparchives.com.au/feature.php?id=700.

Oxford, Gillian. '*Superstar* an artistic and spectacular production'. *Canberra Times*, 30 May 1972.

Rice, Tim. *Oh, What a Circus: The autobiography, 1944–1978*. London: Hodder & Stoughton, 1999.

Scott, Phil. 'Dazzling new production of *Superstar*'. *Sydney Morning Herald*, 30 May 1976.

Scott-Norman, Fiona. 'Musical look at fame and fortune a little too simple'. *Age*, 7 November 2000.

Thompson, Grant. 'Ned Kelly — now he's to be a musical'; *Sydney Morning Herald*, 12 May 1974

Tongue, Cassie. '*Paris: A Rock Odyssey* to hit Melbourne stages'. *AussieTheatre.com*, 27 February 2017.

Verghis, Sharon. 'Moving on — Jon English refuses to rest on his old rocker laurels'. *Weekend Australian*, 28 August 2010.

Vine, David. 'Sitcom promos almost as torrid as our bowlers'. *Canberra Times*, 11 February 1991.

Wahlquist, Gil. 'Judas warm and genuine'. *Sydney Morning Herald*, 29 April 1973.

Walford, Leslie. 'Full-length mink at the hot-dog stand'; *Sydney Morning Herald*, 8 April 1973

— 'After *Superstar* — The super party'. *Sydney Morning Herald*, 13 June 1976.

Wallace, Mark. 'A superstar revival'. *Canberra Times*, 27 July 1992.

Wathen, Jo. 'Jon English: The man with the magnetic eyes'. *Sydney Morning Herald*, 23 August 1987.

Audio, video and TV

After Dark, 9 May 1982, www.youtube.com/watch?v=2N8pkaPEX8g

The Graham Kennedy Show, March 1973, www.youtube.com/watch?v=jkwsL3suc2s

KryztoffTV, 'Jon English talks to Kryztoff about *The Rock Show*', 2 January 2012, www.youtube.com/watch?v=xlBD4z9OKCM

Midday with Ray Martin, 25 September 1985

Midday with Ray Martin, 24 August 1989, www.youtube.com/ watch?v=DT4xNFTH9u0

The Mike Walsh Show, 12 October 1983, www.youtube.com/watch? v=Duz9qKtdhgc

National Film and Sound Archive, Jon English interviewed by Debbie Kruger, 23 November 2009, www.nfsa.gov.au

Rock and Roll Ballroom of the Air, Paddington Town Hall, c. 1975, www.youtube.com/watch?v=j47MlKVVbx8

Shooters: Life Through the Lens, 'Jon English interview and final performance', Governor Hindmarsh Hotel, March 2016, www.youtube.com/watch?v=k_o28ajT5DY

Studio 10, February 2016, www.youtube.com/watch?v=qy1SNgaBLn0

Sweden Rock Festival, 'Jon English interview: Sweden Rock Festival 2013', 8 June 2013, www.youtube.com/watch?v=xBerK_wGpJ4

This is Your Life, 1998, www.youtube.com/watch?v=Cvq5HUeQD00

Today, 19 August 1987, www.youtube.com/watch?v=ZP-8VVjQMGo

Where Are They Now?, '*Jesus Christ Superstar*: Australian cast reunion', 1997, www.youtube.com/watch?v=l4EGO1TxiYk

The World Tonight, 20 August 1990, www.youtube.com/watch? v=cHdB8vqP1M0

Websites

The Australian Live Performance Database, 'Jon English', www.ausstage. edu.au/pages/contributor/2741

Jon English, blogs, jonenglish.com.au (no longer available; provided to the author by Coralea Cameron)

Medical records

Coffs Harbour Health Campus

Newcastle Private Hospital

New South Wales Registry of Births, Deaths & Marriages

JON ENGLISH DISCOGRAPHY

Chart placings are Australian unless otherwise indicated.

Studio albums

Wine Dark Sea (March 1973)
Summer Song / Sweet Lady Mary / Wine Dark Sea / Horsehair and Plastic / Close Every Door / Monopoly / Handbags and Gladrags / Prelude / Tomorrow / Brand New Day / Share the End

Chart peak: #53; charted 3 weeks
Charting singles: Handbags and Gladrags #50

It's All a Game (November 1974)
Turn the Page / Just the Way I Am / He Could Have Been a Dancer / Love Goes on / By Firelight / Space Shanty / Snakeyes / Chained to the Middle / Superstar (You Promised Me) / Hail all Hail to the Revolution (12 Bore)

Chart peak: #4; charted 16 weeks
Charting singles: Turn the Page #20; #2 in Sydney

Hollywood Seven (August 1976)
Hollywood Seven / Walk Across the World / Laughing at the Guru / Money Is / I'm a Survivor / Play with Fire / If You Think You're Groovy / Sandcastles / Lovin' Arms / The Miracle

Chart peak #20; charted 15 weeks
Charting singles: Hollywood Seven #13 / Lovin' Arms #55 / I'm a Survivor #87

Minutes to Midnight (March 1977)
Lay it All Down / Hey Moonshine / Don't Let Me Be Misunderstood / Whole Lot More / A Long Way to Go / Behind Blue Eyes / Everytime I Sing a Love Song / Break Another Dawn / Lady L / Midnight Suite: Part 1 Crosswork; Part II Minutes to Midnight; Part III Comfortable

Chart peak #33; charted 16 weeks
Charting singles: Lay it All Down #46

Against the Wind (with Mario Millo) (1978)
Against the Wind (theme) / Seeds of Fire (Sentencing and Transportation) / Unfinished Theme (Rum for Dignity) / Six Ribbons (The Courtship) / Mary's Theme / The March of the Kings of Laois / Waltz Theme (The Women Are Chosen) / Six Ribbons / Dinny and Ngilgi / Main Theme Major (The Wedding) / Death or Liberty (The Castle Hill Rebellion and Consequences)

Chart peak #10 / #1 Norway / #4 New Zealand / #4 Sweden; charted 18 weeks (Australia)
Charting singles: Six Ribbons #5; #3 in New Zealand

Words Are Not Enough (August 1978)
Give It a Try / Words Are Not Enough / Free Ride / Nights in Paradise / Love is Alive / Sail On / A Love Like Yours / Fantastic (Ain't What It Used To Be) / Hot and Dirty in the City / Same Old Feeling Again

Chart peak #28; charted 13 weeks
Charting singles: Words Are Not Enough #6 / Nights in Paradise #44

Calm Before the Storm (April 1980)
Survivor / Save Me / Carmilla / Down in Frisco / Hot Town / Little By Little / Feel Like Dancing / Sad News / Split / Hope It Turns Out Right

Chart peak #17; charted 17 weeks
Charting singles: Hot Town #11 / Carmilla #27

InRoads (October 1981)

Been in Love Before / Blame it on the Night / Straight from the Heart / You Might Need Somebody / The Shining / Touch and Go / Stranger in a Strange Land / Move Better in the Night / Josephine (Too Many Secrets) / Last Night in Hollywood

Chart peak #58; charted 7 weeks
Charting singles: Straight from the Heart #72 / Josephine (Too Many Secrets) #9 (Norway)

Jokers and Queens (with Marcia Hines) (July 1982)

Jokers and Queens / Ain't Gonna Run / I Heard it Through the Grapevine / This Time / You Were on My Mind / You've Lost that Lovin' Feeling

Chart peak #36; charted 9 weeks
Charting singles: Jokers and Queens #62

Some People (September 1983)

Straight Ahead / Some People (Have All the Fun) / Hell or High Water / Coming Up / Waterloo / Oh Paris / Tempted / I'm Yours / She Was Real / Given Time

Chart peak #35; charted 9 weeks
Charting singles: Some People (Have All the Fun) #50

Dark Horses (May 1987)

Overture / Dark Horses / Treat it Like a Lady / Winds of Limbo / I Can Do Better Than That / The Best in Me / Another Brand New Day / Baby Got Style / Mr Nice Guy / Emotion / Glass Houses

Chart peak #84; charted 7 weeks

Busking (1989)

Always the Busker / Love Hangs by a Thread / Lonely Target / Only Love Can Show the Way / Younger Days / High Windows / Already Gone / Money Money / Why Don't We Spend the Night / We'll Be There

Paris (1990)

Overture / Prelude / A Head Without a Heart / Straight Ahead / Perfect Stranger / A Long Time Coming / Business / The Leader / Any Fool Could See / Thief in the Night / Trust in Your Heart / Come Hell or High Water / No Turning Back / For Better or Worse / Ten Years On / What Price a Friend / Love Has Power / The Beggar / Ulysses Prayer / A Horse With No Rider / Inside Outside / The Balance Shifts / Oh Paris / Finale

Buskers and Angels (1999)

Always the Busker / Out On My Corner / Fancy This / The View Up There / 20-20 Hindsight / Nothing to Hide / One Thing Leads to Another / Nature of the Beast / Life Is Like a Wheel / Splitting Image / Dear Lee / Money Tree / Potential Angels / Try to Be a Hero / What's the View Like Up There? / Roll Daddy Roll / The Guy for Me / Doing Okay / Love is the One Thing / Palm of Our Hands / Fallen Angel / When I Was Younger / Street Beat

Compilations

English History (August 1979)

Get Your Love Right / Wine Dark Sea / Words Are Not Enough / Turn the Page / Minutes to Midnight / Hollywood Seven / Same Old Feeling Again / Lovin' Arms / I'm a Survivor / Play with Fire / Superstar / Brand New Day/ Handbags and Gladrags / Laughing at the Guru / Everytime I Sing a Love Song / Nights in Paradise / Lay it All Down / Sandcastles / Behind Blue Eyes / Six Ribbons

Chart peak #4 / #1 Norway / #3 New Zealand / #17 Sweden; charted 31 weeks (Australia)
Charting (new) singles: Get Your Love Right #27; #3 in New Zealand

Modern English (December 1983)

Hot Town / Beating the Boards / Hold Back the Night / Josephine (Too Many Secrets) / Words Are Not Enough / Get Your Love Right / Jokers and Queens / You've Lost that Lovin' Feeling / Turn the Page / Hollywood Seven / Carmilla / The Shining / Straight From the Heart / I Can't Turn You Loose / Beautiful Loser / Six Ribbons

Chart peak #27

The Best of Jon English (May 1993)

All Together Now / You Might Need Somebody / Some People (Have All the Fun) / Get Your Love Right / Hot Town / Handbags and Gladrags /Always the Busker / Same Old Feeling Again / Carmilla / Lay it All Down / Superstar / She Was Real / Turn the Page / Josephine (Too Many Secrets) / Lovin' Arms / Minutes to Midnight / Words Are Not Enough / Hollywood Seven / Six Ribbons

Chart peak #68

English History II (2001)

Beating the Boards / Overture / Survivor / Turn the Page / All Together Now / Some People (Have All the Fun) / Carmilla / The Shining / Waterloo / Touch & Go / Always the Busker / One Thing Leads to Another / Dark Horses / No Turning Back / Easy Street / Josephine (Too Many Secrets) / She Was Real / Move Better in the Night / Life is Like a Wheel / Glass Houses

Six Ribbons: The Ultimate Collection (May 2011)

Six Ribbons / Turn the Page / Get Your Love Right / All Together Now / Some People (Have All the Fun) / Hot Town / Sandcastles / Handbags and Gladrags / Carmilla / Lovin' Arms / You Might Need Somebody / Survivor / Touch & Go / She Was Real / Another Brand New Day / Wine Dark Sea / Oh Paris / Love Has Power / Beating the

Boards (Live) / Words Are Not Enough / Hold Back the Night / Dark Horses / Minutes to Midnight / Same Old Feeling Again / Josephine (Too Many Secrets) / Jokers and Queens / Hollywood Seven / Always the Busker / Lay it All Down / Share the End / Beautiful Loser (live) / Move Better in the Night / Behind Blue Eyes / Everytime I Sing a Love Song / Glass Houses

Chart peak #23 (March 2016)

Live albums

Beating the Boards (April 1982)
Beating the Boards / I'm a Survivor / Turn the Page / Been in Love Before / Lay it All Down / The Shining / Josephine (Too Many Secrets) / Lovin' Arms / You Might Need Somebody / Get Your Love Right / Words Are Not Enough / Beautiful Loser / Against the Wind/ Six Ribbons / Hot Town / Hollywood Seven / Move Better in the Night / I Can't Turn You Loose / Everytime I Sing a Love Song
Chart peak #24 (Australia) / #33 (New Zealand)

The Rock Show (July 2012)
Hey Hey, My My/The Times They Are a-Changin' / Let There Be Rock / My Generation / Two World Wars/Gloria / San Francisco (Be Sure to Wear Some Flowers in Your Hair)/The Sound of Silence/ California Dreaming / Mercedes Benz/Me and Bobby McGee / Purple Haze/Somebody to Love/White Room / A Whiter Shade of Pale / Handbags and Gladrags / Space Oddity/Rocket Man / Beatles medley / Won't Get Fooled Again/Kashmir / Stairway to Heaven / Guitar riff medley / Lola / See Me, Feel Me/Pinball Wizard / You Took the Words Right Out of My Mouth / Wish You Were Here/Shine On You Crazy Diamond / Rolling Stones medley / Six Ribbons/Turn the Page/Hollywood Seven / Bohemian Rhapsody / With a Little Help From My Friends/Superstar

Tribute album

Spearfish: The English Project (2018)
Never Happen to Me* / Wheels Keep on Turning / Crossing Lines /
Six Ribbons / Assholes and Opinions / Try to Be a Hero / Rhythm of
a Heartbeat* / Renegade / The Shining / Gone (Song for Jon) /
Enola Gay
* Vocals by Jon English

Soundtracks and cast albums
Jon also appeared on the following recordings:

Jesus Christ Superstar (Original Australian Cast Recording) (1972):
chart peak #13
Ned Kelly: A Rock Opera — Studio Cast Recording (1974)
Street Hero (1984)
The Pirates of Penzance (1990)

Sources: Chart information is taken from David Kent, *Australian Chart Book 1970–1992*, Sydney: Australian Chart Book, 1993; and Wikipedia, 'Jon English discography', https://en.wikipedia.org/wiki/Jon_English_discography.

JON ENGLISH THEATRICAL ROLES

Jesus Christ Superstar (1972–73, 1973–74, 1975, 1978)

The Bacchoi (1974)

Phases (1974)

The Pirates of Penzance (1984–86, 1994–95, 2002, 2003)

Rasputin: The Musical Revolution (1987)

Big River: The Adventures of Huckleberry Finn (1989)

The Hunting of the Snark (1990)

The Mikado (1995–96)

H.M.S. Pinafore (1997)

Noises Off (1998)

A Funny Thing Happened on the Way to the Forum (1998–99)

Buskers and Angels (2000, 2009)

Don't Dress for Dinner (2000)

Are You Being Served? (2001)

Paris (2003, 2008)

Dad's Army (2004)

Blood Brothers (2007–08)

The Removalists (2010)

Hairspray (2013)

Spamalot (2014)

Source: The Australian Live Performance Database,
www.ausstage.edu.au

SELECTED LYRICS BY JON ENGLISH

He Could Have Been a Dancer^

(Jonathan James English)

I'm not saying that we did wrong
Or that we were scared and waited too long
I'm just trying to make amends
God knows there'll be other chances someday
It'll happen again
The times weren't right, girl, you must agree
And your dad and your mama would have crucified me
Baby, please stop your crying
I feel bad, too, I ain't lying
Do you think I can sleep at night
With a crime I can't put right?
Do you think in my mind I haven't seen
Some of the things he might have been?

He could have been a dancer
A scholar or a priest
A tinker, a tailor, a candlestick maker
He could have been a man of peace
Just a man

Now, I'm not pretending I don't feel bad
I could have been a proud dad
But these things happen all the time
And oh girl don't let it get at your mind
Maybe later when I've got some work
A little money in the bank
We'll get married in a church
And baby, please stop your crying
I feel bad, too, I ain't lying
Do you think I can sleep at night
With a crime I can't put right?
Do you think in my mind I haven't seen
Some of the things he might have been?

Well, he could have been a dancer
A scholar or a priest
A tinker, a tailor, a candlestick maker
He could have been a man of peace
A man, oh lord
He could have been a dancer
A scholar or a priest
A tinker, a tailor, a candlestick maker
He could have been a man of peace
Just a man, just a man

Six Ribbons^
(Jonathan James English)

If I were a minstrel, I'd sing you six love songs
To tell the whole world of the love that we share
If I were a merchant, I'd bring you six diamonds
With six blood-red roses for my love to wear
But I am a simple man, a poor common farmer
So take my six ribbons to tie back your hair

Yellow and brown, blue as the sky
Red as my blood, green as your eyes

If I were a nobleman, I'd bring you six carriages
With six snow-white horses to take you anywhere
If I were the emperor (Yellow and brown)
I'd build you six palaces (Blue as the sky)
With six hundred servants (Red as my blood)
For comforting fare (Green as your eyes)
But I am a simple man, a poor common farmer
So take my six ribbons, to tie back your hair

If I were a minstrel, I'd sing you six love songs
To tell the whole world of the love that we share
So be not afraid my love, you're never alone, love
While you wear my ribbons, tying back your hair
Once I was a simple man, a poor common farmer
I gave you six ribbons, to tie back your hair

Tooralee, tooralie, all I can share
Is only six ribbons to tie back your hair
Tooralee, tooralie, all I can share
I gave you six ribbons to tie back your hair

Glass Houses^
(Jonathan James English)

Born in forty-nine
Part of a long, long line of roses and wine
And the war clouds had fled and we buried our dead
And future was mine, or so they said

And late in sixty-five
Underneath southern skies, hearin' words from the wise,

Some guy was teaching the past, through a rose-coloured glass
Said the Phoenix will rise from the ashes at last

And build glass houses with ivory towers
On streets paved with gold, where we'll never grow old
And oh, glass houses and ivory towers
Are not what they seem, they're fragile as dreams

And oh, seventy-one
They were handin' out boots and guns to some mother's son
And in seventy-eight, they said sorry, but we made a mistake
Time for some fun, ooh ain't life great

In tall glass houses with ivory towers
The beaches are gold and we'll never grow old
And oh, glass houses, ivory towers
They're fragile as dreams, and never what they seem

You know, nowadays, you go to town
There's glass all around
And they're still building towers
But they're buried deep in the ground
My legacy, starin' at me

Oh, glass houses, ivory towers
They flash like the sun, for everyone
We live in glass houses with ivory towers
Protecting our gold and we're all growin' old

And we're all growin' old

Oh Paris⁺
(Jonathan James English/John Coker)

He learned early if you want somebody, go all the way
So when he met her and he fell in love, he just stole her away
Oh Paris

He crept home in the dead of night and the people say
(You should have known better)
If you love her, man, put up a fight, don't run away
(He should have known better)
Oh Paris

Oh Paris, open your eyes, I ain't tellin' you lies
I said it's just a disguise

And look out Paris
You should have known better
Oh Paris, you should have known better
Oh Paris, you should have known better

Well her people wanted Helen back, with Paris' head in a sack
(They should have known better)
They were lean and sleek and mean and Greek and they want her back
(They should have known better)
Oh Paris

Oh Paris, open your eyes, I ain't tellin' you lies
I said it's just a disguise

And look out Paris
You should have known better
Oh Paris, you should have known better
Oh Paris, you should have known better

They didn't mess around, they want to burn it down
They wanna tear up the town, raze the joint to the ground
They had a thousand longboats and over ten thousand men
And they were all stormin' the walls, again and again and again
Guess they should have known better
Oh Paris, they should have known better
Oh Paris, they should have known better

Troy's too high, too strong to die, to useless force
(They should have known better)
When your spears and swords and your arrows fail, use a wooden horse
(They should have played fairer)
Oh Paris

Oh Paris, open your eyes (for god's sake)
I ain't tellin' you lies (for god's sake), I said it's just a disguise
Look out Paris, you should have known better
Oh Paris, open your eyes (for god's sake)
I ain't tellin' you lies (for god's sake), it's just a disguise
Look out Paris, you should have known better
Oh Paris, you should have known better

Love Has Power[+]
(Jonathan James English/John Dallimore/David Mackay)

There's no surrender
And there's no real goodbyes
While you still remember
The fire in her eyes
Sometimes you suffer
Ah, but you learn to take the falls
And you find out that it's better to love and lose

Than to never love at all

And remember, through the passion and anger
All the heartache and pain

Love has power

Love has power
It can lift you up

Or it can drag you down

No one said life was easy
No one could really explain
Why all the things that bring you pleasure
Are the same things that cause you pain
So just keep your heart open
And try to answer its call
And remember, if your love's not worth dying for
It's worth nothing at all
Nothing at all

Through the heat and the anger
All the destruction and fear

Love has power
Love has power
Enough to lift you up
Enough to drag you down

It's all true
It's my gift to you

Oh, you gotta reach down inside

It's waiting for you

Love has power
Love has power
Enough to lift you up
Love can drag you down
Just remember
Love has power
(Never surrender)

Love has power
Love can lift you up
Love can drag you down
Just remember
Love has power

JON ENGLISH FAMILY TREE

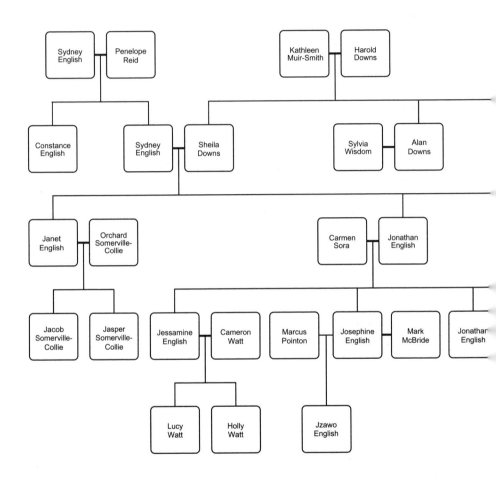

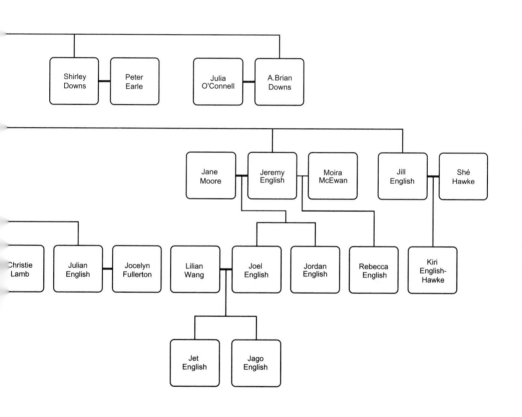